The Diffusion of Information and Communication Technologies

In recent decades, the world has witnessed—unprecedented in terms of speed and geographic coverage—diffusion of new information and communication technologies (ICT). The ongoing Digital Revolution pervasively impacts and reshapes societies and economies and therefore deserves special attention and interest.

This book provides extensive evidence on ICT development patterns and dynamics of this process across developed economies over the period 1980 to the present day. It adopts newly developed methodology to the identification of the 'critical mass' and isolation of technological take-off intervals, which are intimately related to the process of technology diffusion. The statistically robust analysis of country-specific data demonstrates the key economic, social and institutional prerequisites of ICT diffusion across examined countries, indicating the factors that significantly foster or—reversely—hinder the process.

Ewa Lechman is Associate Professor in the Faculty of Management and Economics at Gdańsk University of Technology, Poland.

Routledge Studies in Technology, Work and Organizations

Edited by David Preece
University of Teeside, UK

For a full list of titles in this series, please visit www.routledge.com

The Diffusion of Information and Communication Technologies

Ewa Lechman

LONDON AND NEW YORK

First published 2018 by Routledge

2 Park Square, Milton Park, Abingdon, Oxfordshire OX14 4RN
52 Vanderbilt Avenue, New York, NY 10017

Routledge is an imprint of the Taylor & Francis Group, an informa business

First issued in paperback 2019

Library of Congress Cataloging-in-Publication Data
A catalog record for this book has been requested

ISBN: 978-1-138-20215-3 (hbk)
ISBN: 978-0-367-88957-9 (pbk)

Typeset in Sabon
by Apex CoVantage, LLC

To my daughter, A.

Contents

Figures

Tables

Foreword

'The history of the world is but the biography of great men', wrote the historian Thomas Carlyle in 1841. Most historians now believe that kings and presidents have relatively little impact on ordinary people's lives. Despite the theory living on in journalism, as Simon Kuper critically suggested in the *Financial Times* on the 17th of March of 2017, reality is changing in a way that great men—and even more those (self) supposed so—can really do very little. Demography, climate and technology matter much more. This is not just an encouragement to avoid any fear about the possibility that some political personalities will remain until 2024 or even more, giving the impression to govern the directions the world economy will take. It is just another way to say that the forces of structural changes are always overcoming—and even more nowadays—any attempt to re-introduce a vision of the human and societal development based on the role of a 'special' individuals and/or their capacity to shape (or to limit or address) technological change.

In particular, the speed and the deepness of the most recent technological transformations can no longer be compared with previous industrial revolutions. We are now living in the Fifth Industrial Revolution, based on innovation and diffusion of information and communication technologies (ICT). Their impact on the world economy is modifying old hierarchies based on a bunch of technologies belonging to the previous technological waves. New emerging economies can reduce their distance from the most advanced ones faster. Sometimes they can even advance at a faster speed than the richest countries, at least in some sectors, more directly connected with the ICT. This reality is changing over so frequently, and into unexpected directions, that often it is even impossible to check the relative impact of some specific technology. There is certainly a need for more articulated comprehension of the mass consequences of adopting a series of tools and goods using ICT for the advanced and even more for the emerging economies. Within this framework, the main issue is not—generically speaking—economic development. It is rather a larger diffusion of welfare and of new opportunities for a wider portion of the world population.

This book is a sort of compass permitting navigation into different directions without ever losing the route for the final destination. Ewa Lechman is an economist with the rare capacity to evaluate the effects of ICT in the medium-term—i. e. considering the evolution of at least the last 25–30 years. Time plays a role—and it could not be the opposite—in technological diffusion and in the effects of the adoption of new technologies. More than 35 years ago, by using the concept of 'differential of contemporaneousness', Sidney Pollard suggested in one of his most famous books, *Peaceful Conquest: The Industrialization of Europe, 1760–1970* (London, 1981), that technologies arrive in the same time in different countries, but their effects are diverse because of the level of the previous economic development. This book is a challenge because ICT behave in different ways, and Pollard's vision can finally be reconsidered, basing the new evaluation on very solid foundations. The approach is partly empirical and partly theoretical. The rigorousness of the analysis emerges from the very good balance between the two approaches. This makes the book palatable from many points of view. Economists, but also economic historians, sociologists and technologists can find in the pages of this book several very original results on the impact of ICT in the world economy. Many other readers will also get the confirmation that political personalities at the helm of very important countries in today's world, despite all their efforts, will never be the riders guiding the horse of history. They are hanging 'on to the horse for dear life' as it carries them in directions they could not even imagine, as suggested by the journalist of the *Financial Times*.

Luciano Segreto

Acknowledgements

I wish to acknowledge that this research has been supported by the project no.2015/19/B/HS4/03220 financed by the National Science Centre, Poland.

1   Introduction

The Context

Technology is opportunity; it empowers people and makes things possible. Technological change is beautiful because it is irreversible; although it does not follow a linear pattern, its trajectory is rather marked by abrupt shifts and sometimes long-run stagnation. Technologies are often revolutionary, and in that sense, they enforce the emergence of some turning points in history, generating deep structural changes. David Landes in his influential work *The Unbound Prometheus* writes that '*not everyone likes changes, but those who want the world to be different often yearn for it*' (Landes, 1969, p. X). This provokes thinking that technological progress, to be well understood, needs to be contextualized. To rephrase the latter—technology does not exist in isolation, but it constitutes an essential part of a much larger and complex socio-economic system, which is '*reciprocally influenced by the rate and course of technological development*' (Landes, 1969, p. 5). Understanding the process of technological development allows accounting for the diversity of economic performance of countries, both in the past and in the present time. Purely technical perception of technology is always a huge limitation; it reflects exclusively narrow-minded thinking and does not bring cutting-edge changes to our perception of the outside reality. Technological development has a long history, but regardless of the circumstances, it has always been acknowledged as the prime fundament of change and wealth creation. This is mainly because, in the heart of technological revolutions, there is always global diffusion of knowledge, which substantially underlines radical and profound transformations of social and economic spheres of life, such as movements of labour force from agriculture to industry or services. The importance of technology must not be underestimated. Looking back, one may observe the enormous power and complexity of this phenomenon, and by its profound and detailed analysis, we get better understanding of its changing nature and the role it plays in development over time.

Throughout history, there existed wide gaps among countries in respect to technological development. For ages, the process of inventing things and assimilation of technological novelties have been painfully slow. Knowledge on technology and on how technological advancements could be put to work was not widespread, and these have generated enormous cross-country disparities. Some regions started forging ahead, while the others lagged behind. To some extent, these cross-national inequalities in technological advancement are persistent over time, and looking at the world map, we see heavily backward regions suffering from permanent technological underdevelopment. Before the onset of the Industrial Revolution in the 18th century, technology was diffusing spasmodically, economies were zero-sum systems and economic growth was easily reversible. Hence the pre-industrial societies were virtually locked in a Malthusian trap and unable to escape it. Now, looking briefly at the history of technological change from a purely economic point of few, the aspect of the rate at which different technologies were diffusing worldwide is of seminal importance. The speed of the spread of technological knowledge is far more important than, for instance, asking the question when the new technology emerged (although the latter from the historical point of few is of primary importance). The speed of diffusion of new technologies is crucial for two major reasons. First, it allows finding how fast new technological solutions are being acquired by individuals across the globe, and second, how fast new technologies are embodied in production process, which, in effect, would lead to shifts in productivity and overall welfare. From the economic perspective, the pace of technological change is critical.

Comin et al. (2006) in their exhaustive study on historical technology diffusion[1] covering 115 different technologies in over 150 economies during the last 200 years present arguments in support of the hypothesis that technology *is* the critical factor, which differentiates economic performance of countries. Interestingly, they demonstrate that speed of convergence in levels of technology adoption observed before the year 1925 was crucially different from that reported after 1925. Before 1925, the average rate of convergence was at about 2.4% annually, while after 1925, it increases almost threefold to 6.7% per annum. When discriminating between technologies developed between 1900 and 1925, 1925 and 1950, 1950 and 1975, the average speed of convergence was 1.5%, 5.8% and 7.8%, respectively, which inevitably leads to the general conclusion that the tempo of convergence for new technologies is faster than for old ones. Rapidly proceeding technology convergence suggests that new technologies diffuse at incomparably higher rates compared to old ones.

The rate of technological change we have witnessed since the early '70s of 20th century onwards is the fastest the world has ever experienced. New information and communication technologies (ICT) are rapidly expanding worldwide. The process of diffusion of ICT is overwhelming; it is dynamic, disruptive and distinctive. ICT are shrinking the world. ICT have changed the concept of economy; it connects the unconnected. Today, the technological progress, in terms of its speed and geographic coverage, seems to be an unprecedented phenomenon throughout world history. Never before have so many people had access to such an enormous number of sophisticated technological solutions, which offer to these people unbounded flows of information and knowledge. The ICT Revolution—the Fifth Technological Revolution—gave birth to the remarkable invention; it provided a solid background for the emergence of new complex and numerous linkages within society. Gains that it has generated are not even possible to encapsulate in a brief account.

Tom Standage in his book *The Victorian Internet: The Remarkable Story of the Telegraph and the Nineteenth Century's On-Line Pioneers* (1998) traces back to the second half of the 19th century and claims that the development of the telegraph was the first technology that enabled worldwide communication, thus freeing people from the burden of geographic distance. Interestingly, Standage argues that the development of Internet networks—to a large extent—mirrors the spread of the telegraph network. He also notes that the diffusion of telegraph network was the Internet of Victorian times and enforced the first significant qualitative shifts that the world experienced in terms of ways of communication, while the spread of the Internet network mainly gave way to the huge impulse to quantitative shifts. To some degree, we may agree with this point of view; however, it is important to note that the '*carrying capacity*' of the modern Internet network significantly exceeds the power of the telegraph, and thus its impact on social and economic life has farther reaching implications.

Yet you do not need to be enthusiastic to benefit from ICT. Frances Cairncross writes,

> The advance of the past few decades are now converging. (. . .) technologies such as Internet, mobile telephone (. . .) refine and rearrange (. . .) the coming century, but their broad shape if clear to us.
>
> (Cairncross, 1997, p. vii)

Next, in the same work, she claims,

> This is revolution about opportunity and about increasing human contact. It will be easier than ever before for people with initiative and ideas to turn them into business ventures. It will be easier to discover information, to learn new things, to acquire new skills.
>
> (Cairncross, 1997, p. 26)

It enables fast and low-cost transactions at the same time in different, often geographically isolated, places. It is fast and cheap to distribute among society members, and thus people can easily assimilate ICT. ICT have potential to level the inequalities between those who 'have' and those who 'have-not'. The prospective is promising. Christine Zhen-Wei Qiang, the World Bank economist, writes, 'The mobile platform is emerging as the single most powerful way to extend economic opportunities and key services to millions of people' (World Bank, 2009). However, above all, ICT create social and economic networks, giving positive impulses for intensification of economic activity. It brings market information, financial, educational and health services to remote, underserved regions suffering from infrastructural shortages. New technologies change the ways of doing business, enforce institutional transformation and allow for unbounded and almost costless flows of knowledge and all types of information. Today, economy has no boundaries in time and space. In that sense, new technologies allow challenging information asymmetries—one of the most sever market imperfections and failures disabling its perfect functioning. It is needless to emphasize that it takes time to embody technological change in economic welfare. Even path-breaking inventions do not enforce rapid and abrupt shifts in productivity and an aggregate level of economic outputs. Technology needs time to diffuse across societies and countries, and after to be adopted and effectively used. Undoubtedly, technology matters. Technology matters because it generates extensive structural transformations, enhances productivity shifts and hence changes global economic and social landscapes. For ages, societies made huge efforts to escape their economic and technological backwardness. But connecting people and countries through the ICT network is just the beginning of the long journey towards social and economic wealth. The Industrial Revolution caused global (great) divergence—as noted in Maddison (2007) and then repeated in Comin and Ferrer (2013)—at the beginning of 19th century, when the average per capita income in 'Western countries' was at about 1.9 times higher compared to 'non-Western economies'. Then for the next 200 years, the 'Western countries' were economically growing much faster, so that in at the beginning of 21st century, their average per capita income was 7.2 times higher than in the rest of the World. Angus Deaton, in his book *The Great Escape. Wealth, Health and the Origins of Inequality* (2013), writes,

> The Industrial Revolution (. . .) initiated the economic growth that has been responsible for hundreds of millions of people escaping from material deprivation. The other side of the same Industrial Revolution is what historians call the 'Great Divergence' (. . .) creating the enormous gulf between the West and the rest that has not closed to this day. Today's global inequality was, to a large extent, create by the success of modern economic growth.
>
> (Deaton, 2013, p. 4)

This huge gap in economic wealth was undeniably generated by the uneven spread of achievements during the Industrial Revolution.

However, as claimed by many, the ICT Revolution induced the emergence of Global Convergence and the weakening of core and the strengthening of peripheries; the ICT Revolution allowed for the rise of the rest—the technological rise of economically backward economies.

Getting Value of This Book

What follows is an attempt to contribute to our understanding of the process of the diffusion of new ICT and the paths that it follows as its determinants. In this context, I find several aspects that make me think that this book is important. First, because it empirically confirms what we intuitively know: new ICT are diffusing worldwide at a historically unprecedented pace. It contributes significantly to our understanding of how new technologies are expanding worldwide; it unveils the unique characteristics of this process in extremely heterogeneous countries, and it shows how fast ICT have transformed the world we live in and created totally new forms of networks—networks which do not exclusively matter for inter-personal communication, but also—and maybe above all—for the economy, institutions and many others. This study indents to show that the Fifth ICT Revolution has totally reshaped our thinking about the technological differences existing among world countries. Past technological revolutions, although they neither have brought enormous changes to social and economic spheres of life nor offered technological solutions which could be quickly distributed across all societies, regardless of their physical location, and they did not offer technologies which would be easily accessed and used by all regardless of their skills or material status. Additionally, it allows comparing countries and indicates how well countries are doing compared with others in terms of assimilation and development of ICT. It allows recognizing which countries are forging ahead and which are stagnating or falling behind. Moreover, this book offers the reader a newly developed methodological approach to identify the value of the critical mass that gives rise to the emergence of technological take-off that boosts ICT deployment. This research discusses whether ICT diffusion paths are incremental or abrupt, whether technological change occurs randomly or maybe it is driven by, for instance, technology-oriented state policies.

The central focus of attention of our research is both theoretical conceptualization and empirical investigations. More specifically, we define our research goals as follows:

- explaining the new conceptualization of the critical mass and technological take-off;
- identifying major long-term trends in ICT development;
- development of country-specific ICT diffusion trajectories in respect to four selected core ICT indicators;
- detecting the process of switching from old technologies to new technological solutions offered by the ICT Revolution;
- identifying the critical mass and the emergence of the technological take-off along country-specific ICT diffusion trajectories; and
- examining the seminal factors determining the process of ICT diffusion.

The major empirical goals of this book are very ambitious, not only because it deals with very complex problems of interrelatedness between technology, economy and society but also because we focus on country-specific analysis. Such an approach is time-consuming labour, but it allows the reader to benefit from it and recognize it as the source of new knowledge on the process of spreading new technologies, its dynamics and prerequisites. Additionally, we affirm that the group of high-income and upper-middle-income economies is extremely heterogeneous; those countries vary significantly, not only in terms of their economic performance but also in respect to the market size, legal frameworks or, for instance, the state of development of backbone infrastructure. Our attempt was also to show that if we took the trouble to look more deeply into the problem, we could gain a totally different perspective and ideas of the entire landscape. Henceforth, we are deeply convinced that treating each country as an individual case significantly contributed to our understanding of this complex phenomenon, and this will allow the reader to find the information as satisfactory, and, above all, it is an astonishingly simply way of explaining complicated issues.

Chapter-by-Chapter Outline

The first chapter is the introduction itself. In this part, we provide motivation for this research. We additionally contextualize the problem, define major aims and scopes of our study and explain the consecutive chapters' contents.

Chapter 2 sets out fundamental ideas standing behind technology, innovation and technological progress. In this chapter, intentionally, we locate our consideration on technological development in a broad, historical perspective. We contextualize technological progress, and to this aim, we explain why technology constitutes a fundamental element of complex socio-economic system. In Chapter 2, we also explain the prominent role that technological change plays in long-run economic development and show that the interrelatedness of technology, society and economy is a complex matter involving numerous qualitative and quantitative factors. It briefly pictures how technological progress and uneven diffusion rates have contributed to structural shifts in the world economy, thus determining the changing economic power of nations. It explains why technological breakthroughs have enforced radical transformations of world economic systems and reshaped its economic contours. Next in this chapter, we define the idea of techno-economic paradigm as the concept that captures multidimensionality and interrelatedness of technology, society and economy. In the final part of Chapter 2, we take a brief look at the past five technological surges—technological revolutions the world has experienced for ages. We explain how and why these five technological revolutions have been deeply transforming societies and economies, becoming turning points in human's history. Chapter 2 ends by introducing the Fifth Technological Revolution—the ICT Revolution—and places it in the wider context of the study of past technological surges.

Chapter 3 is entirely devoted to discussing the theoretical framework of technology diffusion, and it presents the process of technology spread as spatial and temporal phenomenon. It begins by defining the process of technology diffusion itself and traces its intellectual foundations. Next, it identifies factors, which potentially precondition the speed of technology diffusion, and it discriminates between driving forces and impediments of this process. It explains the importance of the network effects (network externalities) that enforce rapid diffusion of new technologies. It also briefly discusses major theories (concepts) of diffusion of technology, offers explanations of equilibrium and disequilibrium approaches to technology diffusion modelling and shows the simple concept of sigmoid curve that relatively well describes the technology diffusion pattern. Finally, in Chapter 3, we comprehensively explain the novel methodological approach to identification of the critical mass and the technological take-off as two major prerequisites for ensuring the suitability of the process of technology diffusion.

Chapters 4 and 5 are purely empirical in nature. Chapter 4 presents the results of our empirical analysis of the process of diffusion of new ICT between 1980 and 2015 in 47 high-income and 34 upper-middle-income economies. It portrays country-specific ICT diffusion patterns and summarizes results of logistic growth models showing the in-time dynamics of this process across examined economies. In our research, we concentrate exclusively on four core ICT indicators, which show changes in access to and use of new ICT. These four ICT indicators are as follows: mobile-cellular subscription rate, fixed-broadband subscription rate, active-mobile broadband subscription rate and Internet users (IU). All statistical data are exclusively derived from the World Telecommunications/ICT Indicators database 2016 (20th edition/ December). The results of our analysis allow for discovering major trends in ICT development and unveil the dynamics of this process and changes in cross-national inequalities. By convention, we run countrywide analysis, and such an approach offers a reader a deeper insight into specific paths of ICT diffusion in each country in the scope with our research, and it provides new knowledge on the unique characteristics of this process. Additionally, to complete the picture, we confront the process of mobile-cellular telephony diffusion with fixed (wired) telephony development paths. The results are striking and allow for the identification of the '*fixed-to-mobile technological substitution*' that demonstrates the process of gradual switching from old technology (here, fixed telephony) to new technology (here, mobile-cellular telephony). Analogously, we examine the process of '*fixed-to-mobile technological substitution*' in respect to fixed-broadband and mobile (wireless) broadband networks deployment. Also, in this case, we find that wired networks are being substituted by the wireless technologies offering unbounded access to the Internet network.

Next, in Chapter 5, we use our novel methodological approach and trace countrywide technological take-offs; we calculate the value of the critical mass and the length of the pre-take-off periods regarding ICT diffusion (mobile-cellular telephony and Internet) across all examined high-income and upper-middle-income countries. The time span of this analysis and statistical data on ICT indicators source is analogous as in the previous case. Moreover, in this part of our research, we aim to answer the following question: Under which conditions does the technological take-off occur that allows for breaking out of technological stagnation (leaving the pre-take-off diffusion stage) and into rapid new technologies growth? To this end, we identify country-wide social and economic conditions during the technological take-off intervals. Such an approach, additionally, provides the clear view of whether the technological take-off and critical mass are reached under some specific circumstance (prerequisites) or the unveiled network effects are strong enough to ensure rapid shifts in new technology deployment. In the second part of Chapter 5, we provide additional evidence on mobile-cellular telephony and Internet networks deployment growth across examined countries. With this aim, we trace a set of factors, which potentially may be recognized as those having a statistically significant impact on the process of ICT diffusion. First, we graphically explain the relationship between the level of mobile-cellular telephony adoption and Internet penetration rates *versus* their selected determinants. Second, we present the complementary evidence and use panel regression models to re-examine the hypothesized relationships.

Finally, Chapter 6 summarizes our empirical findings and draws general conclusions.

Note

1. Comin et al. (2006) used Cross-Country Historical Adoption of Technology (CHAT) dataset in their study (see www.nber.org/papers/w15319.pdf).

References

Cairncross, F. (1997). The death of distance: The trends potter's guide to new communications.Harvard Business School Press.

Comin, D. A., & Ferrer, M. M. (2013). *If technology has arrived everywhere, why has income diverged?* (No. w19010). National Bureau of Economic Research.

Comin, D., Hobijn, B., & Rovito, E. (2006). *Five facts you need to know about technology diffusion* (No. w11928). National Bureau of Economic Research.

Deaton, A. (2013). The great escape: Health, wealth, and the origins of inequality. Princeton University Press.

Landes, D. S. (1969). The unbound Prometheus: Technological change and development in Western Europe from 1750 to the present. Cambridge: Cambridge University Press.

Maddison, A. (2007). The world economy: Volume 1: A millennial perspective & Volume 2: Historical statistics. Academic Foundation.

Standage, T. (1998). The Victorian internet: The remarkable story of the telegraph and the nineteenth century's on-line pioneers. London: Weidenfeld & Nicolson.

World Bank. (2009). *Information and communications for development 2009: Extending reach and increasing impact*. Information and Communications for Development Series. The World Bank Group.

2 Technology and Economic Development
Historical Perspective

On the Importance of Technology for Development

> Technological paradigms and trajectories, are in some respect metaphors of the interplay between continuity and ruptures in the process of incorporation of knowledge and technology into (. . .) growth: the metaphor, however should help to illuminate its various aspects and actors to suggest a multi-variable approach to the theory of innovation and technological change.
>
> Giovanni *Dosi (1982)*

Let us start putting all the pieces together by trying to understand (although very superficially) the nature of technology and technological change. Technologies and technological change are complex and multidimensional phenomenon, and thus rigorous formulation of their definition yields difficulties. Although difficult to rigidly define, today, the importance of technological change is widely acknowledged, and many scholars speak in support of the hypothesis that technology and technological knowledge are fundamental elements of development (Rosenberg, 1994), despite the fact that their impact on the economy or society at large is neither immediate nor direct. Today, technology is no longer treated as an unexplained residual (as initially postulated by Solow) but rather is assumed to be the endogenous factor of development, embodying the cumulated knowledge

Mokyr (2005a), in his influential works, provides multiple arguments in support of the thesis that technology is simply knowledge. However, knowledge has always been quite a difficult concept to handle, and, arguably, it is hard to disagree with Mokyr (2005a,b) that knowledge as such is a non-rivalrous good—sharing it with other people does not happen at the expense of diminished knowledge of its original owner. To some extent, technology may also be labeled as a non-rivalrous good, and once it is shared and diffused across society members, each individual can make effective use of it, which does not happen at the expense of the other individual. Put differently, the social marginal cost of knowledge, and thus technology, sharing is zero. Also in his prominent work *The Lever of Riches: Technological Creativity and Economic Progress* (Mokyr, 1992), Mokyr he states that technology is epistemological in nature, meaning that technology as such cannot exist outside people's brains, but rather should be perceived as something that people know. Henceforth, technological change,[1] which emerges as new ideas arrive, is regarded as changes in people's knowledge. The use and adoption of technology, similar to knowledge, allows for the emerging of unique effects of scale to bring benefits to all its users. In the same sense, Fagerberg et al. (2010) define technology as the knowledge which explains how to produce and distribute goods and services. The definition from Fagerberg et al. (2010) coincides with that proposed by Comin et al. (2006), who claim that technology may be defined as a way of accomplishing various things when different techniques and human knowledge are necessary. A similar notion of technology has been proposed by Wilson and Heeks (2000), who suggest that technology is a kind of purposeful activity aiming to apply knowledge by human beings. Such a perception of technology, where it is intimately related to people's knowledge, has far-reaching implications. First, it might suggest that technology embodies human knowledge and, second, that technology serves as a way of transmitting knowledge among individuals (Lechman, 2015). Also, Rosenberg (1974, 1982) argues that technology and technological progress encompass a broad array of human activities, which constitute essential elements of socio-economic systems. In this sense, arguably, it may state that both knowledge and technological progress are inseparable and that technological progress is an outcome of knowledge, but also vice versa (Layton, 1974; Mokyr & Scherer, 1990). Similarly, however in narrower sense, Dosi (1982shows that technology is a unique combination of knowledge, methods, know-how and experience, which, if put together, contribute to growth of productivity and national output. Campbell et al. (2010) claim that the term technology, if broadly defined, refers to '*the development and use of tools, crafts and techniques to solve problems and control/adapt to specific environment*' (Campbell et al., 2010, p. 252). Evenson and Westphal (1995) claim that for technology and technological progress to be properly understood, they should be perceived broadly and encompass all human knowledge on how to do things, with special emphasis on how to produce goods and services, which are highly valued and thus may be traded by people to fulfill their needs. The aforementioned understanding of technology coincides with the view of Dosi (1982), who suggested that technological change should be seen through the lens of growing production possibilities and the increasing number of producible goods. However, in the same work, he also emphasizes that technology is something much broader as '*a set of pieces of knowledge*' (Dosi, 1982, p. 151) encompassing both '*practical*' (related to certain practical problems) and '*theoretical*' (related to knowledge that might be applied to solve some problem, but so far has been not) aspects, and it is strictly associated with all kinds of know-how, methods and procedures, as well as a physical stock of devices.

Societies are usually accustomed to equating technology with simple 'technology products' such as computers and cars; however, one shall bear in mind that 'technologies' and 'technological progress' often bring to societies and economies cutting-edge changes. Introduction of new technologies usually deeply transforms the way both societies and economies act; it enforces significant shifts and transformations, which are often revolutionary. Many technologies, invented through the ages, have been considered 'pervasive technologies', meaning that their wide adoption profoundly reshaped the 'present state of the art'. In respect to technology and technological progress, pervasiveness also means that new technological solutions are thoroughly implemented, and all society members gradually get accustomed to their everyday usage. The implementation of technology involves an ongoing socio-economic process, while the effects of technology adoption are usually indirect and characterized by significant time lags. More often the socio-economic impact of technology is put in a complex context involving not only time but also a wide bundle of social norms and attitudes, political regimes, legal and institutional frameworks and geographical location or country's historical legacy (Kling, 2000).

Olsen and Engen (2007) show that technology is often viewed as simply machines, devices and various tools used for particular production purposes; however, they also underline that, by some scholars, technology is understood as artefacts (Pinch & Bijker, 1987) and thus propose to define technology as '*artefact and knowledge about their operations*' (Olsen & Engen, 2007, p. 2). In works of Dosi and Malerba (1996) and Dosi et al. (1998), we may find the recognition to a large extent that technology has deep social aspects and determinants, and thus both technology and society are inseparable. The latter may be supported by the supposition that technology does not '*arise out of nowhere*' (Olsen & Engen, 2007, p. 2) but rather is an outcome of people's knowledge and practice, interactions between social groups, arising demand and new opportunities, sometimes positive or negative external shock and existing technologies.

In late 1980s, there emerged a remarkable debate contributing to perception and understanding of technology and technological progress. The so-called *the social shaping of technology* approach proposed by MacKenzie and Wajcman (1985, 1999) that allows for the perception of both technology and technological progress from a different perspective and offers broader '*understanding of the relationship between scientific excellence, technological innovation and economic and social well-being*' (Williams & Edge, 1996, p. 1). The social shaping of the technology concept may be claimed as a kind of antidote to another, rather naïve, concept labeled '*technological determinism*', which claims that '*technological development is autonomous in respect to society; it shapes society, but is not reciprocally influenced*' (MacKay & Gillespie, 1992, p. 686). Evidently, technology must not be perceived as being purely deterministic, which would imply that technology simply causes (determines) a set of changes, making certain structures (for instance, social or economic) inevitable (Mattsson, 2007). Technology and technological changes are a rather socially and institutionally embedded process (Dicken,

2007), thus the way technology is used is subjected to the socio-economic context. According to the concept of social shaping of technology, whilst not denying the fact that technology and technological progress affect societies, it is society and its forces which determine the emergence to new technologies. Henceforth, the perception of technology shall not only be exclusively restricted to how it transforms society but also consider the fact that new technology emergence may be an outcome of the process of choice and negotiations between societal groups. When putting the concept of social shaping of technology into the macro perspective, arguably it may be claimed that technology is—at least to some extent—shaped by socio-economic forces, and thus technology is created and after implemented for particular socio-economic objectives (also see Molina, 1989; Law & Bijker, 1992; Bijker, 1995; Bijker et al., 2012). Mowery and Rosenberg (1991) present a convergent view on the relationship between socio-economic systems and technology. They provide arguments that disruptive technological changes are driven and shaped both by economic forces and the stock of past knowledge already embodied in technologies. Arguably, technological inventions may be seen as a process of effective and simultaneous '*coupling at technological and economic levels*' (Mowery & Rosenber, 1991, p. 8), and hence technology is rather '*emphatically not deterministic*' (Dicken, 2007, p. 76).

Another aspect of technological progress and technology itself, which has been raised by Evenson and Westphal (1995), but also may be found in works of Cowan et al. (2000), Håkanson and Nobel (2000) and Rodrik (2000) is their tacitness and circumstantial sensitivity. The tacitness of technology and technological progress, in fact, refers to the issues related to tacitness of knowledge about how processes perform and how to create an efficient system out of it. Also, Pavitt (1999), in his works, claims that technology is '*specific, complex, and partly tacit*' (Pavitt, 1999, p. 3). The stock of knowledge is hardly codifiable or easily transferred between entities. Moreover, the circumstantial sensitivity in respect to technology and technological progress (Westphal, 2002; Kato & Mitra, 2008) seem to be of seminal importance, as it has straightforward implications for whether new technological regimes are accepted by societies and economic systems or not, ensuring social and economic fundaments for rapid assimilation of newly emerging technologies and providing a technology-friendly environment for fast diffusion of new techniques among individuals and throughout the economy with preconditions benefiting from technological progress. Maximizing both social and economic effects that may arise when new technologies arrive is crucial from the long-term perspective. In the same vain, Mokyr (1998) argues that technology, similarly to knowledge, has to be deeply integrated into society to become the source of profits and gains, and thus lead to economic welfare; however, the technology adoption usually does not occur automatically or unconditionally, but only happens in an environment where new technologies may diffuse freely; penetrate various spheres of social, economic and institutional life; and society members assimilate new knowledge embedded in newly arriving technologies. The aspects of the so-called complementary conditions to technology assimilation have also been discussed in works of, inter alia, Ames and Rosenberg (1963) and Fagerberg and Srholec (2008), who emphasized the role of institutional and organizational changes, which are essential for technology to become widespread. Abramovitz (1986), Cimoli and Dosi (1995) and Fagerberg and Srholec (2013) additionally underlined the role of 'social capabilities' and each individuals propensity for learning, thus conditioning the process of new technologies acquisition among society members. Technology as knowledge is transmitted instantaneously to all individuals through the networks created by societies themselves. The process of technology diffusion unveils the unique phenomena labeled as the 'network effects'. The 'network effects' stand for the value of potential connectivity, which, in heterogeneous societies, tends to grow exponentially. It explains the fast-growing number of users of a given technology, which then attracts and multiplies further links. On the grounds of the economy, it means that the increasing number of links among entities is potentially translated into further economic gains. Katz and Shapiro (1985) claim that the 'network effects' demonstrate the increasing utility from usage of a given good or service when accompanied by an increasing number of users of analogous goods or services. Such positive interactions make strong products even stronger and weak ones even weaker, which in effect can lead to the simple substitution of one product by another (McGee & Sammut, 2002). In late the 1990s, Shapiro and Varian (1998) claimed, 'There is a central difference between the old and new economies: the old industrial economy was driven by economies of scale; the new information economy is driven by the economics of networks'. This concept is somehow related to what was stressed in works of Baumol (1986), Perez and Soete (1988) and Verspagen (1991), which stated that a country's ability to adopt new technologies is preconditioned by a wide array of factors. Societies assess and assimilate technological novelties, relying upon 'intellectual' capital (Soete & Verspagen, 1993), institutional, governmental and cultural conditions. Some empirical evidence show that the most prominent factor in a country's ability to adopt and use effectively new technologies are education and skills of the labour force (Baumol, 1989). Countries experiencing significant lacks in these areas probably will never be able to exploit fully the potential that technological change may generate. Thus, these economies may never catch up with richer countries, thus risking permanent lagging behind in terms of socio-economic development. However, the possibilities of forging ahead or falling behind in economic performance because of technological progress are highly influenced by factors which, in fact, might be difficult to capture, and the latter also suggests that the process of adoption and the effective use of new technologies and their contribution to growth and development is far from automatic. Evenson and Westphal (1995) claim that, among scholars and practitioners, there is still little understanding of the nature of and the role of technological progress in the context of development. Still, a unified and commonly agreed upon conceptual framework regarding the latter is lacking, which, to some extent, may be caused by extreme multidimensionality of both processes of technological progress and development.

Looking back at world history, we may learn that technology and world development have always been intimately related. For ages, technology was shaping the contours of the world economy. From the very long-run perspective, the history of world development is marked by the continuously changing economic power of nations and world regions, which to a large extent was determined by technological disruptions and path-breaking innovations giving rise to enormous changes in the global landscape. On the one hand, radical technological surges precondition and predetermine long-term development trajectories, and force the so-called global shifts, which often generate changes in the economic power of countries and the roles they play in the global economic system. On the other hand, it is clearly demonstrated that a country's economic conditions, political regimes, economic systems and legal and institutional environments may provide solid fundaments for the emergence of new technologies and inventions, or reversely, by setting barriers, they hinder the rise of new technologies.

As postulated by many scholars and empirically proven in multiple researches, technology plays a pivotal role in very long-term development process, determining and shaping the development patterns of countries. Such claims have been raised in the contributive works of, inter alia, Solow (1956), Romer (1990), Aghion and Howitt (1992) and Landes (2003), as well as in more recent works of, for instance, Lipsey et al. (2005) and Acemoglu and Robinson (2012). Jared Diamond, in his influential book *Guns, Germs, and Steel: The Fates of Human Societies* (1999) where he intends to explain the pattern of human history during the last 13,000 years and answer the prominent question of why human development took so many different routes in different continents and world regions, clearly emphasizes that already in the year 1500, world regions differed hugely in terms of technological development. Next, he concludes that these past differences in the level of technological development have heavily affected present inequalities among world countries. Put differently, the current level of economic development is, at least to some extent, subjected to the level of technological development in ancient times. Diamond's thesis is also supported by the empirical evidence reported in the extensive research of Comin et al. (2010), which examines the quantitative relationships between technology adoption in ancient times and the present level of development. The very general conclusion from their study is that, surprisingly, today's countries' economic performance is positively correlated with the level of technology adoption in the very old times—1000 BC, 0 AD, and 1500 AD. Their findings are strongly robust and confirm the unique 'technological persistence' across historical epochs (from 1000 BC to 0 AD, from 0 AD to 1500 AD and from 1500 AD to present times) and claim that their findings speak in support of the correctness of the economic growth model where technology is treated endogenously. Another very striking observation is that the past cross-country difference in the level of technology adoption, to a large extent, explains today's cross-national differences not only in regard to the present state of technological advancement but also in terms of *per capita* income. Similar consideration on the role and importance of ancient technology adoption to present development may be found in the works of Mokyr (1992), Rosenberg et al. (1986) and Greene (2000), and most of their findings coincide with those demonstrated in the seminal research of Comin et al. (2010).

Historically, the world economic map has been constantly reshaping, which to a large extent was enforced by continuous technological changes. To some extent, last two millennial were marked by consecutively emerging path-breaking events—usually technological breakthroughs, which abruptly and radically transformed the world economic systems and reshaped its economic contours. The beginning of our millennia was marked by the economic hegemony of Mediterranean countries (the territory of Roman and Greek empires) and also China and India on the other side of the globe. In those times, those regions economically and technologically dominated the entire world. The origins of this economic domination may be found mainly in the relative technological advancement of the Roman Empire and in its effectively functioning institutions, well-developed external trade and division of labour, as well as in its unique social and economic structure (Finley, 1999; Cameron & Neal, 2010). Ancient China and India are also excellent examples of well-performing technological economies. Multiple Chinese inventions, such as paper, compass, porcelain, tea, silk, first forms of paper money and broad adoption of iron in the agricultural sector (Deng, 2011; Wagner, 1993; Temple, 1998) allowed China to gain a dominant economic position in the world. In India, widespread cultivation and use of cotton (Gopal, 1961), similar to China's adoption of iron in the agricultural sector, allowed the country to gain economic power. However, it is important to note that in ancient times, it was not only sophisticated technology which was decisive for economic success but also economic growth and welfare were heavily preconditioned by the size of a country's population. Note that in 1 AD, the Chinese and Indian populations accounted for approximately 60% of total world population, while the European population represented 13% (Maddison, 2007). The latter may suggest that in ancient times, technology was not the prime engine of development; however, its combination with large population size might have led to economic domination. The period between the 5th and 15th centuries—from the collapse of the Roman Empire until the beginning of the first geographic discoveries and the colonial era—is the period of the agrarian revolution and the time of emergence of commodity-monetary economic systems and economically powerful European cities such as Antwerp, Amsterdam, Florence, Venice, Cordoba and Marseille. Moreover, multiple advancements in banking systems maritime insurance were introduced in addition to the spread of universities and growth in intellectual capital, as well as the invention of printing. All of these inventions—although they were not widespread and the diffusion of technology was slow or even spasmodic, especially outside Europe—were important. As Maddison claimed,

> From the year 1000 to 1820, advances in technology (. . .) slower than they have been since, but they were nevertheless a significant component of the growth process. Without improvements in agriculture, the increase in world population could not have been sustained. Without improvements in maritime technology and commercial institutions the opening up of the world economy could not have been achieved. Technical advance in important areas was dependent on fundamental improvements in (. . .) accumulation (. . .) of new knowledge. The long centuries of effort provided intellectual and institutional foundations for the much more rapid advances achieved in the nineteenth and twentieth centuries.
>
> (Maddison, 2007, p. 51)

During the 16th and 17th centuries in Europe, a growing importance of inventions was evident, and although the increases in total industry production and productivity were still slow, that period of time is often labeled '*pre-capitalism*' or '*early capitalism*' (Szpak, 2001; Sanyal, 2014). The slowly rising new economic system gradually overwhelmed a huge part of Europe, providing solid foundations for one of the most prominent '*turning points*' (Acemoglu & Robinson, 2012) in world economic history: the Industrial Revolution. The Industrial Revolution,[2] a newly emerged phenomenon in the 17th century in England, was a total disruption for the well-established economic world order. It enforced radical transformation of economic, social and political systems. It began the end of the Malthusian era of slow, population-dependent, low-productive growth, thus providing the foundation for productivity shifts and hence increases of incomes and personal welfare. This technological surge enhanced the '*global economic takeoff*' and '*takeoff into self-sustained*' (Hobsbawm, 2010) growth that permanently transformed the world economy and socials structures; it began the epoch of technology-driven development. Since the beginning of the 17th century, economic growth is no longer influenced by the size of a country's population; it is productivity driven, and hence it gained in its dynamism, stability, and—most importantly—irreversibility. Importantly, the Industrial Revolution generated the emergence of a new phenomenon labeled '*global shifts*' (Clark et al., 2003; Dicken, 2007), which induced radical changes in economic power of world countries and their share in the global output. Considering the historical economic statistics provided in Maddison (2007), we may conclude that in 1 AD, China and India accounted for nearly 57% of total global production,[3] while Western Europe accounted for only 14%. In 1700 (similar to what was reported for year 1820), although Western Europe progressed economically and its total output accounted for about

22% of the world, the world was still under the economic hegemony of China and India, which produced 46% of global production. However, once the Industrial Revolution arrived, the world economic landscape rapidly changed: We observed loses in economic power in China and India, while Western Europe benefited from the advancements brought by the Industrial Revolution. Western Europe started to forge ahead economically, while Asia and the rest of the world lagged behind. In 1870, Western European countries generated almost 33% of the world's total output, while China and India generated only 29%; then in 1900, it was 34% and 20%, respectively. Additionally, since the end of the 18th century, we observed the growing economic role of the so-called *Western Offshoots* (encompassing Australia, Canada, New Zealand and the United States). The development of this region, however, was mainly driven by the rapidly growing economy of the United States, which was determined by a sound institutional environment and a countrywide diffusion of new technologies. In 1820, the Western Offshoots generated just 2% of the global output, while in 1870 and 1900, it was 10% and 18%. Growing economic domination of the whole Western World[4] resulted in it accounting for 56% of global production in 1960, while China and India generated only 9%. This example manifestly demonstrates that technological shocks may be extremely disruptive in nature, have profound and long-run economic implications and change the economic contours of the world.

Although deep relationships between technology and development are sometimes difficult to quantify or even exemplify, we know quite intuitively that they exist. To some extent, economic theories of technological changes tend to consider the latter as the famous '*black box*' (Rosenber, 1982). However, despite the rising difficulties in formalizing the conceptual framework regarding the interplay between technologies and development, the problem of interdependency between these two in terms of fostering development is deeply rooted in modern economic theory. The theoretical background of the problem analysis is broad and mainly refers to the stream of neoclassical growth theories and macroeconomic determinants of growth. Schumpeter (1943) treated technological change as the heart of the process of economic growth and development. Early neoclassical models and concepts—e.g. Solow (1956)—treat technological advancement as crucial and exogenous factors of long-run economic growth. In his works, Solow assumes that technology is a public good, freely available to everyone at no cost. However, based on such an assumption, the long-run GDP per capita growth generated by technology adoption (in cases of developing countries) shall be equal. But the works of Schumpeter and Kaldor reveal the problem of a different initial condition for development, thus the growth rates differ across countries crucially. In the same vein, there appeared seminal works of Arrow (1962), who claimed the technological change to be an endogenous factor. Other significant contributions of the theoretical and empirical kinds were made by Uzawa (1965), Phelps (1966) and Shell (1967). All authors mentioned earlier stressed the importance of technological changes and permanent growth of technologies as determinants of significant shifts in labour-force skills and abilities which should positively influence growth rates of national income. Along with the previous work, there emerged a remarkable literature on strictly endogenous growth models—e.g. works from Lucas (1988), Romer (1990), Grossman and Helpman (1991) and Aghion and Howitt (1992)—in which the role of technologies in fostering economic growth was highly emphasized. In line with the literature explaining technology as a factor of economic growth, there emerged another stream in the economic theory, which combines the previous work with the hypothesis of catching up when referring to economically backward countries. The idea of implementing technology into broad development theories, in this sense, was undertaken in works of Gerschenkron (1962), Abramovitz (1986) and Maddison (1991). Gerschenkron argues that developing countries mainly operate below the world technology (innovation) frontier, and by copying (imitating) the developed technologies, they gain an opportunity to converge (catch up) with developed countries in terms of economic development. The '*technological congruence*' that represents a lack of appropriate technology to enter a development path has also been stressed in the works of Abramovitz (1994). Gerschenkron (1962) writes, '*Borrowed technology, so much and rightly stressed by Veblen (Veblen, 1915), was one of the primary factors assuring a high speed of development in a backward country*'. Clearly, the process of technological progress and diffusion of technological solutions fully accounts for their nature. Certain features of newly emerging technologies, absorptive capacities of society, knowledge and skills, information asymmetries, channels of diffusion and further adoption and state policies all have highly conditioned diffusion rates, thus creating a friendly environment for technology diffusion or, reversely, posing barriers to the process. Despite the aforementioned, the technology diffusion can be described as a long-run process, which results in a broad spread of different kinds of innovations. It is widely agreed that the process enhances deep changes in economic structures, fosters economic growth and development and contributes to the overall welfare of societies. All of these accelerate countries' development processes, often shifting them from stagnation and changing them into dynamic economies. It is important to note that technology's impact on economic performance is claimed to exhibit in the long-run perspective and, in addition, its easily visible impact is limited and hardly quantifiable, while the remarkable impact of technological development on countries' economies can only be confirmed when it converts into human development (Lechman, 2014).

Techno-Economic Paradigms—The Beautiful Metaphors

Technology and socio-economic systems are fundamentally inseparable (Rosenberg, 1982), and they are linked by two-way causality (Lechman,

2015). Contextualizing the process of technological change is seminal for understanding a bundle of changes and shifts it usually generates both society- and economy-wide. Henceforth, exploring, and then further conceptualization, the interactions between the emergence of new technologies and social and economic development patterns is undeniably needed. Undoubtedly, at a very general level, new technologies are usually disruptive in their nature, and hence often bring the Schumpeterian-type creative destruction across societies and economies. Regardless of whether the process of replacement (substitution) of old technological solutions by the newly emerged ones is smooth or, reversely, it is marked by abrupt and rapid surges, it has far-reaching socio-economic implications.

In the context of major transformations being generated on social and economic grounds as long-term effects of the technological revolution, it may be articulated through the society- and economy-wide use of new technological solutions as they diffuse and, hence, are systematically adopted for multiple purposes. This multidimensionality and interconnectedness among technological revolution, society and economy is captured in the previously discussed concept of techno-economic paradigms. Put differently, technological breakthroughs give rise to new techno-economic paradigms.

Apparently, developed in the late '70s and '80s of 20th century, ideas of technological paradigms and techno-economic paradigms, thanks to their intellectual richness, demonstrated a very fresh and stimulating contribution to the debate on the interconnectedness between technology and economy. Their influence in respect to the theoretical framework additionally consists of showing the way toward shifting from static to dynamic analysis of interactions between technological change and socio-economic development (Von Tunzelmann et al., 2008). Finally, and even more importantly, the concept of techno-economic paradigm links formal economic modeling and history; it bridges various ideas and notions, and shows broad perspective and context, allowing for more profound and insightful interpretation of present and past events. The concept of techno-economic paradigms is a way to conceptualize the array of interactions that occur between the process of technological changes and social and economic development. Generally speaking, techno-economic paradigms may be perceived as unique ideas combining technology, society and economy, thus enabling us to explore the intimate interdependence and casual-relationships among them. Techno-economic paradigms constitute a useful conceptual framework, allowing for the analyzing of the relationships between technological changes and socio-economic development. The concept of the techno-economic paradigm, initially proposed by Perez (1986) and then augmented and modified in works of Freeman and Perez (1986, 1988) and Perez (2002, 2003, 2009a), is apparently closely related to the idea of technological paradigms developed by Dosi (1982). Fundamentally, both technological and techno-economic paradigms rely on Kuhn's concept of the scientific paradigm (Kuhn, 1962), which denotes a way of perceiving the world and defines key problems to be solved. Kuhn also argues that the old paradigms are replaced by the new once, when the first is no longer recognized as providing possible and adequate solutions to the problems encountered. Kuhn (1962) also claims that the change in existing paradigms—the paradigm shift—denotes radical changes in current concepts and ways of perceiving and explaining the reality.[5] Dosi (1982, 1988) writes that the proposed Kuhn scientific paradigm may be *'approximately defined as an "outlook" which defines the relevant problems, a "model" and a "pattern" of inquiry'* (Dosi, 1982, p. 152). In this vein, Dosi (1982)[6] defines the 'technological paradigm' as a *'model' and a 'pattern' of solutions of selected technological problems based on selected principles derived from natural sciences and on selected material technologies'* (Dosi, 1982, p. 152). In other work from Dosi et al. (1994), we read that technological paradigms are strictly related to the knowledge of problem solving in specific fields of technology. Johnston (1970), prior to Dosi (1982), offered another definition of the technological paradigm and states that it should be rather perceived as a bundle of principles widely accepted on certain grounds of technology. In a similar vein, Gibbons and Johnston (1974) suggest that technology and technological development are periodical in nature, which to some extent coincides with the view of Kuhn, who underlines the revolutionary nature of science and hence technology. Arguably, it may also be claimed that technological paradigms define a set of needs that should be fulfilled in a certain techno-economic context, and in this sense, technological change and economic development are linked and precondition each other. As argued in Van den Ende and Dolfsma (2005) and Sinclair-Desgagné (2000) new technological paradigms arise from advancement and development in science, and the accumulation of, inter alia technological, knowledge; they even speak in support of the very radical hypothesis that technological knowledge constitutes the major, if not the only, factor enforcing the emergence of new technological paradigms. The latter coincides with the view of Dosi (1988), who notes that fundamental advances in science and in closely related 'general' technologies constitute a solid background for the emergence of new technological paradigms. Technological paradigms may also be recognized as a homogenous sphere of technology, which is socially and economically contextualized, demarcating a certain field of research, which is aimed at developing inventions.

By convention, the technological paradigm provides a unique framework designed to conduct research, and this research once materialized, often generates great discontinuities along technological development trajectories.[7] Those discontinuities on the technological development paths, manifested because of the novel technological paradigms are usually strictly associated with radical innovations introduced to the socio-economic systems, which enforces profound economy-wide changes. The diffusion process of inventions developed within the new technological paradigm exclusively drives those changes, but they may also be a consequence of gradual switching from one technology to another. Such changes, on the one hand, if implemented effectively, enhance productivity shifts and generate benefits both on social and economic grounds, but on the other hand, they may generate temporal turbulences, instabilities and uncertainties.

The concept, proposed by Perez (1986), of the techno-economic paradigm, although fundamentally and conceptually related to the idea of Dosi's technological paradigm, presents a relatively higher level of generality. As far as the technological paradigm is concerned, in its generic sense, it is relatively narrowly defined; the techno-economic paradigm (or meta-paradigm) is a '*synthetic definition of macro-level systems of production, innovation, governance and social relations*' as suggested by Freeman and Pérez (1988) and then repeated in Cimoli and Dosi (1995, p. 255). Freeman and Pérez (1988) also propose to label the techno-economic paradigm as a 'technological revolution', which encompasses the emergence of radical and incremental innovations. Perez (1983) also argues that technology and economy are inseparably connected and henceforth these phenomena must not be explored separately. Technology shapes economy and vice versa, and thus the idea of techno-economic paradigms constitute a perfectly integrated approach to analyze and understand correctly the relationship between economy and technological change. Techno-economic paradigms allow for generalizing and contextualizing the process of technological changes, which is usually characterized by high dynamism and pervasiveness. Those pervasive effects are visible throughout the economy and society, and become even more identifiable and quantifiable as new technologies diffuse countrywide. In works from Perez (1983, 2002, 2003, 2004), it is widely acknowledged that the concept of techno-economic paradigm goes far beyond the purely technical perception of technological changes, but rather it emphasizes the fact that technology reshapes economic systems, economic and social structures and norms and attitudes. In this respect, Green et al. (1999) consider the embodiment of the quantum leap in potential productivity as a major feature of the techno-economic paradigm concept.

Broadly perceived, the techno-economic paradigm unveils the interactions between technological change and socio-economic development. The techno-economic paradigm is a

> set of best practice principles for efficiency (. . .) applicable to all (. . .) industries and serving to overcome maturity and increase productivity across the whole economy through more efficient equipment, better organizational models and much wider market reach.
>
> (Perez, 2009b, p. 781)

The techno-economic paradigm is '*a quantum jump in potential productivity*' and '*an overarching logic for the technology system of a period*' (Perez, 2004, p. 229).

The key to building solid foundations to understand the concept of techno-economic paradigms is to know the way they arise and how the techno-economic systems are shaped and evolve along time path. Therefore, we account for the origins of Schumpeter's thoughts, which locate the technological change in the centre of modern economic growth theory (Schumpeter, 1934, 1939). Surprisingly, Schumpeter in his seminar works, claimed technology—similarly to institution—to be an exogenous factor of economic growth and development. Technological change, however, was then endogenized by the neo-Schumpeterian school of economic thought, which proclaimed that technological change should be rather seen as an endogenous factor determining economic growth and development (Magnusson, 1994; Hanusch & Pyka, 2007). The neo-Schumpeterian economy recognizes economic development as an innovation-driven, dynamic process, where both qualitative and quantitative transformations are basically enforced by technological change. Not surprisingly, Hanusch and Pyka (2007), state '*Innovation plays a similar role in Neo-Schumpeterian Economics like prices do in Neoclassical Economics*' (Hanusch & Pyka, 2007, p. 1).

The technological change is not purely technical (engineering) phenomenon, but it is rather involved in complex socio-economic systems. Also, it is important to note, new technological solutions do not emerge randomly or in isolation from other, already existing, technologies; they are path dependent and emerge in specific social, institutional and economic environments. Comprehensive understanding of the rhythm of technological change as a time-related and socio-economically contextualized process is essential to exploring the concept of the techno-economic paradigm fully.

Technological change is strongly dependent on the emergence of innovations. As has been already emphasized, the rise of innovations is not a random process, but it is shaped and predetermined by the whole context including institutional and economic environment, legal regulations, social norms and social attitudes towards innovations and, even more importantly, already existing technological solutions. All these create a set of interactions, expressing the relationships between technology, society and economy, which have been labeled by Schumpeter (1939) as '*clusters*', while Freeman (1982, 1992), and also repeated in Freeman and Soete (1997), claims that his type of interconnectedness creates a '*technology system*'. New '*technology systems*', once they appear in the 'techno-economic space', demonstrate strong and long-term impacts on ways of doing business that shape individual countries' social and economic contours. The initial concept of the 'technology system' has been broadened and conceptualized in the works of Freeman (1987, 1995) and Lundvall (1988, 2007) as a 'national system of innovation'.[8] Lundvall (2007) proposes to define the 'national system of innovation' in revolutionary terms, as he claims that this concept would allow the identification of systems that create '*diversity, reproduce routines and select firms, products and routines*' (Lundvall, 2007, p. 14). In the same vein, Lundvall and Johnson (1994) claim that the national system of innovation' transforms production structure, technology and institutions, and thus generates significant externalities and competitive advantages for all agents in a given economy.

Similarly, as particular innovations gradually form systems of innovation, the national systems of innovations interconnect into one system and give rise to the emergence of technological revolutions. In this vein, Perez (2009b) writes, '*On first approximation a technological revolution can be defined as a set of interrelated radical breakthroughs, forming a major constellation of interdependent technologies*' (Perez, 2009b, p. 5). The emergence of the technological revolution is enforced when radical innovations[9] are introduced; henceforth, these innovations diffuse and overwhelm the society and economy. Radical innovations do not actually fit already installed institutional, organizational and economic systems, for they reshape them, initiate a new technological course and are embodied in a truly new product and/or process. Radical innovations may emerge at any point in time; they usually substitute the 'old' technology and initiate the birth of new industry in an economy. Grinin and Korotayev (2015) consider the Industrial Revolution as '*a process of active development of technology, especially designed to save labor in different areas*' (Grinin & Korotayev, 2015, p. 52). Undeniably, technological revolution gives a positive impulse to wealth creation economy-wide; it provides a wide array of novel infrastructure and allows for organizational improvements, thus enforcing productivity shifts. Technological breakthroughs not only bring purely technically new solutions to society and economy, meaning that their influence is not purely technological, but also introduce innovations on organizational grounds and then induce significant social, economic and institutional changes. Once a technological revolution appears, it is gradually assimilated in the economy and social system, which generates great surges of development and these are then followed by transformations and modifications in social, institutional and economic spheres of life. Technological revolutions diffuse; they expand across societies and economies and, hence, generate the '*great surges of development*' (Perez, 2002). 'Each (. . .) revolution has driven *a great surge of development* that takes a half of century or more to spread unevenly across the economy' (Pereze, 2004b, p. 21). Each *great surge of development*, as a time-related process, unveils certain regularities, and it encompasses two consecutive periods (phases): the *installation* period and *deployment* period. The initial (*installation*) phase is sometimes compared to the Schumpeterian 'creative destruction', which means nothing more than the fight of new ideas (technologies) against the old concepts (technologies). Schumpeter writes, '*The process of industrial mutation (. . .) that incessantly revolutionizes the economic structure from within, incessantly destroying the old one, incessantly creating a new one*' (Schumpeter, 1943, p. 83). To some extent, the period of *installation* is an experimental period, during which new technologies try to evade the market and are either accepted or rejected by socio-economic systems. These times of creative destruction are extremely turbulent and marked by periods of instability, during which the old regimes are being gradually eliminated from the market, while the new regimes and technological solutions abruptly irrupt and pervasively evade existing social, organizational, financial and institutional frameworks. The *installation* period is additionally marked by fast diffusion of innovations, and, hence, they are assimilated and then adopted by a constantly growing number of new users. During the *installation* phase, new industrial, new modes of production and infrastructure, new ways of doing business or even new products and inputs are widely articulated. The *installation* period sets up a new common sense (Perez, 2014) across the society and economy, and this period often generates huge inequalities among countries. In other words, the world becomes more differentiated and polarized because of sequentially emerging technological revolutions. The *installation* period is then followed by the *deployment* phase, which historians also label the 'golden age'. The deployment period is a prosperous epoch, unleashing extensively the impact of installed countrywide innovations during the installation phase. The deployment phase is also a period during which the gains and benefits offered by the new socio-economic paradigm are fully unveiled, and when, at least to some extent, huge inequalities (within and among countries) are reduced. Also, during this phase, significant productivity increases are noted, and thus it may be claimed that the full potential of certain technological revolutions have converted into growth of peoples' wealth. The growth of wealth is thus enhanced by technological revolutions, during which there have been 'installed' and assimilated innovations within social, economic and institutional frameworks.

Great Technological Surges

> Since man first forged metal tools and started farming for his food, thus emerging from the stone age, no event in human history has had a greater impact than the Industrial Revolution of the eighteenth and nineteenth century.
>
> Grinin and Korotayev (2015)

> The Industrial Revolution remains one of the history's greatest mysteries.
>
> Gregory Clark (2003)

A clear implication of understanding the issues involved in both technological and economic changes, as well as recognizing the causal-relationships between these two, is to take a brief look at the past great technological revolutions. This brief look at past technological surges provides an excellent knowledge of how and why technology, economy and society are interrelated, and also how new technologies and the diffusion of novel technological knowledge may reshape the way economies and societies are functioning. So far, the world has witnessed five technological revolutions, and each of these has radically restructured the global economy and societies.

Before the First Technological (Industrial) Revolution emerged, the world economy was relatively stagnant in terms of dynamism of economic growth and development. That is not to say that before 1800 economic growth did not occur, but the rates of growth were indecently low; the growth was rather spasmodic and easily reversible, and some even claim that it was nonexistent. According to estimates from Maddison (2001), in Western Europe, between the years 1000 and 1500, the average annual per capita growth of GDP was at about 0.13%, while between 1500 and 1820, it was 0.15%. But what yields even more attention is that the pre-industrial economies and societies were the zero-sum systems, meaning that the growth of wealth of one individual could occur *only* at the expense of someone else. Pre-industrial economies were locked in the Malthusian trap, and, hence, the growth of output could be generated exclusively by the increase of population, meaning that the growth of productivity was close to zero. In Malthusian societies, the increases in quality of life were barely detectable; the rate of economic progress was negligible, and people were living in permanent subsistence. Any kind of technological progress generated short-run benefits, but in the long term, all of these were lost because of the increasing population. Hence the Malthusian economy was rather paradoxical, as short-run productivity growths never led to long-term improvements in living standards. Until 1800, the average quality of life, approximated by personal income, was not higher than in 100,000 BC (Clark, 2003), which suggests that until the beginning of the19th century, the world did not change much in terms of income and economic growth. That is not to say that before the year 1800 no type of change occurred in the world economy, but those changes were neither profound nor sustainable enough to improve humans' welfare.

Surely, those pre-industrial societies still made some inventions which paved the road ahead. But the knowledge of those inventions was diffusing extremely slowly; henceforth, it was not the lack of inventions themselves which impeded the economic growth, but rather the lack of widespread knowledge of them and how to use them to enhance productivity shifts. Before the Industrial Revolution, knowledge was mainly tacit and poorly transmittable, and a huge part of discovered techniques was just a positive effect of experiments from trial and error. Those inventions were not systematic, but mostly random (Komlos, 2000; Mokyr, 2001). It was not an issue of the number of inventions, as it is obvious that they existed. Gilfillan in Mowery and Rosenberg (1991, p. 21) claims, '*Long and influential tradition in the history of technology stresses the crude, trial-and-error, hit-or-miss nature of technological progress*'. Those pre-modern societies developed a kind of '*culture of improvements*' (Friedel, 2007), developing quite a range of useful techniques but without actually understanding how and why they worked. To some extent, the pre-industrial technological development was informal, not codified and rarely transmitted among individuals.

However, bearing in mind the economic importance of inventions and the technological progress as such, the knowledge of how it works must be shared. Thus the critical issue is not the amount of inventions, but the diffusion of them, which preconditions how many society members find out about technological novelties and then assimilate and use them in everyday life. Pre-industrial socio-economic systems were not effective in terms of diffusing knowledge, and thus technological change was not widespread and poorly codified. Mokyr (2002), in his contributive book *The Gift of Athena*, which is repeated in Mokyr (2005b), writes,

> The short answer as to why the West is so much richer today than it was two centuries ago is that collectively (. . .) societies know more. (. . .) effective deployment of that knowledge (. . .) cause for a rapid growth of Western economies.
>
> (Mokyr, 2005b, p. 287)

Szirmai (2005) states that prior to the 20th century, technological inventions usually were not strictly based on scientific knowledge, but rather the development of multiple inventions was closely related to practical experience and experiments aiming to improve the way things were produced. He also raised one very interesting observation: Today, 21st- century technology is mostly related to scientific knowledge, and he claims, '*Technology stands halfway between science (abstract knowledge about fundamental laws and regularities of the natural environment) and production techniques (specific application of technology in products and processes, singular ways of doing particular things)*' (Szirmai, 2005, p. 132).

As already claimed, economic growth did not start at the beginning of the Industrial Revolution. It *did* exist before. However, the economic growth before this path-breaking revolution was of a different kind than the growth which is reported afterward. Before, economic growth differed both in terms of its quantity and quality. According to estimates (see Mokyr, 2001), between 1760 and 1830, the estimated rate of growth was at about 0.5% *per capita per annum*. That was not much, but it was not the rate of growth which was the problem. That pre-industrial growth, as it was not technology-led and productivity-based, was easily reversible, and the economic history was marked by short periods of growth which after a while tended to stagnate. That kind of growth was also mainly local, meaning limited to just a few areas (usually urban) and industries; it was also predominantly subjected to institutional and legal regulations, such as commercial relations, credits or other enforceable contracts (Greif, 2006). As argued by Mokyr (2001), and such views are also supported by Clark (1987, 2003), pre-industrial era (also labeled pre-modern) was subjected to *negative feedback*. By *feedback* he meant that the output of a system in time t_0 becomes automatically the input into the same system in time t_1, which generates productivity increases. But, unfortunately, in the epoch of pre-modern growth this *feedback* was *negative*, meaning that '*each time economic growth of any kind took place, its results after a while became negative inputs in that process and worked to slow it down and end it*' (Mokyr, 2001, p. 297).

Since the onset of the First Technological (Industrial) Revolution, the world has passed the periods of miraculous transformations. It all started in middle of the 18th century in England, and many point out the year 1760 as the critical period—as the breakthrough year. The period between 1765 and 1790 is called the 'years of miracles' (Mokyr, 1992) in terms of technological progress.[10] And despite the fact that the diffusion of those new inventions was relatively slow, and the golden ages of boosting productively were to come later, most important is that after 1790, the economic growth did not slow down, but it was maintained. That was the unique qualitative change that the First Industrial Revolution brought to the world economy and initiated the era of modern economic growth (Kuznets, 1973). Kuznets's theory of modern economic growth endogenized technology and started to treat it as the seminal determinant of economic growth, which is also generated by the economic system itself as a kind of response to market demand and forces that shape it. The view is also supported by Galor and Weil (2000, p. 809), who suggest, '*The event that separates Malthusian and post-Malthusian regimes is the acceleration of the pace of technological progress*'. In a similar vein, Clark proclaims, '*Around 1800, in northwestern Europe and North America, man's long journey in the Malthusian world ended. (. . .) A new era dawned*' (Clark, 2003, p. 193). He also uses a metaphor naming the Industrial Revolution as the '*materialist crossing of the Jordan*'.

Exact dating of the First Technological Wave is hardly possible, but by convention, the period between the 1770s and the 1830s to the 1840s is widely acknowledged as the time of this path-breaking event in economic history. Apparently, this revolution brought to economic life multiple fundamental changes, which irreversibly transformed the way that socio-economic systems function. The prime thing is that during the First Industrial Revolution, both micro- and macro-inventions were introduced, which changed the system of cottage production into a system of factory production (Freeman & Soete, 1997); henceforth, this period is also labeled the Early Mechanization. But this mechanization and switching from cottage to factory production was firstly unveiled in the textile sector. The mechanized cotton industry emerged where massive application of machinery was common and became a powerful way of generating far-reaching consequences not only of the economic type but also social, organizational and institutional. '*The cotton industry presented the most dramatic example of rapid transition from a traditional, loosely organized, geographically dispersed, putting-out system of production, (. . .) to (. . .) managed and centrally located factory system using large-scale machinery*' (Teich & Porter, 1996, p. 17). The cotton industry was no longer a hand-tool-dependent technology but became machinery dependent instead. However, those tremendous changes in England were not limited just to the revolution of the Spinning Jenny and the cotton/textile industry. During the First Industrial Revolution, there were also remarkable innovations in iron-producing techniques as well as the steam engine. These were seminal in terms of long-run progress of the English economy. Not only because they allowed for the mechanization of production but also these inventions enhanced the emergence of new industries. In England, there appeared canals and waterways, turnpike roads and water power (highly improved waterwheels), which were used in industries. In that sense, these inventions were disruptive, because they totally transformed the structure and, even more importantly, the potential of the new economy of England. It was a breakdown with medieval and feudal structures—guilds, associated monopolies and tolls—and the beginning of individual entrepreneurship and small-scale manufacturers (Grubler, 1994). From the very long-run perspective, the Industrial Revolution, however, was also important for a different reason. It was important because it gave birth to the first *networks*, which freed the movement of people, products, capital, information and knowledge.

However, these first achievements of the Industrial Revolution were limited to England (although some signs of it were also traceable in Belgium and France), and to a large extent, they did not diffuse worldwide. Still, the period of 1770–1830 was the era of slow growth, and the full potential of this revolution remained unleashed and was not demonstrated in national accounts and statistics. At the moment of the introduction of innovations, no radical impact on the economy and society at large was detected. According to various estimates, before the 1820s, the growth in England was modest at best (Williamson, 1984)—at about 0.33% per capita per annum. That was not very impressive, and, evidently, the growth of productivity and income enabled by the Industrial Revolution did not appear right after its arrival. English society had to 'wait' nearly 100 years to see the real gains in income and increasing living standards, which were enabled by the rise of this technological breakthrough. Still, in 1760, and several decades after, the English economy demonstrated relatively few signs of growth, but since the 1860s, a significant outburst in economic growth is noted, as the 'first wave' of innovations was then followed by the Second Technological Revolution—the period between the 1830s and the 1870s, when all knowledge and technology were finally unveiled in the statistics of the dynamics of economic growth. The times of significant economic speed up arrived, and hence the epoch of modern growth was there. This epoch is also labeled the 'Age of Steam and Railways', as steam engines and steam-powered railways predominantly enhanced countries' development. Those were also times of growing importance of railways, universal postal and telegraph services, great ports, great depots and international shipping. Henceforth, the various types of networks allowing for growing interconnectedness among individuals, but above all among enterprises, were expanding fast. Development of those networks was of seminal significance for economic expansion of England. One the one hand, a growing number of competing small firms determined the economic expansion of England; on the other hand, those were times of emergence of large companies with unprecedented size (Freeman & Soete, 1997). Iron and coal started to play a major role in the growth of industries and hence in dynamizing economic growth itself. According to Jones (2013) estimates, between 1830 and 1890, in Britain, the steam engine was doing the work of about 600 million people; while during this period, there were only four million employees. In 1861, in England, the share of population employed in agriculture dropped to 21%. The British economy was undergoing profound restructurization, and growth of productivity in industry and agriculture ensured the path of stable growth of personal income and shifted huge masses of English society from subsistence to better living. Those shifts of material well-being which occurred during the First and Second Technological Revolution were unprecedented, and never before had people benefited so much in such a short time.

Historians have labeled the period between the 1880s and 1908 as the Third Technological Revolution; it was the 'Age of Steel, Electricity and Heavy Engineering'. It was an epoch of the extensive use of cheap steel, copper and cables, paper and electrical equipment. Civil engineering and heavy chemistry were fast developing. It was also a time of further expansion of transportation and communication networks such as shipping and steel streaming (using the Suez Canal); expanding worldwide railways, bridges and tunnels; worldwide telegraph; national analog telephony; and, above all, electricity networks. The Third Technological Revolution was marked by expansion of giant companies, cartels and trusts. Mergers and acquisitions were common, and these monopolistic tendencies led to the rise of the first antitrust legal regulations. Next, the period between the beginning of the 20th century and the 1970s, was the Fourth Technological Revolution. It was the 'Age of Oil, the Automobile and Mass Production'. Ford plants, roads and highways and airports were in diffusion across Europe and the United States. It was also the time when the electricity network became commonly deployed in increasing numbers of homes. The world became overwhelmed by the expansion of the analog telephony, telegram and cablegram. Telecommunication networks, both wired and wireless, determined changes in modes of mass communication both within and between societies. During the first part of the 20th century, numerous multinationals emerged and foreign direct investment started to play a significant role in determining economic growth and development.

Needless to say, because of the achievements of the industrial revolutions since the 19th century onwards in England, economic growth was predominantly generated by small but highly productive investments in knowledge, which expanded throughout society members. For the first time in economic history, knowledge, and hence technology, was not exclusively tacit, but became more and more codified, which enhanced its diffusion among societies and induced gains in welfare because of shifting efficiency of the overall economy. Grinin and Korotayev (2015) describe the First Industrial Revolution as

> Profound revolution that transformed the continent with societies based on agriculture and with predominantly illiterate populations with high mortality and fertility into an urbanized industrial region densely

covered by railroads, telegraph and telephone lines; as a result of this revolution Europe transformed from a society of peasants and landowners into a society of (. . .) literate citizens with low mortality rates. (. . .) these societies were moving towards democratization, equal rights and the gradual rise of living standards.

(Grinin & Korotayev, 2015, p. 76)

Very importantly, growth was no longer dependent exclusively on population and land, but rather it started to be technology and productivity driven. As Clark remarked (2002, 2007), before 1800, the economic growth in England was effectively preconditioned by the land *per person*, and in 1760, the farmland rent constituted about 23% of the total national income. In 2000, it was just 0.2%. Land, as resource, did not dominate the 'growth equation' anymore. It was an enormous qualitative change. Looking at the industrial revolutions from the very long-run perspective, another interesting observation arises. Undeniably, this path-breaking event enforced the global economic '*take-off*', and since the beginning of 18th century, the world's gross output outbursts and starts to grow at an unprecedentedly high pace. Examining, even very superficially, historical economic statistics provided in Maddison (2007), it is quite evident that in terms of *per capita* income, the world grew enormously after the 17th century. In the year 1500, the average *per capita* income in the developed world was about 704 US$;[11] in 1700, 907; in 1820, 1,132; and in 1998, it reached 21,470, which shows that over barely 180 years, the average per capita income increased about 19 times (sic!). Despite the fact that the just cited numbers are at best rough approximations, they envisage the radical change in speed of economic growth compared to that encountered before the 18th century. Just to repeat—modern economic growth boosted thanks to the stock of knowledge accumulated during the 17th and 18th centuries, but also a century before. This rise of the Western world and the beginning of its preeminence worldwide reshaped the global economic countries. Such a change in the *tempo* of economic development had far-reaching consequences, and not only of the economic kind. The industrial revolutions contributed to the explosion of social and institutional development. Significant falls in infant mortality accompanied by rising life expectancies enforced the transformation of demographic structures, giving birth to the first demographic transition. Again, according to Maddison (2007), the statistics we see during the first part of the 18th century show the life expectancy was about 35 years, while the infant mortality rate was195 deaths per thousand. In 1999, life expectancy and the infant mortality rate were was approximately 77 and 6, respectively. These extensive changes are also reflected in the changing urbanization and the number of large cities. To compare, see, for instance, Bairoch et al. (1988) or Bairoch and Braider (1991). The impact of the Industrial Revolution may be additionally noticed through the changes in city life (i.e. growth in urbanization, but at the same time, there were increases in inequalities among rich and poor citizens; sudden growth of population living in cities; the emergence of slums), rural environments and transportation systems (i.e. toll roads, canals and railroads), working conditions (i.e. emergence of new types of jobs, but also highly paid jobs; increasing women's engagement in the formal labour market—but at substantially lower wages than men) and society as such (i.e. rise of middle class).

However, all that is gold does not glitter. The economic rise of the Western world in the 18th century undeniably reduced inequalities within societies, but increased inequalities between them. The developmental contrasts among countries were becoming more and more visible.[12] This phenomenon of growing cross-country income inequalities was called the Great Divergence and is extensively discussed in multiple research: see, inter alia, works of Allen (2001), Clark (2003), Ocampo et al. (2007), Williamson (2008), Pomeranz (2009) or, more recently, Antunes and Fatah-Black (2016) or Baten (2016). However, the story does not end there. Around the 1970s, there emerged the Fifth Technological Wave—the ICT Revolution.

Fifth Technological Wave—ICT Revolution

The Fifth Technological Revolution, which emerged in 1971 when the first microprocessor was developed by Intel and saw daylight in Santa Clara in California, gave rise to the new techno-economic paradigm, within which we observe path-breaking inventions and radical restructuration of economic life. The Fifth Technological Revolution, also called the ICT Revolution or the ge of Information and Communications', changed the way people communicate and interact, and thus changed societies. ICT are mainly digital technologies, as they allow for converting the real-world information and knowledge into binary numeric systems (forms). Introduction of ICT also meant gradual switching from analog to digital technologies (Toumazou & Hughes, 1993). Since the second half of the 20th century, the world has witnessed the gradual installation of a new backbone infrastructure, such as cable, fibre optics, radio, satellites, multiple-source and flexible-use electricity networks and high-speed physical transport links. It has also witnessed broad dissemination of new or redefined industries, offering, inter alia, cheap microprocessors, computers and software, telecommunications or computer-aided biotechnology and new materials, which facilitate unbounded flows of information and knowledge at extremely low costs, even among physically separated agents. The Fifth Technological Revolution offered to people totally new modes of communication, generating the rise of new kinds of societal and economic networks. These changes are profound and undoubtedly revolutionary.

To some extent, the Fifth Technological Revolution shares at least two distinctive features with past technological revolutions (Castaldi & Dosi, 2007). First, it introduced technologies, which are pervasive and cutting edge and thus led to profound shifts in societies and economies. Second, the newly established techno-economic regime enforces organizational, legal and institutional changes. However, the ICT Revolution is also very different from its predecessors. Throughout the ages, the tempo of diffusion of technological change and technological novelties was incomparably lower than it is observed worldwide with regard to ICT (Comin et al., 2006). ICT are diffusing worldwide at an unprecedented rate, and even economically backward countries have not been omitted by the *ICT tornado*. Undeniably, ICT may be claimed as the prime enabler of globalization, as it allows for unbounded flows of information and knowledge. The physical distance between agents does not hinder contacts. ICT enables social and economic interactions without physical contact—for example, face-to-face contacts are no longer necessary. By definition, ICT have brought socio-economic transformation, thus allowing people to communicate free from spatial and temporal contexts.

ICT are complex in nature and may have various applications, and thus they may be viewed and defined differently. In this vein, it may be claimed that ICT are intended to use the electronic processing of information, communication and transmission of data. Hargittai (1999) perceives the ICT mainly through the lens of the Internet network, arguing that these types of ICT allow for the emergence of global networks; the retrieval and dissemination of all kinds of knowledge and information are also of seminal importance from the societal point of view. She claims that the Internet determines the rise of the unique network of people, who become not only connected but also inter-dependent. The World Bank (Rodriguez & Wilson, 2000) defines ICT as '*set[s] of activities which facilitate by electronic means the processing, transmission and display of information*'. In a similar vein, Marcelle (2000) argues that ICT may be claimed as unique sets of goods, applications and services, which are used to produce, process and transmit all types of information and knowledge throughout societies and economies. Kiiski and Pohjola (2002) underline the unique feature of ICT that enabled unbounded and massive flows of information worldwide, but they also stress that the ICT networks facilitate market interactions between physically separated agents. According to the UNESCO (2002) definition, ICT are a combination of informatics technology with other technologies—especially communication technologies. The previous definition implies that ICT combine technological applications of informatics society-wide and the whole stock of hardware and software which are designed to process information within organizational and other human aspects, which has far-reaching economic (i.e. commercial or industrial), social, political and institutional implications. Broadly defined, the ICT encompass all equipment and services which are related to broadcasting, computing and telecommunications, and all equipment that allows capturing and displaying information electronically (UN, 2004). ICT enable information processing and communication by electronic means. International Telecommunication Union (ITU) defines ICT as '*technologies and equipment that handle (e.g., access, create, collect,* store, transmit, receive, disseminate) information and communication' (ITU, 2014). ICT are technologies supporting a wide variety of information-related activities, and these activities positively contribute to the development of communication channels; even more important, because of ICT, communication may occur in real time, even across long distances. Freeman and Louçã (2001) and Pérez (2010) emphasize that all changes introduced within the new techno-economic paradigm (ICT paradigm) have been triggered by an innovation with a social- and economy-wide impact. The inventions of the Fifth Technological Revolution—digital technologies, enhanced methods for codifying data and, thus, knowledge and all sorts of information—became easily and quickly distributable and transmittable. In other words, the newly emerged technology system—ICT—allowed for the converging of four basic operations—namely, reproduction of data from one format to another, fast transmission of data, computation and storage without data loss.

Along with the onset of the Digital Revolution, multiple radical innovations involving the application of novel technologies, or combination of them, were introduced to society and the economy, thus paving the road ahead. The rise of new products, new services, new industries or business models and new types of networks have generated disruptive effects in the whole socio-economic systems. ICT are, undeniably, 'pioneering technologies' leading to technological breakthroughs. ICT are totally *disruptive* new technologies, and, henceforth, they deliver transformational change to the markets. ICT 'shake-up' the whole economy; they bring a bundle of different values that were unavailable before. They modify the economic landscape. ICT produce cross-cutting effects in all sectors of the economy, and thus they are *pervasive* (ubiquitous). Pervasive technologies (ICT) are permanently available and network connected; they enrich interactions among entities, and they provide effectiveness, efficiency and empowerment.

Because of their disruptiveness and pervasiveness, ICT produce cross-cutting effects in all sectors of the economy, and thus ICT may be claimed General Purpose Technologies (GPTs hereafter). Bresnahan and Trajtenberg (1995) define General Purpose Technologies as technologies which are pervasive, possess huge potential economy-wide and technical improvement, and as GPTs evade socio-economic systems, they bring long-term productivity gains (Jovanovic & Rousseau, 2005). As GPTs spread across economies and societies, they change not only the structure of the economy but also enforce higher development dynamics. GPTs are also characterized by their technological dynamism (Bresnahan & Trajtenberg, 1995), meaning that continuous innovation efforts are made, thus increasing their in-time efficiency. GPTs are 'prime-movers' of the economy; they produce positive externalities and welfare if their diffusion is not restricted by an institutional framework or low-absorptive capabilities of economic agents. GPTs pave the road ahead and open up new opportunities: '*As GPTs appear (. . .) there is a spell, a growth, with rising output, real wages, and profits*' (Helpman & Trajtenber, 1996, p. 4).

ICT are unique technologies for several reasons. ICT are easily installable and quickly distributable among society members; they spread worldwide even in geographically remote and underserved regions. As ICT diffuse across space, they 'go beyond geography'. Cairncross (2001) writes about the 'death of distance' and claims that because of the widespread use of this new type of technology, communication and market activities have become distance-free. This 'death of distance' is one of the greatest manifestations of this rapid and astonishing change that takes place now across the world. *'Wireless communication (. . .) is killing location, putting the world in our pocket'* (Cairncross, 2001, p. 2). ICT may be easily acquired at very low prices, and hence even low-income societies are not excluded from this type of technology. Although the fact that in some countries the cost of using more sophisticated technologies still remains high, most ICT tools are accessed and used at very low prices, which makes them affordable for people living in permanent material deprivation. What is of even more importance is the marginal cost of an additional user of ICT tools is close to zero, which is why the growth of the number of users does not require any additional investment in hard infrastructure. ICT are easily imitable and deliverable (Lechman, 2015); to use and benefit from ICT, not much knowledge is needed from the final consumer; henceforth, they are rapidly adaptable by low-skilled, poorly educated or even illiterate people. Many claim that ICT are *'for all'* because they diffuse by omitting multiple barriers—financial, societal, linguistic, educational and geographical. To some extent, it might be even claimed that only institutional constraints may hinder wide spread of ICT. Compared to 'old' technologies offered in the past four technological revolutions, ICT have certain advantages. Above all, ICT enforce the emergence of worldwide network linking physically separated agents (Valente, 1996; Castells et al. 2009), and so modern economic development is driven by economies of networks (Shapiro & Varian, 1999). Katz and Shapiro (1985) and Economides (1996) underline the seminal importance of the *'network effects'*, which, first, demonstrate the potential of increasing connectivity, and, second, unveil growing utility of certain networks as the number of user's shifts. Next, as already discussed, ICT free people and market activities from physical location and thus enhance the growth of economic activities among previously marginalized and peripheral regions. The latter, if accompanied by massive flows of information, provides solid fundaments for increasing economic activity, economic inclusion and productivity shifts.

ICT do not exist in isolation, but rather they are installed, adapted and used in certain social, economic and, above all, institutional and political contexts. However, it is widely acknowledged that ICT may be the prime engines of development and may fundamentally reshape and restructure industries, ways of doing business and working methods. They offer broad, effective, cheap and timely information and knowledge sharing, as well as multiple generic advantages. ICT may work in support of networking, communicating with isolated agents, building people's interactivity and increasing interdependency of actors.

Led by general intuition, we claim existence of causal chains between levels of ICT adopted and countries' abilities to enter the pattern of long-term economic development, which in consequence would allow them to catch up with the best-performing economies. We assume that ICT, because of their unique features such as the ability to spread among countries at a high pace and at low cost, requiring minimal skills for usage, provide a solid background for gains creation. On the country level, such gains are accounted as GDP per capita growth going along with the country's ability to diminish the economic development gap between low- and high-developed economies. Using ICT as catalyzing factors for growth might play a critical role in developing and economically backward countries. The near-ubiquitous spread of ICT offers unprecedented opportunities for low-income countries to take off on the development path, mainly by deploying ICT tools for effective economic reforms. ICT can play a critical role in development processes by broadening access to information and all kinds of knowledge, which results in the improvement of people's empowerments and participation in socio-economic life. New technologies enable a significant reduction in high information asymmetries. Reduction in such asymmetries improves access to economic activities for multitudes of agents, thus fostering participation, inter alias, in the labour market of previously disadvantaged societal groups. Wide adoption of ICT helps to overcome intensive constraints to growth that developing counties may experience. The significant impact of ICT on economy in developing countries might be enabled by the creation of positive links between market agents, thus providing opportunities for more flexible work and providing new contacts, which—in effect—results in rising economic activities with potential increases in productivity, firm efficiency or cost reduction. In this vein, ICT bring to developing markets new business models, disruptive innovations, capital-labour substitution and improved goods and services. These account for the growing competitiveness of low- and lower-middle-income countries in the globalized market by offering them new markets or simply enlarging those already in existence. The full potential of new technologies can be easily unleashed when deploying them as economic development accelerators in least-developed countries. The complexity of development goals that these countries have to deal with requires adoption of adequate tools, and as stated by many, ICT are perceived as such. Least-developed countries permanently will lack financial resources, good infrastructure, free and easily access to educational and health-care systems, sound governments and remain in poverty traps unless a breakthrough-like explosion of ICT occurs.

Now ICT deployment is receiving growing attention. By many, ICT are simply perceived as tools (enablers) which foster economic growth and development. Arguably, new ICT bring to developing countries opportunities to fight rural and urban poverty by improving economic performance and the ability to compete in global markets; they provide a means for exploiting an unused labour force and increasing social capital. At the same time, new ICT create better ways for information flows, which open new possibilities for economic cooperation on a larger scale. The nexus between new technologies and achievements of certain 'development goals' is recognized, and it is based on mutually shared objectives, which are efficient, scalable and affordable, as well as a pervasive delivery of goods, services and information flows between people, government and firms. ICT bring to developing countries wide opportunities. These are not always captured in GDP statistics, and exploration of links between technology adoption (diffusion) and economic development might not be straightforward. The impact of ICT on economic activities is neither automatic nor homogenous across countries; it is conditioned by a bundle of factors which are often of the qualitative kind. These might be religions, social structures, traditions and many others. Even though their influence might not be direct or clearly visibly, they might constitute significant constraints for effective usage of ICT. Also, we observe a kind of 'delay' in the detection of the impact of new technologies on economic development. Positive effects of ICT usage, encompassing, inter alia, the rise of productivity may be identifiable with considerable time lags. These lags are accounted as the 'delay hypothesis' (David, 1990), which reflects the time needed for adoption of new technologies along with acquiring enough skills for their effective usage. Arguably, the full potential of new technologies in boosting economic growth might be revealed rather in the long-run perspective, while the evidence exhibited in the short run can be somehow misleading and not very conclusive.

Between the 12th and 18th centuries, the process of the gradual rise of the Western world occurred, and the First Industrial Revolution broke the economic hegemony of Asia. The upswing of the West and the rise of modern economic growth in the 17th and 18th centuries have reshaped the contours of the world economy permanently. Everything changed. A new order was established. Unexpectedly, the First Industrial Revolution caused the Global Divergence. The West started forging ahead, while the rest fell behind. However, the Fifth Technological Revolution allowed for the emergence of the Global Convergence, thus weakening the core and strengthening the economic peripheries. The ICT Revolution may encourage the rise of the rest and potentially diminish enormous development and technological divides.

Notes

1. Freeman and Pérez (1988) distinguish four types of technological change: incremental innovations, which usually encompass small-scale and progressive modifications of already existing products; radical innovations, which drastically and abruptly transform already existing products and process; changes of the technology system, which occurs when, because of technological changes, extensive transformations of the production process are reported, often leading to

the emergence of a new sector in a national economy; and, finally, changes in the techno-economic paradigm, which encompass totally revolutionary changes both on the ground of technology itself and in the entire economic system.

2. For broader discussion on Industrial Revolution, see Sect. 2.3.
3. The author's estimates are based on data derived from PWT 8.1 (accessed September 2016). See also for methodological aspects and world regions classification.
4. Western Europe and Western Offshoots.
5. Kuhn's work on defining and perceiving the paradigms, although influential, was initially criticized as being adaptable exclusively on the grounds of natural science and having relatively little relevance to social science. However, practically, the Kuhnian concept of paradigms has been extensively used on the grounds of social science, especially sociology and economy. See, for instance, works of Blaug (1975), Folbre (1986), Ramstad (1989), Argyrous (1992), Feiner and Roberts (1995), Palley (2005) or Coates (2005), just to cite few.
6. In the work of Nelson and Winter (1982), we find the term 'technological regime', which coincides with the Dosi's 'technological paradigm'.
7. Technological trajectories are defined as a pattern of problem solving within certain technological paradigms (Dosi, 1982). Dosi (1988) also defines the technological trajectory, initially proposed in work of Nelson and Winter (1977), which he understands as the development along the specific paths of actual technological paradigms. Put differently, technological trajectory indicates the direction of development along given technological paradigms. Broadly perceived, technological paradigms as technological trajectories are closely interrelated and indicate the direction of the technological change. Technological trajectories are also labeled 'technological regimes' or 'natural trajectories' (Nelson & Winter, 2009), 'technological guideposts' (Sahal, 1981), 'dominant designs' (Utterback, 1978) or 'technological corridors' (Georghiou et al., 1986).
8. The concept of the 'national system of innovation' has been modified and adjusted to the needs of regional studies. The developed notion of thee 'regional/sectoral system of innovation' may be traced in works of, for instance, Cooke et al. (1997), Arocena and Sutz (2000), Cooke (2002), Malerba (2002).
9. By contrast, incremental innovations are basically improvements and adjustments to already existing products and/or process. Although incremental innovations do generate productivity shifts and thus contribute positively to economic growth, they do not enhance such radical and revolutionary changes as radical innovations do.
10. Historically, it is important to bear in mind the fact that the rise of the First Technological Revolution was not sudden and unexpected. Clark (2007) underlines that the First Technological Revolution was an evolutionary process. To some extent, the First Industrial Revolution was a continuation of the process of multiple inventions which began in 15th and 16th centuries in Europe, but also in numerous scientific breakthroughs in mathematics, astronomy and cartography, just to cite few, between the 11th and 15th centuries (see, for instance, Singer, 1941; Braudel, 1973; Lilley, 1973). By some scholars, the period between 11th and 16th centuries is labeled the Early Industrial Revolution (see, for instance, Cipolla, 1973; Pawson, 1979; Faler, 1981).
11. International dollars in 1990.
12. According to Maddison (2007), in the developer world in 1700, the average per capita income was at about 907 US$; in 1820, 1,130; and in 1998, 21,470. To compare analogously in undeveloped world, in 1700 it was 551; in 1820, 573; and in 1998, 3,102. Thus in 1700, the developed/undeveloped world ratio was 1.65; in 1820, 1.97; but in 1998, 6.92 (sic!).

References

Abramovitz, M. (1986). Catching up, forging ahead, and falling behind. *The Journal of Economic History, 46*(2), 385–406.

Abramowitz, A. I. (1994). Issue evolution reconsidered: Racial attitudes and partisanship in the US electorate. *American Journal of Political Science*, 1–24.

Acemoglu, D., & Robinson, J. (2012). Why nations fail: The origins of power, prosperity, and poverty. Crown Business.

Aghion, P., & Howitt, P. (1992). A model of growth through creative destruction. *Econometrica, 60*(March), 323–351.

Allen, R. C. (2001). The great divergence in European wages and prices from the Middle Ages to the First World War. *Explorations in Economic History, 38*(4), 411–447.

Ames, E., & Rosenberg, N. (1963). Changing technological leadership and industrial growth. *The Economic Journal, 73*(289), 13–31.

Antunes, C., & Fatah-Black, K. (Eds.). (2016). *Explorations in history and globalization*. Routledge.

Argyrous, G. (1992). Kuhn's paradigms and neoclassical economics. *Economics and Philosophy, 8*(2), 231–248.

Arocena, R., & Sutz, J. (2000). Looking at national systems of innovation from the South. *Industry and Innovation, 7*(1), 55–75.

Arrow, K. (1962). Economic welfare and the allocation of resources for invention. In *The rate and direction of inventive activity: Economic and social factors* (pp. 609–626). Princeton: Princeton University Press.

Bairoch, P., Batou, J., & Chevre, P. (1988). The population of European cities: Data bank and short summary of results. *Librairie Droz, Geneva*.

Bairoch, P., & Braider, C. (1991). *Cities and economic development: From the dawn of history to the present*. Chicago: University of Chicago Press.

Baten, J. (Ed.). (2016). *A history of the global economy*. Cambridge: Cambridge University Press.

Baumol, W. J. (1986). Productivity growth, convergence, and welfare: What the long-run data show. *American Economic Review, 76*, 1072–1084.

Baumol, W. J. (1989). Reflections on modern economics: Review. *Cambridge Journal of Economics* (Oxford University Press), *13*(2), 353–358.

Bijker, W. E. (1995). Sociohistorical technology studies. In S. Jasanoff, G. Markle, J. Peterson & T. Pinch (Eds.), *Handbook of science and technology studies*. Cambridge, MA: MIT Press.

Bijker, W. E., Hughes, T. P., Pinch, T., & Douglas, D. G. (2012). *The social construction of technological systems: New directions in the sociology and history of technology*. Cambridge, MA: MIT Press.

Blaug, M. (1975). Kuhn versus Lakatos, or paradigms versus research programmes in the history of economics. *History of Political Economy, 7*(4), 399–433.

Braudel, F. (1973). *Capitalism and material life, 1400–1800* (Vol. 1). HarperCollins.

Bresnahan, T. F., & Trajtenberg, M. (1995). General purpose technologies 'Engines of growth'?. *Journal of Econometrics, 65*(1), 83–108.

Cairncross, F. (2001). The death of distance: How the communications revolution is changing our lives. Harvard Business Press.

Cameron, R. E., & Neal, L. (2010). Historia gospodarcza świata: od paleolitu do czasów najnowszych. Książka i Wiedza.

Campbell, P. J., MacKinnon, A., & Stevens, C. R. (2010). *An introduction to global studies*. John Wiley & Sons.

Castaldi, C., & Dosi, G. (2007). Technical change and economic growth: Some lessons from secular patterns and some conjectures on the current impact of ICT technologies. documento presentado en el seminario "Crecimiento, productividad y tecnologías de la información"(CEPAL, Santiago de Chile, marzo).

Cimoli, M., & Dosi, G. (1995). Technological paradigms, patterns of learning and development: An introductory roadmap. *Journal of Evolutionary Economics*, 5(3), 243–268.

Cipolla, C. M. (Ed.). (1973). The Fontana economic history of Europe: The industrial revolution (Vol. 3). Collins/Fontana.

Clark, G. (1987). Why isn't the whole world developed? Lessons from the cotton mills. *The Journal of Economic History*, 47(01), 141–173.

Clark, G. (2002). Land rental values and the agrarian economy: England and Wales, 1500–1914. *European Review of Economic History*, 6(3), 281–308.

Clark, G. (2003). *The great escape: The industrial revolution in theory and history*. University of California, Davis, Working Paper, September.

Clark, G. (2007). The long march of history: Farm wages, population, and economic growth, England 1209–18691. *The Economic History Review*, 60(1), 97–135.

Clark, G. L., Gertler, M. S., & Feldman, M. P. (2003). *The Oxford handbook of economic geography*. Oxford: Oxford University Press.

Coates, D. (Ed.). (2005). *Varieties of capitalism, varieties of approaches* (pp. 1–25). New York: Palgrave Macmillan.

Comin, D., Easterly, W., & Gong, E. (2010). Was the wealth of nations determined in 1000 BC?. *American Economic Journal: Macroeconomics*, 2(3), 65–97.

Comin, D., Hobijn, B., & Rovito, E. (2006). *Five facts you need to know about technology diffusion* (No. w11928). National Bureau of Economic Research.

Cooke, P. (2002). Regional innovation systems. *The Journal of Technology Transfer*, 27(1), 133–145.

Cooke, P., Uranga, M. G., & Etxebarria, G. (1997). Regional innovation systems: Institutional and organisational dimensions. *Research Policy*, 26(4), 475–491.

Cowan, R., David, P. A., & Foray, D. (2000). The explicit economics of knowledge codification and tacitness. *Industrial and Corporate Change*, 9(2), 211–253.

David, P. A. (1990). The dynamo and the computer: An historical perspective on the modern productivity paradox. *The American Economic Review*, 80(2), 355–361.

Deng, Y. (2011). *Ancient Chinese inventions*. Cambridge: Cambridge University Press.

Diamond, J. (1999). Guns, germs, and steel: The fates of human societies. WW Norton & Company.

Dicken, P. (2007). Global shift: Mapping the changing contours of the world economy. SAGE Publications.

Dosi, G. (1982). Technological paradigms and technological trajectories: A suggested interpretation of the determinants and directions of technical change. *Research Policy*, 11(3), 147–162.

Dosi, G. (1988). Sources, procedures, and microeconomic effects of innovation. *Journal of economic literature*, 1120–1171.

Dosi, G. Freeman, C., Nelson, R., Silverberg, G., & Soete, L. (Eds.). 1988. *Technical change and economic theory*. London: Francis Pinter and New York: Columbia University Press.

Dosi, G., & Malerba, F. (1996). Organizational learning and institutional embeddedness. *Organization and Strategy in the Evolution of the Enterprise*, 1–24.

Dosi, G., Malerba, F., & Orsenigo, L. (1994). Evolutionary regimes and industrial dynamics. *Evolutionary and neo-Schumpeterian approaches to economics*, 203–229.

Dosi, G., Teece, D. J., & Chytry, J. (1998). Technology, organization, and competitiveness: perspectives on industrial and corporate change. Oxford University Press.

Economides, N. (1996). The economics of networks. *International Journal of Industrial Organization*, *14*(6), 673–699.

Evenson, R. E., & Westphal, L. E. (1995). Technological change and technology strategy. *Handbook of Development Economics*, *3*, 2209–2299.

Fagerberg, J., & Srholec, M. (2008). National innovation systems, capabilities and economic development. *Research Policy*, *37*(9), 1417–1435.

Fagerberg, J., & Srholec, M. (2013). Knowledge, capabilities and the poverty trap: The complex interplay between technological, social and geographical factors. *Knowledge and the Economy*, *5*, 113–137.

Fagerberg, J., Srholec, M., & Verspagen, B. (2010). Innovation and economic development. In *Handbook of the economics of innovation* (Vol. 1, pp. 833–872). Elsevier.

Faler, P. G. (1981). Mechanics and manufacturers in the early industrial revolution: Lynn, Massachusetts 1780–1860. SUNY Press.

Feiner, S., & Roberts, B. (1995). Using alternative paradigms to teach about race and gender: A critical thinking approach to introductory economics. *The American Economic Review*, *85*(2), 367–371.

Finley, M. I. (1999). *The ancient economy*. Berkeley, CA: University of California Press.

Folbre, N. (1986). Hearts and spades: Paradigms of household economics. *World Development*, *14*(2), 245–255.

Freeman, C. (1982). *The economics of industrial innovation*. University of Illinois at Urbana-Champaign's Academy for Entrepreneurial Leadership Historical Research Reference in Entrepreneurship.

Freeman, C. (1987). Technology policy and economic policy: Lessons from Japan. London: Frances Pinter.

Freeman, C. (1992). The economics of hope: Essays on technical change and economic growth. London: Frances Pinter.

Freeman, C. (1995). Innovation, changes of techno-economic paradigm and biological analogies in economics. *Revue économique*, *42*(2), 211–231.

Freeman, C., & Louçã, F. (2001). As time goes by: The information revolution and the industrial revolutions in historical perspective. Oxford: Oxford University Press.

Freeman, C., & Perez, C. (1986). *The diffusion of technical innovations and changes of techno-economic paradigm*. Science Policy Research Unit University of Sussex.

Freeman, C., & Perez, C. (1988). Structural crises and adjustments. In G. Dosi, C. Freeman, R. Nelson, G. Silverberg & L. Soet (Eds.), *Technical change and economic theory* (pp. 38–66). London: Pinter.

Freeman, C., & Soete, L. (1997). *The economics of industrial innovation*. Psychology Press.

Friedel, R. D. (2007). A culture of improvement: Technology and the Western millennium. Cambridge, MA: The MIT Press.

Galor, O., & Weil, D. N. (2000). Population, technology, and growth: From Malthusian stagnation to the demographic transition and beyond. *American Economic Review*, 806–828.

Georghiou, L., Metcalfe, J. S., Evans, J., Ray, T., & Gibbons, M. (1986). *Post-innovation performance*. London: McMillan.

Gerschenkron, A. (1962). *Economic backwardness in historical perspective: A book of essays* (No. HC335 G386). Cambridge, MA: Belknap Press of Harvard University Press.

Gibbons, M., & Johnston, R. (1974). The roles of science in technological innovation. *Research Policy*, 3(3), 220–242.

Gopal, L. (1961). Textiles in ancient India. *Journal of the Economic and Social History of the Orient*, 4(1), 53–69.

Green, K., Hull, R., McMeekin, A., & Walsh, V. (1999). The construction of the techno-economic: Networks vs. paradigms. *Research Policy*, 28(7), 777–792.

Greene, K. (2000). Technological innovation and economic progress in the ancient world: MI Finley re-considered. *The Economic History Review*, 53(1), 29–59.

Greif, A. (2006). Institutions and the path to the modern economy: Lessons from medieval trade. Cambridge: Cambridge University Press.

Grinin, L., & Korotayev, A. (2015). Great divergence and great convergence: A global perspective. Springer.

Grossman, G. M. & Helpman, E. (1991). *Innovation and growth in the global economy*. Cambridge: MIT Press.

Grubler, A. (1994). Industrialization as a historical phenomenon. In *Industrial ecology and global change* (pp. 43–68).

Håkanson, L., & Nobel, R. (2000). Technology characteristics and reverse technology transfer. *MIR: Management International Review*, 41(4), 395–420.

Hanusch, H., & Pyka, A. (2007). Principles of neo-Schumpeterian economics. *Cambridge Journal of Economics*, 31(2), 275–289.

Hargittai, E. (1999). Weaving the Western Web: Explaining differences in Internet connectivity among OECD countries. *Telecommunications Policy*, 23(10), 701–718.

Helpman, E., & Trajtenberg, M. (1996). *Diffusion of general purpose technologies* (No. w5773). National Bureau of Economic Research.

Hobsbawm, E. (2010). *Age of revolution: 1789–1848*. UK: Hachette.

ITU. (2014). World Telecommunication Development Conference 2014, Document WTDC14/4-F, ITU, 2014.

Johnston, R. D. (1970). The internal structure of technology. *The Sociological Review*, 18(S1), 117–130.

Jones, J. R. (2013). The Anglo-Dutch wars of the seventeenth century. Routledge.

Jovanovic, B., & Rousseau, P. L. (2005). General purpose technologies. *Handbook of Economic Growth*, 1, 1181–1224.

Kato, A., & Mitra, A. (2008). Imported technology and employment: Evidence from panel data on Indian manufacturing firms. In *High-tech industries, employment and competitiveness* (pp. 180–194). Routledge.

Katz, M. L., and Shapiro, C. (1985). Network externalities, competition and compatibility. *The American Economic Review*, 75(3), 424–440.

Kiiski, S., & Pohjola, M. (2002). Cross-country diffusion of the Internet. *Information Economics and Policy*, 14(2), 297–310.

Kling, R. (2000). Learning about information technologies and social change: The contribution of social informatics. *The Information Society, 16*(3), 217–232.

Komlos, J. (2000). The Industrial Revolution as the escape from the Malthusian trap. *Journal of European Economic History, 29*(2), 307.

Kuhn, T. 1962. *The structure of scientific revolutions.* Chicago, IL: University of Chicago Press.

Kuznets, S. (1973). Modern economic growth: Findings and reflections. *The American Economic Review, 63*(3), 247–258.

Landes, D. S. (2003). The unbound Prometheus: Technological change and industrial development in Western Europe from 1750 to the present. Cambridge: Cambridge University Press.

Law, J., & Bijker, W. E. (1992). Postscript: Technology, stability and social theory. In W. E. Bijker & J. Law (Eds.), *Shaping technology/building society: Studies in sociotechnical change* (pp. 290–308). MIT Press.

Layton, E. T. Jr. (1974). Technology as knowledge. *Technology and Culture, 15*(1), 31–41.

Lechman, E. (2014). ICT diffusion trajectories and economic development: Empirical evidence for 46 developing countries. In *ICTs and the millennium development goals* (pp. 19–39). US: Springer.

Lechman, E. (2015). ICT diffusion in developing countries: Towards a new concept of technological takeoff. Springer.

Lilley, S. (1973). Technological progress and the Industrial Revolution 1700–1914. In C. M. Cipolla (Ed.), *The Fontana economic history of Europe: The industrial revolution.* Glasgow: Fontana.

Lipsey, R. G., Carlaw, K. I., & Bekar, C. T. (2005). *Economic transformations: General purpose technologies and long-term economic growth.* Oxford: Oxford University Press.

Lucas, R. (1988). On the mechanics of economic development. *Journal of Monetary Economics, 22*, 3–42.

Lundvall, B. Å. (1988). Innovation as an interactive process. In *Technical change and economic theory.* Anthem Press.

Lundvall, B. Å. (2007). National innovation systems—analytical concept and development tool. *Industry and Innovation, 14*(1), 95–119.

Lundvall, B. Ä., & Johnson, B. (1994). The learning economy. *Journal of Industry Studies, 1*(2), 23–42.

Mackay, H., & Gillespie, G. (1992). Extending the social shaping of technology approach: Ideology and appropriation. *Social Studies of Science, 22*(4), 685–716.

MacKenzie, D., & Wajcman, J. (1985). *The social shaping of technology: How the refrigerator got its hum.* Open University Press.

MacKenzie, D., & Wajcman, J. (1999). *The social shaping of technology.* Open University Press.

Maddison, A. (1991). Dynamic forces in capitalist development: A long-run comparative view (Vol. 2). Oxford: Oxford University Press.

Maddison, A. (2001). *The world economy: A millenial perspective.* Development Centre of the Organization for Economic Cooperation and Development.

Maddison, A. (2007). The world economy: Volume 1: A millennial perspective & Volume 2: Historical statistics. Academic Foundation.

Magnusson, L. (1994). *Evolutionary and neo-Schumpeterian approaches to economics* (Vol. 36). Springer Science & Business Media.

Malerba, F. (2002). Sectoral systems of innovation and production. *Research Policy*, *31*(2), 247–264.

Marcelle, G. M. (2000). Transforming information and communications technologies for gender equality. UNDP.

Mattsson, H. (2007). Locating biotech innovation: Places, flows and unruly processes. Uppsala University.

McGee, J. & Sammut, T. A. (2002). Network industries in the new economy. *European Business Journal*, *14*(3), 116–131.

Mokyr, J. (1992). The lever of riches: Technological creativity and economic progress. Oxford: Oxford University Press.

Mokyr, J. (1998). The political economy of technological change. In M. Berg & K. Bruland (Eds.), *Technological revolutions in Europe* (pp. 39–64). Edward Eldgar.

Mokyr, J. (2001). The Industrial Revolution and the economic history of technology: Lessons from the British experience, 1760–1850. *The Quarterly Review of Economics and Finance*, *41*(3), 295–311.

Mokyr, J. (2002). The gifts of Athena: Historical origins of the knowledge economy. Princeton: Princeton University Press.

Mokyr, J. (2005a). Long-term economic growth and the history of technology. In S. N. Durlauf & P. Aghion (Eds.), *Handbook of economic growth* (pp. 1113–1180). Elsevier.

Mokyr, J. (2005b). The intellectual origins of modern economic growth. *The Journal of Economic History*, *65*(2), 285–351.

Mokyr, J., & Scherer, F. M. (1990). Twenty-five centuries of technological change: An historical survey (Vol. 35). Taylor & Francis.

Molina, A. H. (1989). *The social basis of the microelectronics revolution*. Edinburgh: Edinburgh University Press.

Mowery, D. C., & Rosenberg, N. (1991). *Technology and the pursuit of economic growth*. Cambridge: Cambridge University Press.

Nelson, R. R., & Winter, S. G. (1977). In search of useful theory of innovation. *Research Policy*, *6*(1), 36–76.

Nelson, R. R., & Winter, S. G. (1982). The Schumpetcrian tradeoff revisited. *The American Economic Review*, *72*(1), 114–132.

Nelson, R. R., & Winter, S. G. (2009). *An evolutionary theory of economic change*. Cambridge, MA: Harvard University Press.

Ocampo, J. A., Jomo, K. S., & Vos, R. (Eds.). (2007). *Growth divergences: Explaining differences in economic performance*. Zed Books.

Olsen, O. E., & Engen, O. A. (2007). Technological change as a trade-off between social construction and technological paradigms. *Technology in Society*, *29*(4), 456–468.

Palley, T. I. (2005). From Keynesianism to neoliberalism: Shifting paradigms in economics. In A. Saad-Filho & D. Johnston (Eds.), *Neoliberalism: A critical reader* (pp. 20–29). University of Chicago Press.

Pavitt, K. (1999). Technology, management and systems of innovation. Edward Elgar Publishing.

Pawson, E. (1979). The early industrial revolution: Britain in the eighteenth century. BT Batsford Limited.

Perez, C. (1983). Structural change and assimilation of new technologies in the economic and social systems. *Futures*, *15*(5), 357–375.

Perez, C. (1986). Las nuevas tecnologías: una visión de conjunto. *Estudios Internacionales*, *19*(76), 420–459.

Perez, C. (2002). Technological revolutions and financial capital: The dynamics of bubbles and golden ages. Edward Elgar Publishing.

Perez, C. (2003). Technological change and opportunities for development as a moving target. In *Trade and development: Directions for the 21st century* (p. 100).

Perez, C. (2004). Technological revolutions, paradigm shifts and socio-institutional change. In E. S. Reinert (Ed.), *Globalization, economic development and inequality: An alternative perspective* (pp. 217–242).

Perez, C. (2009a). Technological revolutions and techno-economic paradigms. *Cambridge Journal of Economics, 34*(1), 185–202.

Perez, C. (2009b). The double bubble at the turn of the century: Technological roots and structural implications. *Cambridge Journal of Economics, 33*(4), 779–805.

Pérez, C. (2010). Technological dynamism and social inclusion in Latin America: A resource-based production development strategy. *Cepal Review, 100,* 121–141.

Perez, C. (2014). A new age of technological progress. In *Owning the future: How Britain can make it in a fast-changing world.* London: Policy Network and Rowman & Littlefield International, Ltd with the support of Lord Bhattacharyya and the Warwick Manufacturing Group. Available at: www.policy-network.net/publications/4712/Owning-the-Future.

Perez, C., & Soete, L. (1988). Catching-up in technology, entry barriers and windows of opportunity. In G. Dosi et al. (Eds.), *Technical Change and Economic Theory* (pp. 458–479). London: Pinter Publishers.

Phelps, E. S. (1966). Models of technical progress and the golden rule of research. *Review of Economic Studies, 33,* 133–145.

Pinch, T. J., & Bijker, W. E. (1987). The social construction of facts and artifacts: Or how the sociology of. In W. E. Bijker, T. P. Hughes, T. Pinch, & D. G. Douglas (Eds.), *The social constructions of technological systems: New directions in the sociology and history of technology* (p. 17). MIT Press.

Pomeranz, K. (2009). The great divergence: China, Europe, and the making of the modern world economy. Princeton: Princeton University Press.

Ramstad, Y. (1989). 'Reasonable value' versus 'Instrumental value': Competing paradigms in institutional economics. *Journal of Economic Issues, 23*(3), 761–777.

Rodriguez, F., & Wilson, E. J. (2000). *Are poor countries losing the information revolution.* The World Bank Infodev. Available at: www.infodev/library/wilsonrodriguez.doc.

Rodrik, D. (2000). Institutions for high-quality growth: What they are and how to acquire them (No. w7540). National Bureau of Economic Research.

Romer, P. (1990). Endogenous technological change. *Journal of Political Economy, 98*(October): S71-S102.

Rosenberg, N. (1974). Science, invention and economic growth. *The Economic Journal, 84*(333), 90–108.

Rosenberg, N. (1982). *Inside the black box: Technology and economics.* Cambridge University Press.

Rosenberg, N. (1994). Exploring the black box: Technology, economics, and history. Cambridge University Press.

Rosenberg, N., Birdzell, L. E., & Mitchell, G. W. (1986). *How the West grew rich* (pp. 113–143). Popular Prakashan.

Sahal, D. (1981). Patterns of technological innovation. Addison-Wesley.

Sanyal, K. (2014). Rethinking capitalist development: Primitive accumulation, governmentality and post-colonial capitalism. Routledge.

Schumpeter, I. S. (1943). *Capitalism: Socialism and democracy*. London: Allen & Unwin.

Schumpeter, J. A. (1934). The theory of economic development: An inquiry into profits, capital, credit, interest, and the business cycle (Vol. 55). Transaction Publishers.

Schumpeter, J. A. (1939). Business cycles: A theoretical, historical, and statistical analysis of the capitalist process. McGraw-Hill.

Shapiro, C. & Varian, H. R. (1999). *Information rules: A strategic guide to the network economy*. Cambridge, MA: Harvard Business School Press.

Shell, K. (1967). A model of innovative activity and capital accumulation. In K. Shell (Ed.), *Essays on the theory of optimal economic growth* (pp. 67–85). Cambridge: MIT Press.

Sinclair-Desgagné, B. (2000). Technological paradigms and the measurement of innovation. CIRANO.

Singer, C. (1941). A short history of science to the nineteenth century. Courier Corporation.

Soete, L., & Verspagen, B. (1993). Technology and growth: The complex dynamics of catching-up, falling behind and taking over. In A. Szirmai (Ed.), *Explaining economic growth*. Elsevier.

Solow, R. M. (1956). A contribution to the theory of economic growth. *The Quarterly Journal of Economics*, 70(1), 65–94.

Szirmai, A. (2005). *Socio-economic development*. Cambridge: Cambridge University Press.

Szpak, J. (2001). *Historia gospodarcza powszechna*. Polskie Wydawn. Ekonomiczne.

Teich, M., & Porter, R. (1996). *The industrial revolution in national context: Europe and the USA*. Cambridg: Cambridge University Press.

Temple, R. K. (1998). The genius of China: 3,000 years of science, discovery, and invention. Prion Books.

Toumazou, C., & Hughes, J. B. (1993). Switched-currents: An analogue technique for digital technology (No. 5). Iet. London: Peter Peregrinus Ltd.

UNESCO. (2002). *Information and communication technology in education*. UNESCO Division of Higher Education, France.

United Nations. (2004). Report of the International Telecommunication Union on information and communication technologies statistics. Economic and Social Council, March 2004.

Utterback, J. M. (1978). *The dynamics of product and process innovation in industry*. Center for Policy Alternatives, Massachusetts Institute of Technology.

Uzawa, H. (1965). Optimum technical change in an aggregate model of economic growth. *International Economic Review*, 6, 18–31.

Valente, T. W. (1996). Social network thresholds in the diffusion of innovations. *Social Networks*, 18(1), 69–89.

Van den Ende, J., & Dolfsma, W. (2005). Technology-push, demand-pull and the shaping of technological paradigms-Patterns in the development of computing technology. *Journal of Evolutionary Economics*, 15(1), 83–99.

Veblen, I. (1915). *Germany and the industrial revolution*. New York: BW Huebsch.

Verspagen, B. (1991). A new empirical approach to catching up or falling behind. *Structural Change and Economic Dynamics*, 2(2), 359–380.

Von Tunzelmann, N., Malerba, F., Nightingale, P., & Metcalfe, S. (2008). Technological paradigms: Past, present and future. *Industrial and Corporate Change*, 17(3), 467–484.

Wagner, D. B. (1993). *Iron and steel in ancient China* (Vol. 9). Brill.

Westphal, L. E. (2002). Technology strategies for economic development in a fast changing global economy. *Economics of Innovation and New Technology, 11*(4–5), 275–320.

Williams, R., & Edge, D. (1996). The social shaping of technology. *Research Policy, 25*(6), 865–899.

Williamson, J. G. (1984). Why was British growth so slow during the industrial revolution? *The Journal of Economic History, 44*(3), 687–712.

Williamson, J. G. (2008). Globalization and the Great divergence: Terms of trade booms, volatility and the poor periphery, 1782–1913. *European Review of Economic History, 12*(3), 355–391.

Wilson, G., & Heeks, R. (2000). Technology, poverty and development. *Poverty and Development into the 21st Century*, 403–424.

3 Technology Diffusion
Conceptual Aspects

Technology Dynamics

> Technology moves at a certain speed, and in certain direction, and the study of innovation helps us understand these laws of motion.
>
> Mokyr (2010)

> When a successful new product or process technology appears, that appearance initiates a process by which the number of users or owners of that technology increases absolutely and/or relatively over time for a period of time. That rate of increase may be slow (and even in some cases nonexistent) or fast. (. . .). It is this process by which new technology spreads that is refereed to here as the diffusion of new technology.
>
> Paul Stoneman and Giuliana Battisti (2010)

Technologies rise, diffuse, saturate and decline. And although technology diffusion is not of a simple linear but rather non-linearly proceeding phenomenon, it evolves and changes over time, and its evolutionary trajectory is characterized by certain regularities. Technology diffusion is not instantaneous, but over time, a distributed phenomenon. At the very beginning, when new technologies emerge, they generate a kind of disorder which may increase initial uncertainty and unstable relationships, as well as chaos. Usually, new technology causes turbulences.

Diffusion of technology is in the core of technological change; its pattern and speed are marked by uncertainty and, sometimes, random fluctuations; it generates disorder within well-established social, organizational and economic systems. To some extent, understanding the process of disorder and order is essential to understanding the process of technological change followed by the diffusion of new technologies across societies. Technology and economy cannot be recognized as equilibrium systems, but they are usually marked by discontinuities, abrupt ups and downs and permanent disequilibrium. This disequilibrium is more of a characteristic feature of dynamic techno-economic systems rather than its failure. The long-term lack of equilibrium is, however, a positive aspect of this techno-economic dynamism, as it stimulates changes and shifts, giving rise to new ideas and concepts which are consecutively embedded into disruptive and pervasive innovations that change economic contours of countries.

The process of diffusion refers to expansion, spread, propagation and dissemination. Technology diffusion stands for the transfer of information, knowledge and ideas over economies and societies regardless of their heterogeneity and complexity. Without diffusion, innovations would have never become widespread, and thus their social and economic influence would remain negligible and without any significant feedback. Because of diffusion, innovations may become useful for each individual, and this makes the process of diffusion of seminal importance. Rogers (1983), in his influential book *Diffusion of Innovations*, analyzes the process of diffusion from sociological perspective, and he claims that technology diffusion occurs through communication channels over time and among society members, and hence social networks and communication systems play a key role in the process of new technologies dissemination. Rogers (1983) emphasizes the prominent role of interpersonal communication, what was then labeled 'the word-of-mouth' effect, as the shaping factor of the diffusion process. The role of 'the word-of-mouth' effect and 'two-step communications' has also been stressed in works of Mansfield (1961, 1971), as these two effects allow exchanging knowledge on newly introduced technologies and learning about their advantages. According to David (1986), the process of diffusion becomes less random as people acquire technological novelties driven by their anticipated profitability and belief that the new technology is superior to the old one. Geroski (2000), Stoneman (2001) and Saviotti (2002) additionally argue that people rarely make their decisions independently; they are led by their cognitive capacities and 'mass behavior' that is culturally and morally affected. All these determine the strength of the 'domino effect' that perpetuates the speed of new technology dissemination society-wide. Dosi (1991), similarly to Mansfield (1968), Romeo (1975) or Ray (1983), underlines the instantaneousness of the process of diffusion, arguing that time is inherently involved while the pace of new technology dissemination is determined by the unique features of the technologies.

Also, it may be defined as the 'mechanism that spreads successful varieties of products and processes throughout an economic structure and displaces wholly or partially the existing inferior varieties' (Sarkar, 1998, p. 131). This time-related and dynamic process allows for putting into extensive use predominantly radical innovations (the process of emergence of invention, by definition, is prior to diffusion), which as claimed by Freeman (1991) are mainly discontinues events, but actually they are in the very center of a wide variety of diffusion studies. The process of technology diffusion preconditions how fast 'pioneering technologies' are being adopted and used by economic agents, spread among individuals and hence put to productive and organizational use. Technology diffusion reflects the process of spreading new inventions across individuals and companies. Also, it may be defined as the process of spreading innovations through the population and potential adopters (Rogers, 1983). Grübler and Nakićenović (1991) argue that the process of diffusion translates the enormous potential encapsulated in radical innovations into real economic change. In a similar vein, Peres et al. (2010) consider the process in the wider socio-economic context and write that 'innovation diffusion is the process of market penetration of new products and services, which is driven by social influence. Such influences include all of the interdependencies among consumers that affect various players with or without their explicit knowledge' (ibid., p. 92). Such an approach to the process of technology diffusion goes far beyond its purely mechanical aspects and emphasizes that the process of propagation of new ideas and knowledge embodied in innovations is, first, socially and economically driven and preconditioned, and, second, to a large extent, it is endogenously led. Many claim that the process of technology diffusion is—to a large extent—deterministic and mechanical in its nature (see, inter alia, works of Geroski, 2000 or Ismail, 2015) and may occur unintended by individuals. However, when going deeper, detailed study of the process of technology diffusion unveils its complexity, temporal and unique characteristics, as well as multiple interdependencies that it generates across societies and economies. Undeniably, technology diffusion results in multilevel adaptation of technological novelties and thus underlines social, organizational and, overall, economic processes. Ausubel (1991) notes that diffusion in itself demonstrates some countervailing effects, as it forces homogenization (as similar technologies are used by increasing the number of users) and, reversely, it drives heterogenization of individuals and/or companies, which, because of adoption of new technologies, diversify their economic activities.

As raised by (Grübler, 1991), diffusion is not a unary process. He also defines this process in a rather non-standard way as a '*sequence of replacements*' of old technologies by new ones. In the same vein, Hall (2004) writes that diffusion describes the process which allows for adopting new technologies, or replacing old ones with the new ones. The definition offered by Grübler and Hall, however, coincides mostly with the notion of technological substitution (see, for instance, works of Fisher & Pry, 1971; Bhargava, 1989; Mahajan & Muller, 1996 or Morris & Pratt, 2003), which is recognized as the process of gradual switching from the 'old type' to the 'new type' of technology as new technological solutions are evading the market. A roughly similar perception of technology diffusion may be traced in the work of Foray and Grübler (1990) and Foray (1997), who state, '*Diffusion process can thus be considered as a series of competitions at given times between a technology A, which is in the middle of transformation, and other technologies*' (Foray & Grübler, 1990, p. 408).

In a general sense, technology diffusion may be defined as a time- and space-related dynamic and non-linear process, initially generating disorder in socio-economic systems, leading to the introduction of cutting-edge and disruptive innovations to the market which finally transform societies and economies.

Technology diffusion combines imitative and repetitive activities, but, undeniably, these two are seminal for new technologies to become widespread, broadly accessed and well used. Diffusion is rarely a smooth and orderly process, but it is rather marked by uncertainty, especially visible in its early phases. Forces driving its speed and extent change over time and thus determine if the diffusion process succeeds or, reversely, is hindered because of an unfriendly environment and thus societies remain 'locked' in the 'low-level trap'. Most likely, these are societal, economic and, above all, institutional factors which constitute a unique constellation of factors determining the speed of diffusion. Attewell (1992), Swanson and Ramiller (1997, 2004) and Moore (2002) also underline that diffusion occurs usually in an unsmooth fashion, while the diffusion trajectory is often marked by abrupt ups and downs.

Technologies do not diffuse into a vacuum (Grübler, 1991) but rather they interact with social, economic and institutional environments, and these interactions reflect their elasticity and complexity and predetermine the rate of diffusion and its long-term consequences. Nathan Rosenberg in his contributive work *Perspectives on Technology* (Rosenberg, 1976), writes,

> In the history of diffusion of many innovations, one cannot help being stuck by two characteristics of the diffusion: its apparent overall slowness on the one hand, and the wide variations in the rates of acceptance of different inventions, on the other.
>
> (Rosenberg, 1976, p. 191)

Undeniably, the speed at which technologies diffuse and are accepted by new users is crucial, mainly because it preconditions the emergence of its socio-economic effects. If diffusion is spasmodic and for a long time the technology is neither accessed nor used by society, its positive impact is significantly weakened and arises with huge time lags. These variations of acceptance rates as well as cross-country differences in speed of diffusion of certain technologies account for several factors, which are of sociological, economic, institutional or historical nature.

Effective adoption of new technologies is a multistage process, and especially in its early phase, it is marked by huge uncertainty. It is right to say that uncertainty is inherent to the process of technology diffusion, while there may be multiple areas of these uncertainties recognized (Stoneman & Battisti, 2010), and they are associated with institutional and legal frameworks, which may impede the diffusion of innovations, costs of adoption of new technological solutions, size of sunk cost, access to information and interpersonal communication channels with its inherent slowness (Rogers, 1983), social attitudes toward risk taking and social capabilities to assimilate innovations, agents' decision-making processes under uncertainty and their risk aversion (the trade-offs between risk and potential benefits arise). Finally, the process of technology diffusion may be endogenously and exogenously driven. The first would mean that diffusion is mostly a self-propagating process where the number of contacts between users and non-users is not restricted and may grow rapidly. However, it may occur that new technological solutions are acquired in a more passive way, as economic agents may be forced to adopt and put into use new technologies and/or are externally influenced, which, for instance, may reflect the implementation of certain economic policies and strategies. Each time the process of new technologies begins, to be effective, pervasive and overwhelming must be driven by low-cost and widely available input. To give an example from the past, in the 19th century, the propagation process of railway networks was enabled by the availability of cheap coal, while the spread of electric networks was facilitated by the availability of cheap iron. Today, behind the Fifth Technological Revolution stands the cheap microprocessor (Freeman & Pérez, 1988). That is why new path-breaking technologies may diffuse worldwide. However, behind the successful spread of new technologies there also stand factors, closely related to the accessibility of low-cost inputs, changing the structure of relative costs, which offers economic actors future benefits and sustainable productivity gains. If the latter is unveiled, the process of technology diffusion is reinforced and leads to the emergence of economies of scale and hence new opportunities to adopt new technological solutions arise, which, in effect, further drive the rapid diffusion of technologies. New technologies, once they become widespread, take root in collective consciousness (Perez, 2004) and become new 'common sense' for all. Fast propagation (diffusion) of new technologies may, however, be weakened by several external factors, and hence it does not always flow smoothly. Social, economic, institutional or political obstacles often constitute the self-slowing factors, which makes the process of technology diffusion a painstaking process. There are usually institutions in countries which by generating internal resistances impede the appearance of positive externalities and hence hinder the diffusion process. Changes of established frameworks, modes of acting, routines and practices are often spasmodic and diminish positive effects that might be demonstrated quickly if the diffusion of new technologies was unrestricted. Unfortunately, social pressure and high demand are not always sufficient to ensure an unbounded spread of newly embodied knowledge. The external environment conditioning the rate and diffusion patterns is not only subjected to uncertainty but also to limited information about the potential benefits that new technology may offer and costs of its adoption and/or switching from old to new technological solutions. The factors mentioned earlier refer to both consumers (demanders) and producers (suppliers) who undertake decisions on whether to acquire and offer to the market new technologies or not. Is new technology a real improvement? Will it generate profits on the micro- and/or macro-level? If so, will these benefits arrive immediately or with time lags? It is important to note that consumers demonstrate enormous heterogeneity on one hand, but on the other hand, their propensity to imitate others is notable. The micro-behavior of each individual is fundamental, as it may effectively encourage or, reversely, hinder further propagation of new technologies. Positive or negative social and economic feedback constitute important factors that determine the diffusion time path of new technologies, as unveiling network effects (positive externalities) have a huge 'modeling' power regarding diffusion trajectories and the speed of it (for more discussion, see Sect. 3.2). To a large extent, the rate of diffusion is determined by the decisions made by both sides of the market; however, Hall (2004) makes an interesting observation: '*The decision to adopt a new invention is that at any point in time the choice being made is not a choice between adopting and not adopting but a choice between adopting now or deferring the decision until later*' (Hall, 2004, p. 8).

The diffusion process, usually initiated right after successful commercialization of emerged innovation(s), may in effect determine the rise of new products, services or industries. The early stage diffusion process is marked by the experimentation period (Nakićenović, 1991) and a high degree of diversity regarding the number and variety of new products and services introduced to the market. Importantly, during the initial diffusion phase, the spread of new technology may be both user and producer led, which, as claimed by Sahal (1981), is predominantly driven by the learning process of both sides of the market and adaptability and usability of new technological solutions and it is determined by the extent to which new technologies substitute old ones (Hall, 2004). Moreover, the early diffusion phase is also the time of strong competition among companies trying to gain the market. High pressure for price drops, which is accompanied by significant cost reduction as production becomes more standardized and consecutive incremental innovations are introduced, finally results in the specific 'shaking out' (Nakićenović, 1991), and only a few firms survive. The early diffusion phase is of crucial importance. It is a time of temporally disordered market frictions and sometimes crises and painful adjustments. The course of this phase is mostly dependent on social and institutional responses, assimilation capabilities, propensity to risk taking and attitudes towards novelties, and succession of substitution along market niches (Grübler, 1991) if the diffusion process eventually 'succeeds' or 'fails'. Possibly, social high risk aversion, impeding institutions and legal frameworks may effectively hinder the spread of technological novelties and hence the future adoption of new technology is blocked. These societies remain in the trap, which is difficult to escape from. Such an unfortunate scenario is sometimes encountered in peripheral regions and/or countries that are usually economically lagging behind. These time lags in adoption of new technologies clearly demonstrate that the diffusion process is not only time but also space attributed. The race of the spread on innovations in world peripheries may be seen as the 'Schumpeterian bandwagons' (Scrase & MacKerron, 2009; Rohlfs, 2003) of technologies, which diffuse worldwide, however, with significant time lags.

> Use a model that makes sense and enjoy that fact that some simple relationships are deep and important.
>
> Ausubel (1991)

It is widely recognized that the world of technology is full of biological and evolutionary metaphors (Devezas, 2005). In theoretical and empirical studies of technology diffusion, we apply models based on the growth-to-limits behavior of bacteria (Ausubel, 1991); we adopt the Voltera-Lotka[1] equation and 'natural law' of growth of species developed by Darwin (1968), models for species selection proposed by Fisher (1930), Gompertz's model modified version of the exponential function—logistic growth function—or Fisher and Pry's (1971) model to describe the process of technological substitution. Needless to say, they all originate from the biological realm, and their adoption in the theory of technology diffusion allows capturing and describing the nature of the technology diffusion process and providing a powerful tool for technological forecasting. These biological metaphors broadly encountered in the diffusion studies are based on one fundamental assumption: both living systems and socio-technological systems share several common features and striking similarities. Such recognition, however, leads to broad adoption of 'evolutionary algorithms' (Devezas, 2005) in the field of technological studies.

The intellectual foundations of contemporary concepts of technology diffusion are deeply rooted in evolutionary paradigms of Darwin (1968), which developed the analytical framework to examine the natural growth, the process of diffusion and the natural selection of species in biological systems. In their works, they have demonstrated the unique ability of species to grow infinitely and to compete and survive in certain environmental conditions. Today, in multiple techno-economic concepts, technologies, for instance, are treated analogously to species in Darwin's theory, and they are claimed to diffuse following the sigmoid path and compete with other technologies to gain market. As argued by Ehrnberg (1995), the simple concept of the sigmoid pattern well describes the process of technology diffusion, despite the fact that it may be marked by several disruptions, discontinuities and disequilibria. The sigmoid pattern (see Figure 3.1)—also labeled S-shaped pattern, S-shaped trajectory, S-shaped time path, S-curve or Gompertz curve[2]—illustrates the technology behavior over time. It is simply generated by plotting the number of new users (new adopters) of a given technology *versus* time, and it provides the insight into changing diffusion dynamics (diffusion rates) along consecutive phases of the diffusion process. The sigmoid shape of the diffusion trajectory additionally allows distinguishing characteristic phases of the process of diffusion of technology and exploring unique features of these phases.

The first seminal observation regarding the S-shaped path approximating the changing (here, growing number) of new users (adopters) of new technology is that the diffusion of new technology does not follow linear patterns, but the process proceeds non-linearly over time.[3] The second important observation is that the process of diffusion is distributed over time. Third, the diffusion is not unary, but rather a multistage process characterized by consecutive equilibria and the specific diffusion life cycle (Grübler, 1991). From the long-term perspective, the diffusion operates within an evolutionary type and

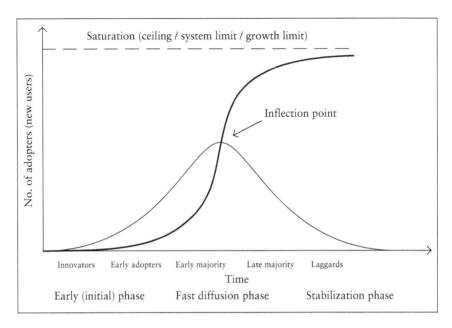

Figure 3.1 Diffusion curve and bell curve[4]

non-equilibrium modes. However, despite its complexity and non-linearity, the diffusion pattern is not a 'random walk', but rather several continual regularities may be recognized in it.

Along the sigmoid diffusion pattern, three characteristic phases may be distinguished. At the very beginning, the process of diffusion is slow, sometimes even spasmodic, and characterized by low speed. During the initial (early) diffusion stage, the number of new users (new adopters) of new technology remains low, and thus a relatively small share of society has access to and uses the new technological solutions (these are only 'inventors' and 'early adopters'; see Rogers (1983)). During the early diffusion phase, the number of contacts between adopters and non-adopters of new technology is small, and thus network growth is impeded; the cost of adoption of new technology may still be high, which effectively hinders its dissemination; the socio-economic environment may be volatile, and so initially the performance of new technology may be poor. At this stage of diffusion, this process—to some extent—is still reversible if impeded by people's high risk aversion or legal constraints. The diffusion path may also be marked by random and irregular fluctuations, but it is a time of adjustment of the social and institutional frameworks so that they can become 'supportive' for new technology. Under favorable conditions, owing to the easiness of contacts and the growing number of new users, the '*domino effect*' is revealed, and hence the diffusion may speed up; the process becomes irreversible. Driven by various market forces, people's positive attitudes towards new technology from which they expect to receive benefits are enhanced by its first users (Rogers calls this group 'early majority'), fast cost reduction of adopting new technological solutions and multiple applicability and usability, and unveiling economies of scale. The number of new users increases rapidly. Once the 'critical mass'[5] along the diffusion trajectory is reached, the curve takes off and enters the fast diffusion phase when the process of diffusion usually proceeds at an exponential rate. The fast diffusion phase is the time of the most disruptive changes, thus overwhelming societies and economies not only because the number of new users of new technology is rapidly growing but also because of the 'expansion' of new technological solutions and their incorporation into organizational and production systems. This is a time of deep structural changes, where new technology is extensively exploited and benefits from its adoption and usage are demonstrated. During the fast diffusion stage, the new types of social and economic networks are established, which, in turn, reshape the ways that economies function. The exact speed of diffusion is different in each case of technology. It is interlinked with incremental improvements associated with certain innovation and determined by new technology appropriability to be adopted and used for multiple purposes (for instance, R&D activities), profitability and economic agents' expectations (Dosi, 1991; Stoneman & Diederen, 1994; Nakićenović & Grübler, 2013).

In terms of mathematical properties of the sigmoid pattern, during the fast diffusion phase, the inflection point of the curve may be identified. The inflection point occurs once the maximum rate of diffusion is reached, and if the diffusion path after the inflection point is the mirror image of it before the inflection point, then the curve is labeled as symmetric. However, new technology does not diffuse at the exponential rate infinitely. Each system has its growth limits and its carrying capacity. Henceforth, once the high share of society has already adopted the new technology, the process of diffusion slows down, and the system heads towards full saturation (see Figure 3.2). The maturity (stabilization) phase is reached, during which the rate of diffusion again becomes slow and no significant growth in the number of new users is reported.

Finally, each technology may enter the phasing out stage, where newly emerging technologies evade the market, and the old ones are gradually substituted by the new ones. Each technological generation, eventually, becomes outdated, and societies switch to the new technologies. '*S-curves are known to cascade with a new one beginning where the last one leaves off. New products replace old products just as new technologies replace old technologies*' (Modis, 2007, p. 870). The time span needed to pass from one phase to another is different in each case, depending on the type of new technology, social-economic conditions and institutional framework, as well as factors such as geographical conditions or dominant region. In various societies, consecutive stages of diffusion last for a different number of years, but still at the macro level, the time path of technology diffusion if portrayed by the

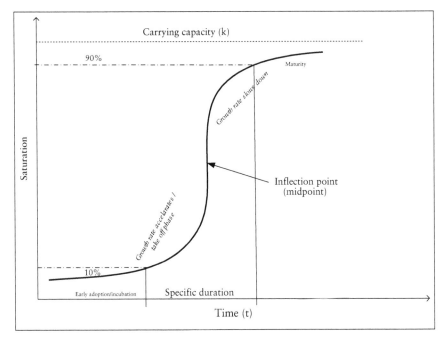

Figure 3.2 S-shaped time path
Source: Lechman (2015).

sigmoid trajectory. As underlined by Grübler (1991) and then repeated in Dopfer et al. (2004), this relatively smooth S-time path does not contradict with the permanently changing environment, or different adoption patterns demonstrated at the micro (or even individual) level.

The regularities of the evolution of different systems, as well as techno-economic systems, where initially slow changes are followed by rapid shifts and next the phase of fast changes ends as the rate of change again slows down, have been observed for decades. It was Pierre-Francois Verhulst, inspired by work of Thomas Malthus on population dynamics, who first used the logistic equation to describe the population growth as the self-limiting process (Kucharavy & De Guio, 2011). Teodore Modis (2007) claims that logistic growth is growth under competition. The logistic equation, some-times also labeled the Verhulst[6]-Pearl[7] equation, is a logistics function which generates the S-shape (see Figure 3.2) curve broadly adopted to display the process of technology diffusion. Today, the logistic equation tracing the S-shaped pattern is one the best recognized sigmoid asymptotic functions, which is broadly used to examine the growth of given variables that are time dependent.

Mathematically speaking, the S-shaped curve is generated by the logistic function (Kudryashov, 2013) of which the generalized form is defined as

$$N(Z) = \frac{expZ}{1 + expZ} = \frac{1}{1 + exp^{-Z}} \qquad (3.1)$$

under the assumption that the number of new technology adopters, N, is determined by more than one explanatory variable, which are captured in Z. We define

$$Z = \alpha + \beta X, \qquad (3.2)$$

where α determines the location of the curve, the β its slope and the X defines the continuous stimulus of the process.

The simplified form of Eq. (3.1), the logistic function that predicts the S-shaped curve, however, including just one explanatory variable, time (t), originates from the exponential growth model (Meyer et al. 1999) that if written as an ordinary differential equation appears as follows:

$$\frac{dY_x(t)}{dt} = a\, Y_x(t), \qquad (3.3)$$

where $Y(t)$ explains the level of x, t denotes time and the parameter α is the growth rate. By introducing e^8 to Eq. (3.3), it can be rewritten as

$$Y_x(t) = \beta e^{\alpha t}, \qquad (3.4)$$

with notation analogous to Eq. (3.3). The additional parameter β in Eq. (3.4) stands for the initial value of x at $t = 0$.

It is important to note that the growth model is, by definition, exponential; henceforth, if left to itself, x tends to grow infinitely in geometric progression. However, the extrapolation of $Y_x(t)$ generated by an exponential growth model leads to unrealistic predictions (see arguments raised by Stone, 1980; Meyer, 1994; Coontz, 2013). To solve the problem of 'infinite growth', the 'resistance' parameter (Cramer, 2003; Kwasnicki, 2013) is added to Eq. (3.4), which introduces the limit of growth.

The adjusted version of Eq. (3.3) follows the logistic differential function:

$$\frac{dY(t)}{dt} = aY(t)\left(1 - \frac{Y(t)}{k}\right) \qquad (3.5)$$

In Eq. (3.5), the additional parameter κ shows the 'limit of growth'—the upper asymptote limiting the potentially infinite growth of Y. Put differently, the κ parameter may be labeled the 'slowing parameter' or the 'negative feedback', which in effect generates the sigmoid trajectory (see Figure 3.2).

The logistic differential equation, Eq. (3.5), can be expressed as the logistic growth function:

$$N_x(t) = \frac{\kappa}{1 + e^{-a(t-\beta)}} \tag{3.6}$$

or, alternatively,

$$N_x(t) = \frac{\kappa}{1 + \exp(-\alpha(t-\beta))} \tag{3.7}$$

where $N_x(t)$ stands for the value of variable x in time period t. The logistic growth function, by definition, is always taking non-negative values, thus $N_x(t) > 0$.

The parameters in Eq. (3.6) and Eq. (3.7) show the following (Lechman, 2015):

- κ—upper asymptote determining the limit of growth ($N(t) \rightarrow \kappa$), also labeled 'carrying capacity' or 'saturation';
- α—growth rate determining the speed (rate) of diffusion; and
- β—midpoint, which specifies the exact time (T_m) when the logistic pattern reaches 0.5κ.

To facilitate interpretation of these parameters and provide a bit of 'economic logic', it is useful to replace α with a 'specific duration' parameter, defined as $\Delta t = \dfrac{\ln(81)}{\alpha}$, which approximates the time needed for x to grow from $10\%\kappa$ to $90\%\kappa$. The midpoint (β) describes the point in time at which the logistic growth starts to level off.

It is important to note that the problem of measurement and approximating technology diffusion time paths is also closely related to various technology (innovation) diffusion models. Technology diffusion models intend to propose realistic representation of the diffusion process and appear as complex and time-evolving phenomena; they provide a theoretical framework that allows for both qualitative and quantitative analysis of this process, assessing the speed of diffusion, developing its time path and identifying the fostering or impeding factors. In late 1950, there emerged first theoretical and empirical works that tackled the issues of technology diffusion. Since the initial path-breaking works of Griliches[9] (1957) and Mansfield (1961), we have observed a growing body of literature trying to conceptualize and capture into formal models the process of technology diffusion. First studies of technology diffusion were formalized as epidemic models of diffusion, which considered the process of technology dissemination analogously to the spread of contagious diseases by infection in the natural environment. Interestingly, epidemic models of diffusion allow for the identification of the presence of empirical regularities (Sarkar, 1998) in the process of technology spread both at the micro- and macro levels, regardless of various socio-economic conditions and the institutional environment. Adoption of epidemic models allows for the exploration of the nature and dynamic of the technology dissemination process, identifying the rate and time needed to achieve high technology saturation of the heterogeneous society. Interestingly, theoretical specifications of epidemic theories of technology diffusion generate the S-shaped pattern (logistic curve), thus approximating development trajectory across society members. However, despite the fact that epidemic models describe the process of technology diffusion relatively well (numerous empirical studies have demonstrated that new technology diffusion follows the logistic curve), they have been widely criticized for their simplicity, restrictive assumptions, remaining silent to 'behavioral' determinants of the process of technology spread, treating economic agents as 'passive'—instead of 'active'—adopters (seekers) of new technologies (Antonelli, 2012) and ignoring multiple external factors preconditioning the dynamics of the process of technology diffusion. This criticism, however, paved the road ahead for the new elaboration of a wide variety of theoretical models intending to formalize and explain the process of technology diffusion. From the 1970s onwards, in theoretical literature, there may be recognized two main strands in technology diffusion studies—namely, the equilibrium and (evolutionary) disequilibrium approaches (models). The first approach to modeling technology diffusion, the equilibrium approach, has its conceptual foundations in the neoclassical school of economic thought, and it is based on several rigid assumptions: equilibrium mechanism, full information and infinite rationality of economic agents. In technology diffusion theoretical specifications, falling into the equilibrium-type models, the process of technology dissemination is characterized by a sequence of shifting state equilibria (Sarkar, 1998), while each entity is perfectly informed and thus information asymmetries do not impede nor interfere with the process of new technologies adoption. Each economic agent is additionally rational, and the process of technology diffusion may be both endogenously driven (see diffusion models based on game theory[10]) or exogenously driven (mainly encountered in probit (rank) diffusion models[11]). The evolutionary disequilibrium approach to conceptualizing technology diffusion based on the process of technology diffusion is disequilibrating rather than equilibrating, and thus diffusion patterns may be marked by discontinuities. The process is strongly endogenous; economic agents' decisions are taken, however, under limited information (information asymmetries may interfere with the process of diffusion spread) and characterized by bounded rationality. The intellectual roots of the paradigm that technology diffusion is a disequilibrating and endogenously driven process may be traced in the contributive works of Charles Darwin and other works on biological evolution. In disequilibrium models of technology diffusion,[12] economic agents (individuals and/or firms) are supposed to behave like spices in the natural environment. However, in the economic environment, there are multiple constraints, such as legal regulations or geographical and infrastructural constraints, which determine the speed of diffusion across society members. Nelson and Winter (2009) and Silverberg et al. (1988) claim that the diffusion process may be defined as an evolutionary, disequilibrium process involving the gradual spread of new technology under uncertainty and incomplete information, bounded rationality and endogeneity of economic structures. This bounded rationality makes economic actors unable to anticipate potential profits to be gained from new technologies, and thus the socio-economic system demonstrates the off-equilibrium behavior until the equilibrium is achieved. Matthews (1984) and Witt (1992) claim that the spread of new technology may be—to some extent—a random process, as individuals do not necessarily take their decisions driven by profits maximization or perfectly informed about the advantages of new technological solutions. The process of technology diffusion is not, however, linear, but rather follows the S-shaped trajectory, which may be disrupted by abrupt ups and downs generated by random exogenous shocks.

The evolutionary models of technology diffusion are intellectually and conceptually related to path-dependence models exhibiting positive externalities (Loch & Huberman, 1999). The positive externalities are defined as benefits generated by the growing number of adopters and users of new technology (innovation), and such perceptions of positive externalities are traced in works of Granovetter (1978), Katz and Shapiro (1985) and Cusumano et al. (1992), and in more recent research from Jaffe et al. (2005), Bergek et al. (2008), Roper et al. (2013) and Hoy and Polborn (2015). In literature, the concept of positive externalities is also recognized as the 'bandwagon effect', presenting the unique consumers' behavior associated with prestige seeking associated with the adoption of new technological solutions. The emerging positive externalities phenomenon also suggests that the growing number of users of new technology automatically increases its usefulness and encourages more people to adopt new technological solutions. The evolutionary models of technology diffusion, to some extent, relate to the 'punctuated-equilibrium' concept initially offered by Gould and Eldredge (1977) that used this term to describe some emerging discontinuities along the evolutionary process. Later, Foster and Young (1990) defined the punctuation as switching between stable equilibria in the system. On the ground of evolutionary models of technology diffusion, the 'punctuated-equilibrium' concept refers to the situation when new technology is being abruptly adopted and thus generates punctuation. Put differently, because of sudden changes and rapid diffusion of new technology, as well as the emergence of positive externalities, the equilibrium switch (punctuation) is observed.

Other authors' claims are that positive externalities are closely related to the notions of network externalities (network effects) and critical mass. See, for instance, works of Allen (1988), Economides and Himmelberg (1995) or Economides (1996). So far, however, the problem of the critical mass has been a rarely explored area of research; henceforth, the consecutive Sect. 3.2 is entirely devoted to the broader explanation of this problem.

Network Effects, Critical Mass and Technological Take-Off

Technology diffusion is a dynamic, time-based, self-propagating and self-perpetuating process. The diffusion process usually occurs in a continuous manner (Liikanen et al., 2004), which is well-described by the logistic growth model (see Eq. (3.6)) and visualized as the S-shaped time patterns (see Figure 3.2). Despite possibly arising discontinuities and irregularities, diffusion is not a random process which cannot be foreseen. In that sense, the diffusion process is a kind of collective phenomenon; it is also path dependent, as its future path and dynamic are conditioned by past events; it proceeds only if a certain 'installed base' of users (innovators) is built up. Moreover, as argued in the previous section, the process of technology diffusion is rather disequilibrating than equilibrating in its nature, and hence it allows for the examination of the evolution of the system. It is important to note that the mathematical form of the logistic growth model, which perfectly reflects the logic standing behind epidemic models and the process of contamination, additionally demonstrates the uniqueness of network externalities. Many claim, compare for instance in works of Stoneman (1983), Markus (1987), Geroski (2000) or Peres et al. (2010), that emerging network externalities are the principal phenomena which characterize the process of technology diffusion and its dynamics. The network externalities, also labeled network effects, are actually analogous to what we call 'imitation effect' in the Bass model (see Bass (1969, 1980), or the 'word-of-mouth' effect (or the 'domino effect') (see Geroski, 2000, Lee et al., 2010). Cabral (2006) writes,

> The network effects, that is, the case when adoption benefits are increasing in the number of adopter. (. . .) suppose that each potential user derives a benefit from communicating with (. . .) others. Such benefits can only be gained if the other users are also hooked up in the network (. . .).
>
> (Cabral, 2006, p. 2)

Put differently, for an individual, the value of a new technological solution, to a large extent, depends on how many people have already adopted it. The latter is especially true when speaking of communication technologies, or other technologies allowing for the spread of knowledge and information.[13] Economides (1996) intends to explain reasons for the emergence of positive network effects, and he points out that this unique effect occurs as market agents value complementarity between different components of a network.[14] Network externalities are a kind of epidemic in social networks. Once the new technology is introduced to the market, it invades and spreads (diffuses) among society members like a contagious disease.

As emphasized in Katz and Shapiro (1985) and David (1985), and then repeated in Shapiro and Varian (1998), Shy (2001) and Keser et al. (2012), the positive social and economic outcomes associated with the society- and economy-wide implementation of new technologies predominantly depend on the number of people, new users, that decide to acquire and use newly emerging technological solutions. If the number of people who wish to pay—new users—buy and adopt new technology is substantial, this effectively drives further growth of the number of additional new users and hence the positive feedback—the network effects emerge. Loch and Huberman (1999) underline that positive network effects encourage broader acceptance of new technology, which under uncertainty that is inherent in the system of diffusion makes people imitate the behavior of others to repeat choices made by innovators and/or early adopters. Henceforth, arguably, we may claim that network effects demonstrate rather imitative effects, or imitative behavior, unveiled throughout the process of the spread of new technologies. The positive feedback arises when society members tend to communicate among themselves and, because of various communication channels, a stock of knowledge on advantages and benefits of new technology is transmitted.

Further, Cabral (1990) claimed that network effects, although they lie in the nature of the process of diffusion, might enforce discontinuities along the technology diffusion trajectory. Indeed, strong positive externalities unveiled during the process of technology diffusion often lead to sudden and unforeseeable 'catastrophe' in the adoption of new technology; the demand explodes, and the system passes from low-level equilibria to high-level equilibria. The 'catastrophe' is like a genuine disruption that occurs after relatively long periods of stagnation or spasmodic change (usually growth) (Sarkar, 1998). The 'catastrophe' enforces radical and permanent change; it punctuates and it shifts the system from the low-level trap.

Network externalities, which are intimately related to the process of technology diffusion and emerge as positive feedback from random contacts among economic agents, effectively enforce rapid growth of the network itself (Valente, 1996; Lechman, 2015). Put differently, the network effects act as positive re-alimentation schema, generate sustainable multiplication of new users of a given technology (Markus, 1987) and thus the number of new users usually starts to grow exponentially. However, it is important to note that these positive network effects may be unveiled only if the socio-economic system reaches a certain critical mass.[15,16] Put shortly, network externalities are the sources of the critical mass. Following Cabral (1990, 2006), we may claim that the emergence of the critical mass is preconditioned by the strength of the network effects and the intensity of random contacts among society members. Only if the network externalities are sufficiently strong can the 'catastrophe' on the diffusion trajectory occur, and this 'catastrophe' point corresponds to the critical mass or the low-level equilibrium point. In the same vein as Cabral, Economides and Himmelberg (1995, 1996) suggest that the critical mass should be recognized as the low-level equilibria point on the diffusion path, which must be reached to sustain further diffusion processes. Technically, Economides and Himmelberg (1995, 1996) have pointed out that the critical mass is the smallest possible, but higher than zero, saturation rate which conditions effective spread of new technologies. Lim et al. (2003) following Rogers (1990) and Schoder (2000), define critical mass as the minimal number of users of new technology ensuring the future rate of adoption to be self-sustaining.

Rogers (1983) proposes analyzing the phenomenon of critical mass from a broader and non-technical (non-mathematical) perspective. He argues that critical mass may be defined as a unique point on technology diffusion patterns, which conditions the diffusion process to become self-sustaining (self-perpetuating). Rogers perceives the process of diffusion as endogenously driven, and hence he demonstrates that rapid spread of technological novelties among society members is driven by networking activities rather than strongly conditioned by prices of changes (mainly shifts) in products and/or services' quality and utility. A similar perception of the critical mass was proposed by Allen (1988), who emphasized social aspects of this problem, arguing,

> Each person has, as it were, an individual vision of what constitutes critical mass (. . .) upon everybody watching while being watched (. . .) critical mass for the group floats it seems on shifting perceptions of what the group outcome may be.
>
> (Allen, 1988)

Assuming that the process of technology diffusion is endogenous implies that reaching the critical mass is an important prerequisite to determine its success of failure. If the critical mass is not reached, and the system is 'locked' in the slow-rate and low-level diffusion trap, the risk of failure arises. Not reaching the critical mass may be caused by multiple factors, such as legal and institutional constraints, impeded spatial dynamics of diffusion, high risk aversion, information gaps and asymmetries or chaotic behavior of individuals. In the case of various impediments, diffusion of technologies and reaching the crucial mass should be stimulated so that the challenge-response type of socio-economic behavior of agents constitutes a strong stimulus for growth of the network. Apparently, if different 'bottlenecks' are overcome, the critical mass is reached, the system is shifted from the low-level equilibria and the number of new users of a given technology starts to grow at the exponential rate; hence, both societies and economies may 'reap the fruits' of implementation and usage of new technologies. Evidently, reaching the critical mass is a *sine qua non* for new technology diffusion. It is noteworthy that the phenomenon of the critical mass, at least to some extent, generates non-linearities along technology diffusion paths. When the critical mass is reached, the diffusion path is usually no longer marked by random fluctuations, but rather the diffusion pattern is more systematic and resembles the S-shaped curve.

Technically, the critical mass is a threshold penetration (saturation) rate that *must* be achieved to encourage other individuals in a given society to acquire new technology. Reaching the critical mass signals the occurrence of technological take-off;[17] henceforth, the critical mass may be defined as the threshold saturation enabling the technological take-off (see Figure 3.3). Once the critical mass is reached, the diffusion will eventually, under favorable conditions, reach the whole population. If the system reaches its critical mass and the unique technological take-off takes place, it determines further patterns of technology diffusion. Golder and Tellis (1997) define the 'take-off' as the point along the diffusion curve at which the empirical curve demonstrates the greatest inflections relative to the initial growth rate. Mathematically speaking, this would be the point along the diffusion path where its second derivative reaches the maximum.

The emergence of the technological take-off constitutes a prerequisite for ensuring the sustainability of the process of technology diffusion (Lechman, 2015). Visual inspection of Figure 3.3 suggests that both critical mass and technological take-off are preceded by the early diffusion phase. The length of the early diffusion phase, which we also label the *pre-take-off stage (phase)* may be measured by the number of years between the time when new technology was introduced to the market for the first time and the time when the critical mass is reached. During the pre-take-off stage, the

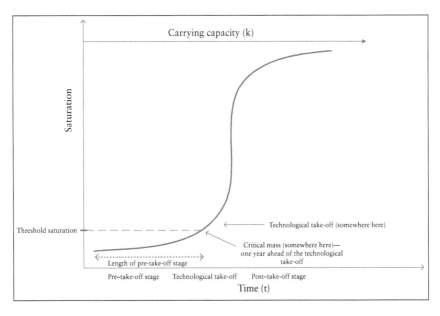

Figure 3.3 Critical mass and technological take-off on the diffusion S-shaped time path

Source: Author's elaboration.

process of the spread of new technology among agents proceeds at a relatively slow rate, which means that the number of new users of technology is increasing spasmodically. Importantly, during the early diffusion stage, the process of spreading new technologies is still—at least to some extent—reversible, meaning that if new technology does not gain enough acceptance among society members, its adoption rate would finally start to decrease, as new competing and more advantageous technology starts to evade the market intensively. Moreover, if during this early phase the diffusion processes is hindered by external factors and the diffusion rate results remain at an extremely low level for a significantly long time period, there emerges a risk of being 'locked' in the low-level (low-saturation) trap from which escape might be difficult.

However, under favorable conditions, once the critical mass is reached and the technological take-off occurs, the diffusion starts to proceed at a high pace, typically at an exponential rate, and the number of users of new technology increases dramatically. Put differently, the technological take-off perpetuates, speeds up the process of diffusion, and hence it radically changes its nature. Technological take-off suggests entering a new phase on the diffusion path. Technological take-off may be also labeled as the transition point (time) from the initial (early, introductory) phase (stage) to the rapid growth phase. Finally, the rate of diffusion slows down, and the system reaches the maturity (stabilization) phase (compare Figure 3.2), during which increases of the number of new users of a given technology, although positive, are usually negligible.

Next in this section, following Lechman (2015), we explain an operational measure to determine when the critical mass is reached and the technological take-off occurs. The novel methodological approach that follows allows for the identification of

- saturation (penetration rate) at which the critical mass is reached;
- time period when the critical mass is reached;
- time period when the technological take-off occurs; and
- length of the pre-take-off stage on the diffusion time path.

We propose the conceptual definition of the *critical saturation (penetration) rate* (critical mass[18]) and define it as the technology- and country-specific *threshold* that once passed provokes the occurrence of the technological take-off, while the *technological take-off* we define as the time period (usually one year) after the critical mass is reached, which once achieved enables the diffusion of technology to proceed at an exponential rate. In other words, the critical saturation rate (critical mass) is reached one year ahead of the technological take-off. The *critical year* denotes the time period when the critical saturation rate is reached, while the *pre-take-off stage* we define as the diffusion phase occurring between the initial year that new technology was first introduced to the market until the critical year.

Determining, in mathematical terms, the critical mass, the technological take-off and the length of the pre-take-off stage in a given economy yields the definition of the following terms:

- technology replication coefficient—$\Phi_{i,t}$,
- marginal growth in technology adoption—$\Omega_{i,t}$,
- level of technology adoption (saturation)—$S_{i,t}$,

where i denotes country and t denotes time. Moreover, we denote the critical saturation (penetration) rate as $\vartheta_{i,t}$, the critical year as T_i^{crit}, the technological take-off as $T_i^{takeoff}$, and the pre-take-off stage as Π_i^y, with analogous notations, where y is the number of years.

Let $S_{i,t}$ be the level of technology adoption in i-country at t-time, and by definition, for each time period, the level of technology adoption is taking non-negative values $S_{i,t} > 0$. Hypothetically, $S_{i,t} = 0$ may occur, but in that case, the given technology is adopted by a none entity. Let us assume, however, that $S_{i,t} > 0$ and the diffusion process is reported, then we may define the replication coefficient as

$$\Phi_{i,t} = \frac{S_{i,t}}{S_{i,t-1}}, \tag{3.8}$$

or, alternatively,

$$S_{i,t} = \Phi_{i,t} [S_{i,t-1}] \tag{3.9}$$

The replication coefficient, $\Phi_{i,t}$, explains the multiplication (replication) of the given technology users, which is demonstrated because of emerging positive network externalities. It also shows the dynamics of the process of spreading new technology over time. To give an example, if $\Phi_{i,t}$ is 5 in i-country and t-time, it shows that in $(t-1)$, each user of a given technology has 'generated' an *additional* four new users of the same technology (in time t we had five users, while in time $t-1$ we had only one user). Assuming that in each consecutive year the saturation rate is higher, hence $S_{i,t-1} > 0$, $S_{i,t} > 0$ and $S_{i,t} > S_{i,t-1}$, then for each time period, the replication coefficient is non-negative, $\Phi_{i,t} \in (0;\infty)$. Arguably, the process of replication of users of a given technology is a 'foundation stone' of the diffusion itself. The value of $\Phi_{i,t}$ determines whether the total number of users of a given technology increases, decreases or is constant over time. If $\Phi_{i,t} > 1$, it shows that in each consecutive year the number of users of technology is growing; if $\Phi_{i,t} < 1$, the number of users of technology is falling, while if—$\Phi_{i,t} = 1$, it is constant and no diffusion is reported.

$$\Omega_{i,t} = S_{i,t} - S_{i,t-1},\qquad\qquad(3.10)$$

Next, we define marginal growth in technology adoption, which is with analogous notations as in Eq. (3.8), and it expresses the change in total number of users of new technology over consecutive years.

It's noteworthy that $\Phi_{i,t}$ and $\Omega_{i,t}$ are intimately related and interdependent. Consider the case when $\Phi_{i,t} > 1$. Then we may write,

$$\Omega_{i,t} = S_{i,t-1}[\Phi_{i,t} - 1]\qquad\qquad(3.11)$$

The interrelatedness of $\Phi_{i,t}$ and $\Omega_{i,t}$ is demonstrated in Figure 3.4. Figure 3.4 also allows for visual identification of the critical mass (critical penetration rate) and technological take-off, which are identified along the S-shaped diffusion curve.

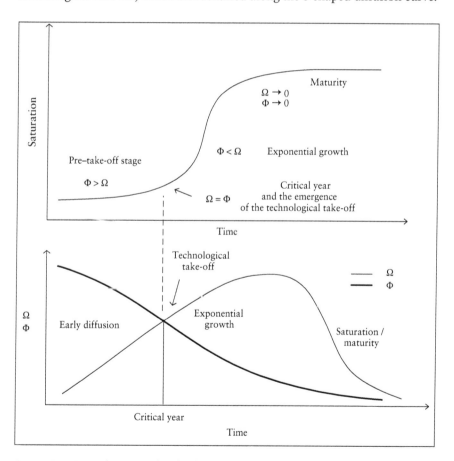

Figure 3.4 Critical mass and technological take-off—theoretical specification
Source: Adapted from Lechman (2015).

The marginal growth in technology—$\Omega_{i,t}$—is determined by the dynamics of the diffusion process, which we express through the replication of the coefficient $\Phi_{i,t}$. First, if $\Phi_{i,y} > 1$, then $\Omega_{i,y} > 0$, and the replication process is sufficiently high and the diffusion proceeds dynamically, which is demonstrated in the increasing number of new technology users ($S_{i,t} < S_{i,t+1}$) Second, if $\Phi_{i,y} = 1$, then $\Omega_{i,y} = 0$ and no replication is reported and the diffusion does not proceed, which results in a constant number of users of new technology ($S_{i,t} = S_{i,t+1} = \ldots = S_{i,t+n}$). And third, f $\Phi_{i,y} < 1$, then $\Omega_{i,y} < 0$ and the replication process is weak and the diffusion is limited; the number of users of new technology is falling ($S_{i,t} > S_{i,t+1}$). Examining the co-movements of $\Phi_{i,t}$ and $\Omega_{i,t}$ values—see Figure 3.4—along the S-shaped diffusion trajectory allows for the detection of critical saturation rate $\vartheta_{i,t}$, critical year T_i^{crit}, technological take-off $T_i^{takeoff}$ and the length of the pre-take-off phase Π_i^y

During the pre-take-off diffusion stage, the replication coefficient is higher than marginal growth ($\Phi_{i,t} > \Omega_{i,y}$). The latter implies that in the initial phase of diffusion, there emerges the gap between $\Phi_{i,t}$ and $\Omega_{i,t}$. However, if the diffusion process is characterized by relatively high dynamism, then the replication process gains in strength so that $\Phi_{i,t} > 1$ and $\Omega_{i,y} > 0$, resulting in a growing number of a given technology users and the emergence of positive network effects. It is noteworthy that as diffusion proceeds, we observe gradual increases in value of the marginal growth of technology, while simultaneously the replication coefficient drops. Eventually, it leads to eliminating the gap between $\Phi_{i,t}$ and $\Omega_{i,t}$; henceforth, eventually $\Phi_{i,t} = \Omega_{i,t}$. The process briefly described in this section may be visually traced (see Figure 3.4) as convergence of paths approximating changing values of $\Phi_{i,t}$ and $\Omega_{i,t}$ over time. If $\Phi_{i,t} = \Omega_{i,t}$ occurs at a given point in time, the paths approximating changing values of $\Phi_{i,t}$ and $\Omega_{i,t}$ finally intersect. *This unique point in time when $\Phi_{i,t} = \Omega_{i,t}$, we label the critical year*[19] T_i^{crit}, *while the saturation in T_i^{crit}, we name the critical saturation rate $\vartheta_{i,t}$, which approximates the critical mass.* Conceptually, the critical year is the specific time period during which the dynamics of the diffusion process transforms radically, meaning from that point onwards, the diffusion proceeds at an exponential rate and the number of users of a given technology increases dramatically. In other words, the early diffusion phase is left behind, and the process of diffusion enters the exponential growth phase.

Identification of the critical year T_i^{crit} allows for the determination of the length of the pre-take-off stage, which is

$$\Pi_i^y = T_i^{crit} - T_i^{1st}, \tag{3.12}$$

where $T_i^{initial}$ denotes the time period when a given technology was first introduced to the market.

Next, we identify the technological take-off $T_i^{takeoff}$, which is the time period during which the rate of the diffusion process is radically shifted, and claim that it occurs during the next two years after the critical mass is reached. Hence we may write,

$$T_i^{takeoff} = T_i^{crit} + 2,$$ (3.13)

with standard notations.

Once the critical mass and technological take-off are reached, the new technology starts to spread at a high—usually exponential—rate. However, eventually, the diffusion slows down as the system heads towards high saturation and enters the maturity phase along the diffusion trajectory, during which $\Phi_{i,t} \to 1$, and $\Omega_{i,t} = 0$.

Hypothetically, if during the early diffusion phase the process of spreading new technology is too weak or impeded by external factors, the network externalities do not emerge and, as a consequence, the critical mass may not be reached and the technological take-off will not occur. Considering the methodological procedure explained earlier, this would imply that the initially emerging gap between $\Phi_{i,t}$ and $\Omega_{i,t}$ is not closed, and paths approximating changes in replication coefficients and marginal growths of technology will diverge rather than converge. If $\Phi_{i,t} = \Omega_{i,t}$ is not reported, then the critical mass is not reached, and the process of technology diffusion is discontinued. In such a case, the unoptimistic scenario, that the diffusion process never speeds up, is that it is possible that the spread of new technology will be restrained and the system will remain locked in the 'low-level' trap.

Finally, it's noteworthy that the emergence of the critical mass and the technological take-off is not unconditional. New technologies do not diffuse into a vacuum. Acquiring technological novelties is not a one-time task, but rather should be perceived as continuous and dynamic, especially in the context of a rapidly changing environment, human knowledge, people's needs and propensities or state policy. Arguably, technology diffusion and the external environment, including a wide variety of social, economic and institutional aspects, remain in a kind of symbiotic relationship.

The critical mass giving rise to the exponential growth of new users of technology, is strongly affected by personal preferences and attitudes of the group of people called by Rogers 'early adopters'. In fact, their willingness to take risks and experiment, and their willingness to pay for technological novelties are decisive factors for the success or failure of the process of technology diffusion. Only if the group of 'early adopters' is new technologies focused and demonstrates high propensity to adopt and use novelties, and is interested in technologically sophisticated solutions, will the process of technology diffusion be successful. Hence reaching the critical mass or not is basically conditioned by the behavior and habits of the 'early adopters'.

Conceptually, the problem of critical mass may be, however, perceived from a significantly broader perspective. For instance, Perez (2004) views the critical mass from the very broad and macro perspective, and she writes,

> When the diffusion of the new paradigm has reached a certain critical mass, imposing its new modernizing logic upon the rest of the productive system, that both the painful consequences of the process of 'creative destruction' and the obstacles to a full and beneficial deployment of the new potential become fully visible.
>
> (Perez, 2004, p. 16)

Socio-economic systems are characterized by unique inertia, which, first, may heavily hinder rapid adoption of new technologies, and, second, increases uncertainty under which potential new adopters operate. Much effort is needed to overcome this system of inertia. What would allow this system to head towards reaching certain critical mass of adopters? Often the whole socio-economic system and its actors require multiple, usually demand-side, incentives to increase their propensity to acquire new technology. The latter preconditions the intensity with which network effects positively affect the process of diffusion and hence reach the critical mass. Henceforth, reaching the critical mass is determined by a unique combination of various prerequisites, encompassing both strictly social aspects, such as social norms and attitudes, as well as economic and institutional factors, inter alia, relative prices, willingness to pay for new technology, availability and relative utility of subsidiary and/or complementary goods and services, fundamental relationship between price and quality of newly offered technological solutions or market regulations. Put shortly, the dynamics of diffusion and diffusion patterns are socially and economically shaped, while the presence of network externalities, shifting the systems from low-level into high-level equilibria, effectively fuels the process of spreading new ideas.

Notes

1. Also known as 'predator-pray' equation used to describe the competition process and the dynamics of biological systems.
2. Named after Benjamin Gompertz (1779–1865), a British mathematician famous for his demographic model of mortality.
3. J. Schumpeter (1934) in his seminal work *The Theory of Economic Development: An Inquiry into Profits, Capital, Credit, Interest, and the Business Cycle* claimed that technological change is characterized by linear progression, meaning that the technology diffusion path is rather a linear type. He argued that new technologies are simply adopted and exploited by the economic system. Schumpeter also argued that being a 'non-user' ('non-adopter') of new technology would be irrational; hence, all rationally behaving economic agents should immediately adopt new technology.
4. Mathematically, the bell curve is the first derivative of the S-shaped trajectory. It shows the expansion of new technology and the stock of knowledge that is

associated with it, which is the consequence of the process of diffusion. The slope of the bell curve decreases as the number of new users of new technology grows, and the inflection point of the sigmoid pattern, by definition, coincides with the maximum of the bell curve.

5. For broader discussion on the concept of 'critical mass', see Sect. 3.2.

6. Pierre François Verhulst (1804–1849) was a Belgian mathematician, who in 1838, published the logistic equation representing growth of individuals in time. He assumed that growth is restricted by the system carrying capacity, showing the maximum number of individuals that the given system can support.

7. Raymond Pearl (1879–1940) was an American biologist, who in late the 1920s, together with Lowell Reed (1886–1960), a researcher in biostatistics, used a similar formula of the logistic equation in biological sciences.

8. Base of natural logarithms.

9. An economist, Z.Griliches, developed the first empirical study in an attempt to capture quantitative aspects of technology diffusion. He studied the 'diffusion' of hybrid corn seed in Midwestern United States. In his study, Griliches underlined the importance of several aspects, determining the process of diffusion of innovations, such as expected profits, geographical conditions, suppliers' activities and easiness of technology transfer, which are characteristics of certain technologies.

10. See Fudenberg and Tirole (1985), Tirole (1988), Reinganum (1981, 1989), Kapur (1995), Karshenas and Stoneman (1993).

11. See David (1969, 1975), Davies (1979), Stoneman and Ireland (1983), David and Olsen (1984), Jovanovic and MacDonald (1993).

12. See Silverberg (1991), Metcalfe (1997), Geroski (2000), Nelson and Winter (2009),

13. Technologies that facilitate communication or the spread of knowledge and information are also named 'network goods', as their utility increases with the growing number of people (network) that use them.

14. Economides (1996) additionally differentiates between two major approaches to network analysis: the macro approach, which attempts to demonstrate the macro consequences of the network externalities, and the micro approach, which intends to identify the root causes of the network effects.

15. Originally, the term critical mass comes from nuclear physics where it denotes the amount of radioactive material needed for a pile to go into a self-sustaining reaction.

16. The term critical mass was introduced to social sciences by Mancur Olson (1965), who defined it as a critical number of new users of new technology who encourage the remaining part of the society to imitate their behavior and hence lead to collective actions.

17. The term 'take-off' has been initially used in economic literature by Walt Rostow, who, in his seminal paper 'The Take-Off into Self-Sustaining Growth' (1956) writes, '*Centering on a relatively brief time interval of two or three decades when the economy and the society of which it is a part transforms themselves in such ways that economic growth is, subsequently, more or less automatic*' (Rostow, 1956, p. 1). Rostow named this transformation the '*take-off*'. Rostow (1956, 1963, 1990) also argues that identifying the '*take-off*' entails seeking to isolate the specific period (interval) in which '*the scale of productive activity reaches a critical level, (. . .) which leads to a massive and progressive structural transformation in economic, better viewed as change in kind than a merely in degree*' (Rostow, 1956, p. 16).

18. The terms critical saturation rate and critical mass are used interchangeably.

19. Technically, for identification of the *exact* time when $\Phi_{i,t} = \Omega_{i,t}$ daily data would be needed. As usual, only annual data is broadly available. By convention, we claim that the critical year is the first year when $\Phi_{i,t} < \Omega_{i,t}$, if $\Phi_{i,t-1} > \Omega_{i,t-1}$.

References

Allen, D. (1988). New telecommunications services: Network externalities and critical mass. *Telecommunications Policy*, 12(3), 257–271.

Antonelli, C. (2012). The economics of localized technological change and industrial dynamics (Vol. 3). Springer Science & Business Media.

Attewell, P. (1992). Technology diffusion and organizational learning: The case of business computing. *Organization Science*, 3(1), 1–19.

Ausubel, J. H. (1991). Rat race dynamics and crazy companies: The diffusion of technologies and social behavior. In *Diffusion of technologies and social behavior* (pp. 1–17). Berlin and Heidelberg: Springer.

Bass, F. M. (1969). A new product growth for model consumer durables. *Management Science*, 15(5), 215–227.

Bass, F. M. (1980). The relationship between diffusion rates, experience curves, and demand elasticities for consumer durable technological innovations. *Journal of Business*, 53(3), S51–S67.

Bergek, A., Jacobsson, S., & Sandén, B. A. (2008). 'Legitimation' and 'development of positive externalities': Two key processes in the formation phase of technological innovation systems. *Technology Analysis & Strategic Management*, 20(5), 575–592.

Bhargava, S. C. (1989). Generalized Lotka-Volterra equations and the mechanism of technological substitution. *Technological Forecasting and Social Change*, 35(4), 319–326.

Cabral, L. M. (1990). On the adoption of innovations with 'network' externalities. *Mathematical Social Sciences*, 19(3), 299–308.

Cabral, L. M. (2006). Equilibrium, epidemic and catastrophe: Diffusion of innovations with network effects. In C. Antonelli, D. Foray, B. H. Hall, & W. E. Steinmueller (Eds.), *New frontiers in the economics of innovation and new technology: Essays in honour of Paul A. David* (p. 427).

Coontz, S. H. (2013). Population theories and their economic interpretation (Vol. 8). Routledge.

Cramer, J. S. (2003). The origins and development of the logit model. In *Logit models from economics and other fields* (pp. 149–158). Cambridge University Press.

Cusumano, M. A., Mylonadis, Y., & Rosenbloom, R. S. (1992). Strategic maneuvering and mass-market dynamics: The triumph of VHS over beta. *Business History Review*, 66(1), 51–94.

Darwin, C. (1859 [1968]). *The origin of species*. London: Murray Google Scholar.

David, P. A. (1969). *A contribution to the theory of diffusion*. Research Center in Economic Growth, Stanford University.

David, P. A. (1975). Technical choice innovation and economic growth: Essays on American and British experience in the nineteenth century. Cambridge University Press.

David, P. A. (1985). Clio and the economics of QWERTY. *The American Economic Review*, 75(2), 332–337.

David, P. A. (1986). Technology diffusion, public policy, and industrial competitiveness. In *The positive sum strategy: Harnessing technology for economic growth* (pp. 373–391).

David, P. A., & Olsen, T. E. (1984). Anticipated automation: A rational expectations model of technological diffusion. CEPR/Stanford University.

Davies, S. (1979). *The diffusion of process innovations.* CUP Archive.

Devezas, T. C. (2005). Evolutionary theory of technological change: State-of-the-art and new approaches. *Technological Forecasting and Social Change, 72*(9), 1137–1152.

Dopfer, K., Foster, J., & Potts, J. (2004). Micro-meso-macro. *Journal of Evolutionary Economics, 14*(3), 263–279.

Dosi, G. (1991). The research on innovation diffusion: An assessment. In *Diffusion of technologies and social behavior* (pp. 179–208). Berlin and Heidelberg: Springer.

Economides, N. (1996). The economics of networks. *International Journal of Industrial Organization, 14*(6), 673–699.

Economides, N., & Himmelberg, C. P. (1995). *Critical mass and network size with application to the US fax market.* NYU Stern School of Business, EC-95-11.

Ehrnberg, E. (1995). On the definition and measurement of technological discontinuities. *Technovation, 15*(7), 437–452.

Fisher, J. C., & Pry, R. H. (1971). A simple substitution model of technological change. *Technological Forecasting and Social Change, 3*, 75–88.

Fisher, R. A. (1930). The genetical theory of natural selection: A complete variorum edition. Oxford: Oxford University Press.

Foray, D. (1997). The dynamic implications of increasing returns: Technological change and path dependent inefficiency. *International Journal of Industrial Organization, 15*(6), 733–752.

Foray, D., & Grübler, A. (1990). Morphological analysis, diffusion and lockout of technologies: Ferrous casting in France and the FRG. *Research Policy, 19*(6), 535–550.

Foster, D., & Young, P. (1990). Stochastic evolutionary game dynamics*. *Theoretical Population Biology, 38*(2), 219–232.

Freeman, C. (1991). Innovation, changes of techno-economic paradigm and biological analogies in economics. *Revue économique, 42*(2), 211–231.

Freeman, C., & Pérez, C. (1988). Structural crises and adjustements. In G. Dosi, C. Freeman, R. Nelson, G. Silverberg & L. Soet (Eds.), *Technical change and economic theory.* London: Pinter.

Fudenberg, D., & Tirole, J. (1985). Preemption and rent equalization in the adoption of new technology. *The Review of Economic Studies, 52*(3), 383–401.

Geroski, P. A. (2000). Models of technology diffusion. *Research Policy, 29*(4), 603–625.

Golder, P. N., & Tellis, G. J. (1997). Will it ever fly? Modeling the takeoff of really new consumer durables. *Marketing Science, 16*(3), 256–270.

Gould, S. J., & Eldredge, N. (1977). Punctuated equilibria: The tempo and mode of evolution reconsidered. *Paleobiology, 3*(02), 115–151.

Granovetter, M. (1978). Threshold models of collective behavior. *American Journal of Sociology, 83*(6), 1420–1443.

Griliches, Z. (1957). Hybrid corn: An exploration in the economics of technological change. *Econometrica, Journal of the Econometric Society, 25*(4), 501–522.

Grübler, A. (1991). Diffusion: long-term patterns and discontinuities. In *Diffusion of technologies and social behavior* (pp. 451–482). Berlin & Heidelberg: Springer.

Grübler, A., & Nakićenović, N. (1991). Long waves, technology diffusion, and substitution. *Review (Fernand Braudel Center), XIV*(2), 313–343.

Hall, B. H. (2004). *Innovation and diffusion* (No. w10212). National Bureau of Economic Research.

Hoy, M., & Polborn, M. K. (2015). The value of technology improvements in games with externalities: A fresh look at offsetting behavior. *Journal of Public Economics*, *131*, 12–20.

Ismail, A. (2015). A review of theoretical approaches on diffusion analysis: Discussing issues involved in the adoption of ICT services in a complex socio-economic context. *Australian Journal of Sustainable Business and Society*, *1*(1), 97–108.

Jaffe, A. B., Newell, R. G., & Stavins, R. N. (2005). A tale of two market failures: Technology and environmental policy. *Ecological Economics*, *54*(2), 164–174.

Jovanovic, B., & MacDonald, G. (1993). *Competitive diffusion* (No. w4463). National Bureau of Economic Research.

Kapur, S. (1995). Technological diffusion with social learning. *Journal of Industrial Economics*, *43*(2), 173–195.

Karshenas, M., & Stoneman, P. L. (1993). Rank, stock, order, and epidemic effects in the diffusion of new process technologies: An empirical model. *The RAND Journal of Economics*, *24*(4), 503–528.

Katz, M. L., & Shapiro, C. (1985). Network externalities, competition, and compatibility. *The American Economic Review*, *75*(3), 424–440.

Keser, C., Suleymanova, I., & Wey, C. (2012). Technology adoption in markets with network effects: Theory and experimental evidence. *Information Economics and Policy*, *24*(3), 262–276.

Kucharavy, D., & De Guio, R. (2011). Application of S-shaped curves. *Procedia Engineering*, *9*, 559–572.

Kudryashov, N. A. (2013). Polynomials in logistic function and solitary waves of nonlinear differential equations. *Applied Mathematics and Computation*, *219*(17), 9245–9253.

Kwasnicki, W. (2013). Logistic growth of the global economy and competitiveness of nations. *Technological Forecasting and Social Change*, *80*(1), 50–76.

Lechman, E. (2015). ICT diffusion in developing countries: Towards a new concept of technological takeoff. Springer.

Lee, M., Kim, K., & Cho, Y. (2010). A study on the relationship between technology diffusion and new product diffusion. *Technological Forecasting and Social Change*, *77*(5), 796–802.

Liikanen, J., Stoneman, P., & Toivanen, O. (2004). Intergenerational effects in the diffusion of new technology: The case of mobile phones. *International Journal of Industrial Organization*, *22*(8), 1137–1154.

Lim, B. L., Choi, M., & Park, M. C. (2003). The late take-off phenomenon in the diffusion of telecommunication services: Network effect and the critical mass. *Information Economics and Policy*, *15*(4), 537–557.

Loch, C. H., & Huberman, B. A. (1999). A punctuated-equilibrium model of technology diffusion. *Management Science*, *45*(2), 160–177.

Mahajan, V., & Muller, E. (1996). Timing, diffusion, and substitution of successive generations of technological innovations: The IBM mainframe case. *Technological Forecasting and Social Change*, *51*(2), 109–132.

Mansfield, E. (1961). Technical change and the rate of imitation. *Econometrica: Journal of the Econometric Society*, *29*(4), 741–766.

Mansfield, E. (1968). Industrial research and technological innovation; An econometric analysis. New York: Norton & Co.

Mansfield, E. (1971). Technological change: An introduction to a vital area of modern economics. Norton.

Markus, M. L. (1987). Toward a 'critical mass' theory of interactive media universal access, interdependence and diffusion. *Communication Research*, 14(5), 491–511.

Matthews, R. C. (1984). Darwinism and economic change. *Oxford Economic Papers*, 36, 91–117.

Metcalfe, J. S. (1997). On diffusion and the process of technological change. In A. Gilberto & N. D. Liso, N. D. (Eds.), *Economics of structural and technological change* (pp. 123–144).

Meyer, P. (1994). Bi-logistic growth. *Technological Forecasting and Social Change*, 47(1), 89–102.

Meyer, P. S., Yung, J. W., & Ausubel, J. H. (1999). A primer on logistic growth and substitution: The mathematics of the Loglet Lab software. *Technological Forecasting and Social Change*, 61(3), 247–271.

Modis, T. (2007). Strengths and weaknesses of S-curves. *Technological Forecasting and Social Change*, 74(6), 866–872.

Mokyr, J. (2010). The contribution of economic history to the study of innovation and technical change: 1750–1914. In B. H. Hall & N. Rosenberg (Eds.), *Handbook of the economics of innovation* (Vol. 1, pp. 11–50). Elsevier.

Moore, G. A. (2002). *Crossing the chasm: Marketing and selling technology project.* Harper Collins

Morris, S. A., & Pratt, D. (2003). Analysis of the Lotka–Volterra competition equations as a technological substitution model. *Technological Forecasting and Social Change*, 70(2), 103–133.

Nakićenović, N. (1991). Diffusion of pervasive systems: A case of transport infrastructures. In *Diffusion of technologies and social behavior* (pp. 483–510). Berlin and Heidelberg: Springer.

Nakićenović, N., & Grübler, A. (Eds.). (2013). *Diffusion of technologies and social behavior*. Springer Science & Business Media.

Nelson, R. R., & Winter, S. G. (2009). *An evolutionary theory of economic change*. Cambridge, MA: Harvard University Press.

Olson, M. (1965). The logic of collective action: Public goods and the theory of groups. Cambridge, MA.

Peres, R., Muller, E., & Mahajan, V. (2010). Innovation diffusion and new product growth models: A critical review and research directions. *International Journal of Research in Marketing*, 27(2), 91–106.

Perez, C. (2004). Technological revolutions, paradigm shifts and socio-institutional change. In E. S. Reinert (Eds.), *Globalization, economic development and inequality: An alternative perspective* (pp. 217–242). Edward Elgar Publishing.

Ray, G. F. (1983). The diffusion of mature technologies. *National Institute Economic Review*, 106(1), 56–62.

Reinganum, J. F. (1981). On the diffusion of new technology: A game theoretic approach. *The Review of Economic Studies*, 48(3), 395–405.

Reinganum, J. F. (1989). The timing of innovation: Research, development, and diffusion. In M. Armstrong & R. H. Porter (Eds.), *Handbook of industrial organization* (Vol. 1, pp. 849–908). Elsevier.

Rogers, E. M. (1983). *Diffusion of innovations*. New York.

Rogers, E. M. (1990, March). The 'critical mass' in the diffusion of interactive technologies. In *Modelling the innovation* (pp. 79–94).

Rohlfs, J. H. (2003). *Bandwagon effects in high-technology industries*. Cambridge, MA: MIT Press.

Romeo, A. A. (1975). Interindustry and interfirm differences in the rate of diffusion of an innovation. *The Review of Economics and Statistics*, *57*(3), 311–319.

Roper, S., Vahter, P., & Love, J. H. (2013). Externalities of openness in innovation. *Research Policy*, *42*(9), 1544–1554.

Rosenberg, N. (1976). *Perspectives on technology*. CUP Archive.

Rostow, W. W. (1956). The take-off into self-sustained growth. *The Economic Journal*, *66*(261), 25–48.

Rostow, W. W. (1963). Economics of take-off into sustained growth. Springer.

Rostow, W. W. (1990). *The stages of economic growth: A non-communist manifesto*. Cambridge: Cambridge University Press.

Sahal, D. (1981). Patterns of technological innovation. Addison-Wesley.

Sarkar, J. (1998). Technological diffusion: Alternative theories and historical evidence. *Journal of Economic Surveys*, *12*(2), 131–176.

Saviotti, P. P. (2002). Black boxes and variety in the evolution of technologies. In C. Antonelli & N. De Liso (Eds.), *Economics of structural and technological change* (pp. 184–212). Routledge.

Schoder, D. (2000). Forecasting the success of telecommunication services in the presence of network effects. *Information Economics and Policy*, *12*(2), 181–200.

Schumpeter, J. A. (1934). The theory of economic development: An inquiry into profits, capital, credit, interest, and the business cycle (Vol. 55). Transaction Publishers.

Scrase, I., & MacKerron, G. (2009). Lock-in. In *Energy for the future* (pp. 89–100). UK: Palgrave Macmillan.

Shapiro, C., & Varian, H. (1998). Information rules: A strategic guide to the. In C. Shapiro, H. R. Varian, & W. E. Becker (Eds.), *Network economy*.

Shy, O. (2001). *The economics of network industries*. Cambridge: Cambridge University Press.

Silverberg, G. (1991). Adoption and diffusion of technology as a collective evolutionary process. *Technological Forecasting and Social Change*, *39*(1–2), 67–80.

Silverberg, G., Dosi, G., & Orsenigo, L. (1988). Innovation, diversity and diffusion: A self-organisation model. *The Economic Journal*, *98*(393), 1032–1054.

Stone, R. (1980). Sigmoids. *Journal of Applied Statistics*, *7*(1), 59–119.

Stoneman, P. (1983). *The economic analysis of technological change*. Oxford and New York: Oxford University Press.

Stoneman, P. (2001). The economics of technological diffusion. Wiley-Blackwell.

Stoneman, P., & Battisti, G. (2010). The diffusion of new technology. In B. H. Hall & N. Rosenberg (Eds.), *Handbook of the economics of innovation* (Vol. 2, pp. 733–760).

Stoneman, P., & Diederen, P. (1994). Technology diffusion and public policy. *The Economic Journal*, *104*(425), 918–930.

Stoneman, P., & Ireland, N. J. (1983). The role of supply factors in the diffusion of new process technology. *The Economic Journal*, *93*, 66–78.

Swanson, E. B., & Ramiller, N. C. (1997). The organizing vision in information systems innovation. *Organization Science*, *8*(5), 458–474.

Swanson, E. B., & Ramiller, N. C. (2004). Innovating mindfully with information technology. *MIS Quarterly*, *28*(4), 553–583.

Tirole, J. (1988). *The theory of industrial organization*. Cambridge, MA: MIT Press.

Valente, T. W. (1996). Social network thresholds in the diffusion of innovations. *Social Networks*, *18*(1), 69–89.

Witt, U. (1992). Evolutionary concepts in economics. *Eastern Economic Journal*, *18*(4), 405–419.

4 Identifying ICT Diffusion Patterns
Linking Models to Data for Technology

Data and Empirical Sample

The Sample

Our research focuses on examining the unique features of the process of ICT diffusion, and we intend to unveil factors determining the pace of spreading new technologies across selected upper-middle- and high-income economies. The time span of the empirical analysis is fully subjected to the availability of ICT data, and thus it covers the period between 1980 and 2015. Our empirical sample consists of 81 countries (see Table 4.1), where 34 are upper-middle-income economies (out of 53 classified as such) and 41 are high-income economies (out of 80 classified as such). By definition, from our empirical research, we have arbitrarily excluded small states and small island states (regardless of data availability) and those economies for which the available time series on ICT indicators were too short or with too many breaks to allow for reliable calculations and estimates. In our study, we have applied the World Bank country classification by income level for the fiscal year 2016; henceforth, all economies where classified into four standard income groups according to gross national income per capita level in 2014. The upper-middle-income economies are those where the annual GNI per capita ranges from 4,126 to 12,735 in current USUS (adopting the Atlas methodology), while high-income economies are those where annual GNI per capita is higher than 12,736 in current US$.

By convention, our analysis concentrates on developed economies. Despite the fact that this group of countries encompasses economies enjoying relatively high per capita income levels, the homogeneity of this group is a bit spurious. In fact, this group of countries is extremely heterogeneous, which makes examining these countries a challenging task. The countries differ significantly not only in terms of per capita income but also in respect to social development and welfare, political regimes and institutional and legal frameworks. They also vary in terms of culture, dominant religion, social norms and attitudes, as well as geopolitical location and population density. All these differences matter and heavily affect each country's individual

Table 4.1 List of selected upper-middle- and high-income economies

Upper-middle-income countries (total 34)		High-income countries (total 47)	
Algeria	Lebanon	Argentina[1]	Lithuania
Angola	Malaysia	Australia	Malta
Azerbaijan	Maldives	Austria	Korea (Rep. of)
Belarus	Mauritius	Belgium	Latvia
Bosnia and	Mexico	Brunei Darussalam	Oman
Herzegovina	Namibia	Canada	Poland
Botswana	Panama	Chile	Portugal
Brazil	Paraguay	Croatia	Qatar
Bulgaria	Peru	Cyprus	Russia
China	Romania	Czech Republic	Saudi Arabia
Colombia	Serbia	Denmark	Singapore
Costa Rica	South Africa	Estonia	Seychelles
Dominican	Surinam	Finland	Slovak Republic
Republic	Macedonia, T.F.Y.R.	France	Slovenia
Ecuador	Thailand	Germany	Spain
Iran (Islamic	Tunisia	Greece	Sweden
Rep. of)	Turkey	Hungary	Switzerland
Jamaica		Iceland	United Arab Emirates
Jordan		Ireland	United Kingdom
Kazakhstan		Israel	United States
		Italy	Uruguay
		Japan	Venezuela
		Netherlands	
		New Zealand	
		Norway	

[1] According to the World Bank country classification, during the period 1987–2017, Argentina was only once classified as a high-income country in fiscal year 2016, thus according to GNI per capita in USUS (Atlas methodology) in 2014 (see World Bank Analytical Classification tables → Country Analytical History sub-table). For the remaining years, Argentina was classified as an upper-middle-income economy (except years 1989 and 1990, when it was classified as a lower-middle-income economy).

Source: Derived from World Bank country classification (accessed November 2016).

social, economic and technological landscape. These differences additionally shape each country's unique characteristics and predetermines its ability to assimilate and effectively use new technologies.

It is noteworthy that treating all these countries as one homogenous group would result in a loss of a huge amount of information, thus not allowing the unveiling of their various unique features. Henceforth, we deliberately disaggregated the evidence and ran country-specific analysis with the belief that such an approach allows for the identification of country-specific ICT diffusion paths, estimates the dynamics of the process, unveils specific features of the technological take-off and its prerequisites and runs detailed analysis of countrywide conditions, which enable fast ICT diffusion.

The Data

Our database consists of annual data for 34 upper-middle- and 47 high-income economies from all world regions, and the sample period spans from 1980 to 2015. To ensure the international comparisons of data, in the case of each country, we have chosen the same sources of statistical data and applied the same techniques of analysis.

All statistics on ICT have been exclusively derived from the World Tele-communications/ICT Indicators database 2016 (WTI 2016; 20th Edition/December[1]). All data, which are available in WTI 2016 (an its past editions), are collected from national bodies, such as ministries, telecommunication authorities and national statistical agencies. These data on ICT are based on common international statistical standards, and that ensures their cross-country comparability, and thus they are characterized by the relatively least scarcity and inconsistency. To examine a country's individual achievements in terms of access to and use of new ICT, we have selected *four* core ICT indicators. These four measures allow for the assessment of a country's ICT performance, which is expressed through the 'lens' of accessibility and usage.

The selected ICT indicators are as follows:

- *Mobile-cellular telephone subscription* per 100 inhabitants ($MCS_{i,y}$, where i denotes country, and y denotes year), which refers to the number of subscriptions to a public mobile-telephone service that provides access to the public switched telephone network using cellular technology. The indicator includes (and is split into) the number of postpaid subscriptions and the number of active prepaid accounts that have been used during the last three months. The indicator applies to all mobile-cellular subscriptions that offer voice communications (definition provided in WTI 2016).
- *Active mobile-broadband subscriptions per 100 inhabitants* ($AMS_{i,y}$, hereafter with analogous notations), which refers to the sum of standard mobile-broadband and dedicated mobile broadband subscriptions to the public Internet. It covers actual subscribers, not potential subscribers, even though the latter may have broadband enabled handsets (definition provided in WTI 2016).
- *Fixed-broadband subscriptions per 100 inhabitants* ($FBS_{i,y}$, hereafter with analogous notations), which refers to fixed subscriptions to high-speed access to the public Internet (a TCP/IP connection) at downstream speeds equal to, or greater than, 256 kbit/s. This includes cable modem, DSL, fibre-to-the-home/building, other fixed (wired)-broadband subscriptions, satellite broadband and terrestrial fixed wireless broadband. This total is measured irrespective of the method of payment. It excludes subscriptions that have access to data communications (including the Internet) via mobile-cellular networks. It should include fixed WiMAX

and any other fixed wireless technologies. It includes both residential subscriptions and subscriptions for organizations (definition provided in WTI 2016).

- *Internet users as share of population* ($IU_{i,y}$, hereafter with analogous notations). This indicator can include both estimates and survey data corresponding to the proportion of individuals using the Internet based on results from national household surveys. The number should reflect the total population of the country, or at least individuals of five years and older. If this number is not available (i.e. target population reflects a more limited age group), an estimate for the entire population is produced (definition provided in WTI 2016).

Additionally, to demonstrate the process of switching from 'old' technologies offering voice communication to 'new' solutions, we use statistical data on fixed-telephone (previously named main telephone lines) subscriptions per 100 inhabitants. The ICT indicator of fixed-telephony ($FTL_{i,y}$, hereafter with analogous notations as in the case of previous ICT indicators) refers to the sum of the active number of analogue fixed-telephone lines, voice-over Internet Protocol subscriptions, fixed-wireless local loop subscriptions, ISDN voice-channel equivalents and fixed public payphones (see definition in WTI 2016).

The ICT indicators on mobile-cellular, active mobile-broadband and fixed-broadband basically reflect the state of development of ICT infrastructure and the possibility of society members accessing these types of new technologies, while the IU indicator rather demonstrates exclusively the state of access to and use of Internet networks by individuals and households through a variety of channels—e.g. fixed-narrowband Internet networks, fixed-broadband Internet networks or mobile networks. Basic data on ICT performance should be used wisely and be carefully interpreted. Despite the simplicity of ICT indicators, their in-depth analysis clearly unveils areas in which countries are doing well and those areas where there is still much room for improvement. Even brief analysis of basic ICT indicators allows for a rise in awareness on which countries are forging ahead or falling behind in respect to certain ICT achievements. When reading and interpreting statistics on ICT, it is important to note that for each country, the following relationship of '*inhabitants > those who have access > users > subscribers*' is true. Usually the number of legal subscribers accounts for the smallest number of people, while the number of users exceeds the number of subscribers, and the number of those who have access to certain technology usually exceeds the number of users. 'Subscribers' are legal owners of a given technology, who are obliged to pay for it, while 'users' are those who simply can use certain technology but not necessarily pay for its usage. Only in the case of mobile-cellular subscribers do we find this simple relationship as untrue, as in many countries, the number of subscribers per 100 inhabitants is higher than 100, which suggests that '*inhabitants < subscribers < (potentially) users*'.

The time span of our empirical research is set for the period 1980–2015; however, regarding various ICT indicators, time series availability varies heavily both across time and space. These differences result not only from difficulties with data collection on the country level but also earlier they were determined by the time of emergence and introduction to the national tele-communication market's new type of technology. The data on fixed-telephony subscriptions are available since early the '70s of the 20th century, when this type of technology for voice communication started to become widely available. Hence, for FTLi,y, the time series offered by WTI statistics cover the longest time span are well balanced (breaks in time series are exception, actually). In the case of data on mobile-cellular subscription, the time series are available since 1980, and the first statistics are for Finland. Next, in 1981, statistics on mobile-cellular subscriptions became available for Japan, Norway and Sweden; then in 1982, they become available for Denmark and United Arab Emirates. During the following years, statistical data regarding this type of ICT were becoming gradually available in consecutive countries, and, finally, since 1997, the dataset is perfectly balanced[2] (no gaps in time series are reported). The first official data on fixed-broadband subscriptions were released in the year 1998 for Belgium, Brazil, Canada, France, Japan, Korea (Rep. of), Netherlands, Singapore and the United States. The next year, in 1999, these data appeared for the next 13 countries, and since 2007, full-time series are reported. Time series on active mobile-broadband are relatively the shortest, as both upper-middle- and high-income economies are available from 2007 onward. However, in high-income economies, the full-time series are available from 2010, while in upper-middle-income economies, the series are only available from 2013. In upper-middle-income countries, in 2007, data on active mobile-broadband subscriptions were available only for four economies—Dominican Republic, Malaysia, Mauritius and Romani—and in 2008, they were available for another three countries. Analogously, in 2007, in high-income economies, similar data were available for 10 countries, while the next year, in 2008, data were available for another 12.

Key Trends in ICT Development

> Information technology is the most dynamic, pervasive, and influential tech-nology of our times. (. . .) this technology will alter our labor, business, gov-ernmental, and other socio-institutional structures.
>
> (H. A. Linstone, 1991, p. 89)

For the last decades, the world has been rapidly and profoundly transform-ing because of the explosive growth of new ICT. Available time series on changing ICT penetration rates suggests that both developing and devel-oped economies have been included in this overwhelming process. Rapidly boosting demand for new technologies offering 'connection with the outside world', mainly because of low-cost, fast and distributable, as well as easily adaptable wireless solutions, has disruptively reshaped the world landscape. The fast spread of ICT has opened new windows of opportunities for technological catching up, leapfrogging other countries technologically or simply escaping from permanent—often historically conditioned—technological marginalization.

This section throws light on the general overview of the process of ICT diffusion in developed countries that has been ostensibly observed for the last three decades. This part of the research uncovers that the process of spreading new ICT is phenomenally rapid and that ICT diffuse worldwide is happening at a historically unprecedented pace. It is also designed to demonstrate several striking facts about ICT diffusion across examined economies, putting special emphasis on drawing a general picture of key trends in diffusion, dynamics of the process and changes in inequality in access to and use of new technologies.

This preliminary evidence of key trends in ICT development in the developed world (34 upper-middle-income and 47 high-income economies) is limited to the period between 1990 and 2015. Here we decided to exclude the years 1980–1989, as complete data on ICT development for this period are available for very few countries. Table 4.2 summarizes the ICT indicators (mobile-cellular subscriptions—MCS, fixed-broadband subscriptions—FBS, active mobile-broadband subscriptions—AMS and Internet users—IU) descriptive statistics for upper-middle- and high-income economies between 1990 and 2015. These empirical results are additionally supported by the graphical evidence displayed in Figure 4.1, demonstrating ICT diffusion trajectories with regard to examined ICT indicators (*average values*[3]).

The results provided in Table 4.2 and demonstrated in Figure 4.1 shed light on how fast and disruptive changes in access to and use of ICT were in developed economies between 1990 and 2015.

Taking a closer look at MCS diffusion paths (see Figure 4.1), both in upper-middle- and high-income economies, some striking similarities are easily observable. Because of relatively good data availability in this case, we developed diffusion paths for the period 1980–2015. First, with regard to the high-income group, three characteristic phases along diffusion patterns can be distinguished—namely, the early (initial) diffusion stage during which the rate of diffusion is low and the growth in ICT penetration rate is spasmodic and easily reversible. During this early stage of diffusion, no significant or rapid shifts in ICT adoption are reported. All examined countries were 'locked' in this initial diffusion stage for approximately 17 years. Second, somewhere around 1996–1997, we observed take-off into exponential growth, thus the phase of rapid diffusion was achieved. During this stage, we note extremely rapid growth in terms of increasing numbers of new users of mobile-cellular telephony. Third, after this period of rapid diffusion, we observed that counties entered the stabilization (saturation) phase, somewhere around the year 2010, when the rate of ICT deployment slowed down. The general characteristics of the 'average' diffusion path drawn for

Table 4.2 ICT summary statistics. High-income and upper-middle-income economies. Period 1990–2015

ICT variable	No. of obs.	Mean	Std. dev.	Min. value	Max. value	Gini index	Atkinson index (for $\varepsilon = 0.5$)	Average annual growth rate[1] (%)
High-income economies								
MCS_1990	35	1.3	1.5	0.005	5.4	0.58	0.30	15.9
MCS_2000	47	43.9	22.6	2.2	76.4	0.29	0.08	
MCS_2015	47	129.3	22.1	81.9	187.3	0.09	0.007	
IU_1990	19	0.3	0.3	0.001	0.8	0.53	0.27	20.5
IU_2000	47	22.5	16.0	1.9	52.0	0.39	0.13	
IU_2015	47	79.9	10.6	58.1	98.2	0.07	0.004	
FBS_2000	28	1.6	1.8	0.01	8.4	0.65	0.37	26.3
FBS_2015	47	27.3	9.9	5.6	44.8	0.20	0.04	
AMS_2009	33	29.4	24.8	1.1	88.6	0.44	0.17	21.6
AMS_2015	47	79.4	29.4	4.5	144.1	0.20	0.04	
Upper-middle-income economies								
MCS_1990	13	0.08	0.1	0.0004	0.5	0.67	0.41	29.6
MCS_2000	33	8.8	6.9	0.2	25.5	0.43	0.17	
MCS_2015	34	123.4	35.2	60.8	206.6	0.15	0.01	
IU_1993	11	0.03	0.04	0.0001	0.1	0.57	0.29	38.1
IU_2000	33	3.6	3.8	0.1	21.4	0.44	0.18	
IU_2015	34	52.1	14.3	12.4	77.0	0.14	0.02	
FBS_2001	15	.05	0.07	0.0009	0.2	0.64	0.36	57.8
FBS_2015	34	11.2	7.1	0.7	31.3	0.34	0.10	
AMS_2009	16	2.8	3.6	0.06	14.5	0.57	0.27	36.4
AMS_2015	34	54.9	19.2	19.3	95.5	0.19	0.03	

[1] Accounts for average values of ICT incicators in respective years.

Source: Author's calculations.

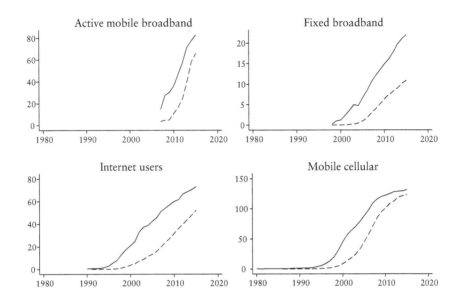

Figure 4.1 General trends in ICT diffusion. Annual averages for the period 1980–2015

Note: The solid line represents high-income economies, and the long-dash line represents upper-middle-income economies. On the Y-axis, absolute values of ICT adoption are represented. For different years, the number of countries included in calculations differs because of the various data availability.

Source: Author's elaboration.

upper-middle-income economies are very similar, however, it's noteworthy that the take-off was reported about four to five years later compared to the high-income group, and the unique 'temporal shift' is observed.

Despite the fact that the 'average' MCS diffusion path results were very similar in both income groups, it is interesting to note that in upper-middle-income economies, the average annual rate of growth was almost twice as high as in high-income economies; in upper-middle-income countries, the MCS penetration rate was growing at about 30% per year, while in high-income economies, it was only growing at 16% annually. However, despite these striking differences, in 2015, the average MCS penetration rate was similar in analyzed country income groups, 129% and 123% in high-income and upper-middle-income economies, respectively. In 1990, the average MCS penetration rate for the group of high-income economies was 1.3%, while for upper-middle-income economies it was only 0.08%.

Regarding the key trends in fixed-broadband network expansion, the evidence summarized in Table 4.1 and in Figure 4.2 again suggests that for

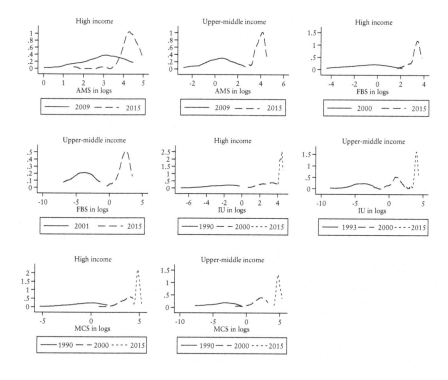

Figure 4.2 Changes in ICT distributions. Period 1990–2015

Note: On the Y-axis, there are Kernel densities, and on the X-axis, there are logged values of absolute data on ICT indicators. For different years, there are a number of countries included in calculations that differ because of various data availability and Kernel = epanechnikov.

Source: Author's elaboration.

both income groups the 'averaged' FBS diffusion paths are similar. However, reversely to what was observed for MCS diffusion, the initially diffusion stage is barely detectable. It seems that in this case the immediate take-off took place, and all in developed countries the fixed-broadband networks were expanding fast from the very beginning. It is interesting to note, that analogous observation may be drawn with regard to 'averaged' IU diffusion trajectories. Neither in the case of upper-middle- nor in high-income economies was the early diffusion stage reported, but, in fact, it turned out to be very short, and the take-off did not emerge rapidly. Still, with regard to 'average' FBS and IU diffusion paths, a unique 'temporal shift' is detected between analyzed country income groups. Interestingly, the fastest average annual growth was reported for upper-middle-income economies in respect to fixed-broadband penetration rates; it grew at almost 58% annually (sic!).

In high-income economies, the analogous rate of change was at about 26% per year. Also, the average annual growth of the number of new users of the Internet network was substantially higher in upper-middle-income economies compared to those high-income economies (see Table 4.1). It is important to emphasize here that in respect to the average penetration rate for FBS and IU, in 2015, large differences are evident; for instance, in high-income economies, the average FBS penetration rate was slightly above 27%, while at the same, the share of individuals using the Internet was almost 80%. Evidently, in both income groups, the expansion of fixed-broadband networks was not that successful, as one could imagine. Clearly, the fixed-broadband networks were not that successful in gaining new users worldwide, as it was reported, for instance, for mobile-cellular telephony. Actually, in 2015, all examined countries were still located in the beginning of the rapid diffusion stage (compare FBS diffusion curves in Figure 4.2), and what is an even more striking observation, the IU penetration rates far exceeded the FBS penetration rates. The latter may be, however, easily explained when looking at the active mobile-broadband diffusion paths (see Figure 4.2 and Table 4.1). When examining the AMS diffusion trajectories in respect to both country income groups, the initial stage of diffusion may not be detected but rather the immediate take-offs are reported. The time series showing changes in adoption of mobile broadband are relatively short; the data were first available in 2007. However, the picture displayed in Figure 4.2 provides evidence that this type of technology spread miraculously across the examined countries. In 2015, in high-income economies, the average AMS penetration rate was almost 80%, while in the upper-middle-income economies, it was about 55%. These numbers, however, perfectly coincide with average IU for both income groups: 80% and 52% for high-income and upper-middle-income economies, respectively. The latter suggests that in examined economies, access to mobile broadband may be claimed as a technological solution which effectively enhances wide access to the Internet network. According to ITU (2015) estimates, the mobile-broadband market is the most dynamically developed segment of ICT services. Access to mobile-broadband technology does have enormous power to empower people in terms of access to the Internet network. The emergence of such technology has radically transformed the way individuals access the Internet, thus freeing people from the necessity of having a fixed network is a fundamental change. Since 2007, its worldwide penetration has increased 12 times and continues to grow at a high pace, offering individuals unlimited opportunities to 'connect with the outside world'. Needless to say, unlike fixed networks that have very limited reach and require costly backbone infrastructure, mobile-broadband technology has become the prime way that people access the Internet network.

The empirical evidence briefly discussed earlier unveiled another interesting feature of the process of ICT diffusion. Apparently, all ICT indicators were growing more rapidly in the upper-middle-income economies when compared to the high-income economies (compare annual growth rates in

Table 4.1), which suggests that in relatively poorer countries, ICT diffuse faster than in the richer ones. Poorer countries, however, just imitate and assimilate ready-made technological solutions. Imitating is faster and easier than creating innovations. In Figure 4.2, we have plotted respective density curves for each ICT indicator for upper-middle- and high-income economies separately for two different years: the first year when data on respective ICT indicators were available and for 2015 (the final year of our analysis). For better visualization, all density plots are for logged values of respective ICT indicators. This picture is additionally complemented with the evidence drawn in Figure 4.3 where we have visualized changes in cross-country inequality in access to and use of ICT between 1980 and 2015.

Needless to say, across the examined economies, the pace of diffusion of ICT was shaping the general landscape in this respect. As stated previously in this section, between 1990 and 2015, we have observed enormous shifts in access to mobile-cellular telephony and mobile-broadband networks, and seen growing use of Internet networks. Despite the fact that fixed-broadband networks were not growing rapidly enough to meet the societies' demands for 'staying connected', these needs have been met by broadly expanding wireless networks. Undeniably, all of these factors provide a very positive view and speak in support of the hypothesis on the success of new ICT in the developed world.

One might have an impression that in developed economies, ICT are spreading fast and do not meet any type of constraints or limits. Moreover, this impression might even be enforced when confronted with elementary empirical evidence on changes in cross-country distribution of ICT and in cross-national disparities in this respect. Empirical data provided in Figures 4.2 and 4.3, as well as in Table 4.2, perfectly explain 'improvements' in terms of growing or falling inequities in access to and use of ICT.

Figure 4.2 clearly demonstrates in-time evolution in distribution and inequalities in respect to examined ICT indicators. In Figure 4.2, we have plotted separately density functions for each analyzed ICT indicator for selected years, and each single graph supports the evidence on rapidly falling cross-country inequalities with regard to ICT. Regarding mobile-cellular telephony (MCS) we have drawn density lines for years 1990, 2000 and 2015 for upper-middle- and high-income economies separately. For both country income groups, in 1990, the MCS density line results are highly platykurtic, which suggests enormous cross-country inequalities in access to mobile-cellular telephony. Next, in 2000, the MCS distribution becomes slightly mesokurtic, and, finally, in 2015, it gets a perfect leptokurtic shape, indicating effectively diminishing cross-national gaps with regard to access to mobile-cellular telephony. For both country income groups, in 2015, the inequalities in access to MCS disappeared, and this conclusion is supported by the values of Gini and Atkinson coefficients, additionally visualized in Figure 4.3, calculated for the respective years (see Table 4.2). To give an example, in high-income economies in 1990, the Gini and Atkinson coefficients were

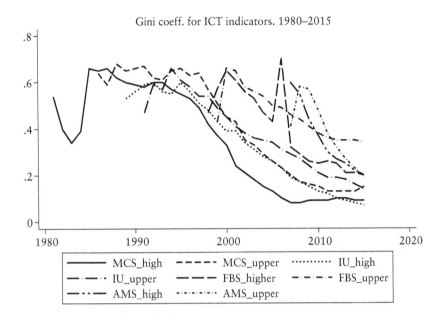

Figure 4.3 Changes in inequality (Gini coefficients time trends) in access to and use
of ICT. Period 1980–2015

Note: For different years, the number of countries included in the calculations differs because
of various data availability.

Source: Author's elaboration.

0.58 and 0.30, respectively, while in 2015, the coefficients dropped to 0.09
and 0.007, suggesting an almost perfect cross-country equality in access to
mobile-cellular telephony. These numbers, however, might be slightly misleading. When comparing inter-country gaps in absolute terms, the picture
that arises is substantially different from what might have been expected.
This example speaks for itself. Considering high-income economies in 1990,
the absolute gap in MCS penetration was at 5%pp (the maximum MCS penetration rate was for Sweden and the minimum for Croatia), while in 2015,
the gap grew to 105,4%pp (sic!; the maximum MCS penetration rate was for
the United Arab Emirates and the minimum was for Canada). Considering
growth in Internet penetration (approximated by IU variable) rates between
1990 and 2015 across examined economies, it is apparent that these changes
are quite similar to what was observed in the case of mobile-cellular telephony.
Figure 4.2 plots density curves for IU variables for 1990, 2000 and 2015
in high-income economies and for 1993, 2000 and 2015 in upper-middle-
income economies. Again, enormous transformation in the shape of density

curves is clearly visible. During the initial years of analysis, the respective IU-density plots were highly platykurtic, and then in 2015, they became leptokurtic, thus providing arguments in support of the hypothesis on rapidly falling cross-country inequalities in Internet penetration rates. Additionally, when taking a closer look at the Gini and Atkinson coefficients for the respective years and country income groups, we observed radical drops in their values. For instance, in high-income economies, the Gini coefficient decreased from 0.53 in 1990 to 0.07 in 2015, which again confirms the previous conclusions concerning gradually disappearing inequalities in this regard. Gains from such changes are obvious, but still, when considering the cross-country gaps in absolute terms, the picture is different. For instance, in 1996, among high-income economies, the best performing country in terms of Internet penetration rates was Norway at18%, while the worst performing country was Argentina at 0.14%. In 2015, the best performing country was Iceland and the worst performing country was—again—Argentina. They reached 98% and 69%, respectively. In upper-middle-income economies, analogous gaps are even more striking. In 1997, the best performing country (with the highest Internet penetration rate) was Tunisia, while the worst performing country was Algeria. Internet penetration rates in those countries reached 2.3% and 0.005%, respectively. Next, in 2015, the best performer was Turkey and the worst performer was—again—Algeria. Their IU indicators achieved values 77% and 12.4%, respectively. The situation is thus not very different from what we observed for mobile-cellular telephony. On the one hand, rapid diffusion of ICT enhanced radical decreases in cross-country inequalities, thus the distribution of ICT became more equalized, but on the other hand, the absolute divides between 'top/bottom' countries grew enormously.

Available time series for FBS and AMS cover a relatively short time span, 2000–2015 and 2007–2015, respectively. AMS data for 2007 are available for very few countries; henceforth, we plot respective curves and calculate inequality coefficients starting from 2009. Not surprisingly, in both country income groups, respective FBS density plots (see Figure 4.2) suggest significant drops in cross-country disparities; however, for high-income economies, this change seems to be more radical compared to upper-middle-income economies. Similarly, in the case of AMS density plots, the evidence demonstrates diminishing cross-national differences in access to mobile-broadband technology. Only in the case of high-income economies does the density curve drawn for 2015 show that this group of countries is internally divided into two subgroups: first where access to AMS grew substantially between 2009 and 2015, enforcing drops in cross-country inequalities, and second encompassing economies which seem to lag behind in respect to increasing access to mobile broadband. This supposition may be supported by the fact that in high-income economies, the Gini coefficients were 0.44 and 0.20 in 2009 and 2015, respectively, thus the 'Gini_2015/Gini_2009' ratio was 2.2, while in the upper-middle-income group, the analogous ration resulted in 3.0, suggesting more radical drops in inequalities.

Figure 4.3 displays trends in Gini coefficients for respective ICT indicators and additionally visualizes the process of radical drops in cross-country inequality in access to and use of various forms of new ICT, which undeniably has been enforced by rapid diffusion of ICT and significant shifts in ICT penetration rates across examined economies. This picture, together with descriptive and inequality statistics summarized in Table 4.2, allows for the realization of how pervasively new ICT were expanding across developed economies for the last three decades. Furthermore, it helps us to understand that between 1990 and 2015, the cross-national distribution of ICT was becoming more and more equalized. This supposition may be additionally supported by the evidence that falling cross-country inequalities in access to and use of ICT may be additionally confirmed by changes in coefficients of variations[4] calculated for respective years and in two examined country income groups (see Table 4.3). Table 4.3 additionally demonstrates the magnitude of the absolute (digital) gap between 'top and bottom' countries for consecutive ICT indicators. Paradoxically, drops in value of the coefficients of variation calculated for respective ICT indicators are accompanied by an increase in the absolute digital divide (digital/ICT gap). Coefficients of variations for each ICT indicator change in the opposite direction to

Table 4.3 Core ICT indicators—coefficients of variation and absolute (digital) gap. High-income- and upper-middle-income economies. Period 1990–2015

ICT variable	Coeff. of variation	Absolute (digital) gap[1]
High-income economies		
MCS_1990	1.17	5.375 %pp. [Sweden—Croatia]
MCS_2015	0.16	105.4 %pp. [United Arab Emirates Canada]
IU_1990	0.98	0.778 %pp. [Israel—Austria]
IU_2015	0.13	40.1 %pp. [Iceland—Seychelles]
FBS_2000	1.52	8.39 [Latvia—Korea (Rep. of)]
FBS_2015	0.36	39.2 %pp. [Switzerland—Oman]
AMS_2007	1.37	39.2 %pp. [Singapore—Oman]
AMS_2015	0.36	104.9 %pp. [Finland—Brunei Dar.]
Upper-middle-income economies		
MCS_1990	1.56	0.5 %pp. [Malaysia—Algeria]
MCS_2015	0.28	146.5 %pp. [Maldives—Angola]
IU_1991	0.86	0.01 %pp. [South Africa—Thailand]
IU_2015	0.27	64.6 %pp. [Azerbaijan—Angola]
FBS_2000	1.41	0.06 %pp. [Brazil—Iran]
FBS_2015	0.61	30.6 %pp. [Belarus—Angola]
AMS_2007	0.79	3.2 %pp. [Romania—Dominican Republic]
AMS_2015	0.34	76.2 %pp. [Costa Rica—Angola]

[1]Absolute digital gap is calculated by a simple difference in absolute values of the ICT penetration rate in the 'top country' and the 'bottom country'.

Source: Author's calculations.

absolute digital gaps—coefficients of variations fall, while absolute ICT gaps grow. To give an example, in the group of upper-middle-income economies in 1990, the absolute 'mobile-cellular gap' was just 0.05 %pp (the 'top country'[5] was Malaysia, while the 'bottom country'[6] was Algeria), but in 2015, it grew to 146.5 %pp (the 'top country' was Maldives, and the 'bottom country' was Angola). For the remaining ICT indicators in examined country income groups, the tendencies are analogous, as in the cited example. In each case, we find that despite falling cross-country variations (relative inequalities) in access to and use ICT, the absolute gaps are growing. At the beginning of the analyzed period, all countries were ICT-poor and technologically disconnected; then in 2015, a huge majority of them became ICT rich and technologically connected. *However, have these countries become more equal or unequal in respect to ICT deployment?*

Inequalities are a multifaceted phenomenon. Probably, many people think that technological inequalities, broadly labeled digital divide[7] (digital gaps), automatically disappear as growing ICT penetration rates are reported worldwide. But, in fact, things are far more complicated. The disappearance of inequalities might be a myth, and despite the fact that fast worldwide diffusion of new technologies did help societies to escape technological isolation and backwardness, this phenomenal process has also generated new forms of inequalities.

Hence, would the drop in technological inequalities be illusive, or would growing access to ICT generate different forms of exclusion and isolation? Undeniably, insufficient pressure on fast deployment of new technological solutions in some countries may cause growing digital divides (Warschauer, 2004). ICT penetration rates differ substantially among countries. In effect, those economies where ICT diffusion pace is slower will finally begin to lag behind. The danger of being left behind grows as other countries rapidly advance in deploying new technologies. If significant differences in ICT deployment rates are maintained for a long time, cross-country differences in ICT penetration rates increase, and thus the absolute digital gap grows. To some extent, the emergence of this type of divide is random and hardly predictable from a worldwide perspective. Evidently, social capability to adapt and/or create new knowledge and institutional and economic readiness are critical to ensure digital and technological inclusion for all society members.

The existence of digital divides cannot be neglected. Paradoxically, opposite of expectations, the rapid spread of various forms of new technologies does not close the technological gaps. Of course, what cannot be denied when analyzing technological inequalities using the classical inequality measures such as the Gini coefficient, for instance, is that cross-country ICT inequalities are falling. Put differently, technologies tend to be more equally distributed among economies. Also, it is not a standard interpretation in this study that some nations have ICT now and the others will have it latter. It could be argued that this is not the case. When looking at basic ICT access and usage statistics, at first sight, it becomes obvious that in 2015, almost all countries had already adapted various forms of new technologies. It was not the case that some countries were totally excluded from access to any type of ICT, but ICT was already there. What was easy to notice, however, was that because of the different speeds of ICT diffusion, in 2015, the ICT penetration rates differed significantly across countries. A new type of divides emerged.

Finally, the digital divide is not a *binary* phenomenon; its notion should not be limited to the simple division of people who 'have' and those who 'have-not'. It is not that simple. Some may also have an impression that inequalities and divides are the same, that both terms are drawing a rigid line between those who are included and those who suffer from exclusion. However, it is hard not have an impression that inequalities mostly should be interpreted in relative terms. Unequal cross-country distribution of ICT does not automatically imply that there exist societies with *no* access to new technologies. That is not necessarily the case. But divides should be rather interpreted in absolute terms. Digital gaps go far beyond this naïve understanding of issues, as digital gaps combine a broad array of factors, impediments, barriers and constraints. These barriers do are not necessarily financial ones. Today, ICT may be accessed and used at a very low cost; wireless solutions allow users to reach societies in geographically isolated areas; thus, we should not attach overriding importance to the financial aspects of the physical availability of basic ICT tools. Digital gaps are often unveiled in terms of language, content, basic education and skills, literacy and social attitudes. To some extent, digital divides are in people's minds and thus are difficult to combat and overcome.

Drawing ICT Profile of Countries

> Knowledge (. . .) can only have economic importance is it can be shared, that is, communicated and used by people (. . .). The critical characteristic of knowledge is not only its size (that is, how much does this society know) but its diffusion (who and how many members of this society know what is known?) and (. . .) access cost.
>
> (J. Mokyr (2001, p. 299)

In Sect.4.2, we have briefly presented a general overview of the phenomenal process of ICT diffusion in the developed world, which was observed for the last decades. It demonstrated rapidly changing ICT penetration rates across high-income and upper-middle-income economies between 1980 and 2015, and radically dropping relative cross-country technological inequalities. Interestingly, the paths visualizing growing access to mobile-cellular telephony or to infrastructure allowing for Internet connection (such as fixed-broadband and/or mobile-broadband networks) have been relatively similar in both country income groups. Would this suggest that new ICT diffuse across societies regardless of per capita income, institutional and legal frameworks, social norms and attitudes or geographical conditions? If the latter is true, we might state that the process of diffusion of ICT is endogenously driven, and—to some extent—it is a self-perpetuating (self-sustaining) process.

Faced with the challenge of examining the process of new technology spread, and to justify our supposition on the endogenous character of the process of ICT diffusion, we take a closer look at the process in each of the analyzed economies. To this aim, we deliberately disaggregate the evidence, presented earlier in Sect. 4.2, and we draw country-specific ICT diffusion profiles. The empirical evidence we demonstrate next encompasses 47 high-income and 34 upper-middle-income countries for which we develop countrywide diffusion patterns by graphically presenting development paths in respect to changing access to and use of mobile-cellular telephony, fixed broadband and mobile broadband, and the share of population using (and thus having access to) the Internet network. To provide the in-depth insight into each country's transforming ICT profile, in each case, we use the longest available time series in respect to certain ICT indicators. Henceforth, for different countries, the time span of analysis may vary according to data availability and time series completeness. Drawing individual country ICT profiles gives a clear picture of diffusion trajectories in each of the examined economies, which allows for drawing extensive and well-justified conclusions. It additionally allows for the unveiling of country-unique characteristics regarding the process of ICT spread, but it also allows for the identification of some similarities and regularities in this respect.

To ensure the clarity of presentation of our results, we divide Sect.4.3 into two parts: Sect.4.3.1 demonstrates the evidence on mobile-cellular networks diffusion and Sect.4.3.2 explains the patterns of growing Internet penetration rates.

Mobile-Cellular Telephony Diffusion

The first part of Sect.4.3 is fully dedicated to describing the results of our analysis of mobile-cellular telephony diffusion patterns between 1980 and 2015. Figures 4.4 and 4.5 display country-specific MCS diffusion paths, while Table 4.4 summarizes the results of estimated logistics growth models that explain the unique features of this process in each economy.

Figures 4.4 and 4.5 graphically display countrywide mobile-cellular telephony diffusion patterns for the period of 1980–2015. The value of this graphical evidence is additionally enhanced by logistic growth estimates. The results of which are summarized in Table 4.4. As mentioned before, because of the various availability of ICT data, for different countries, the time span of analysis may differ. In each picture visualizing the process of MCS diffusion, purposely, we have added lines demonstrating changes in fixed (wired)-telephony penetration rates, which enriches the whole picture by demonstrating the unique process of 'fixed-to-mobile telephony

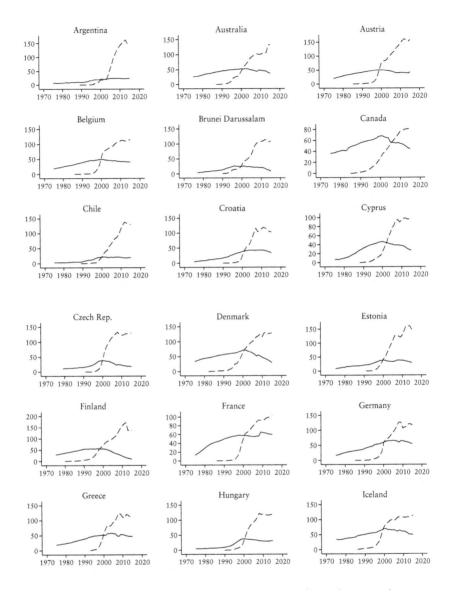

Figure 4.4 MCS and FTL diffusion paths. Country-specific evidence. High-income economies. Period 1975–2015

Note: Solid line represents mobile-cellular telephony diffusion path, dash line represents fixed-telephony diffusion line. On the X-axis, we see the time, and on the Y-axis, we see the MCS and FTL penetration rates (expressed in number of subscribers per 1000 inhabitants).

Source: Author's elaboration.

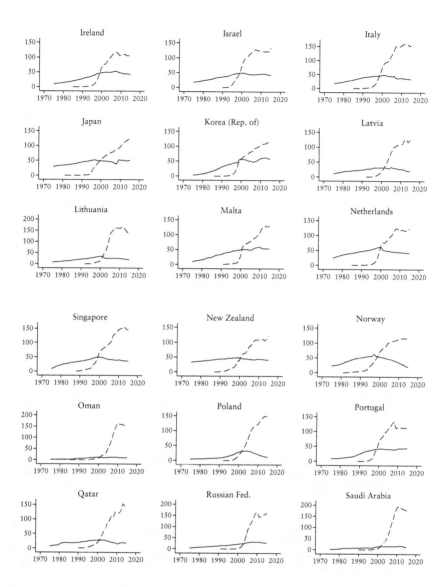

Figure 4.4 (Continued)

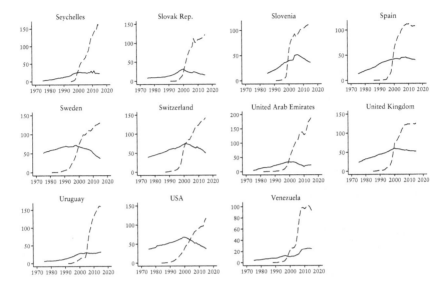

Figure 4.4 (Continued)

substitution'. The term 'fixed-to-mobile telephony substitution'[8] has been proposed by Lechman (2015) and defines the unique process of gradual switching (substituting) from old technology (fixed telephony) to new technology (mobile telephony).

During the period of 1980–2015, developed countries experienced unprecedented diffusion of mobile-cellular telephony in terms of pace. In high-income economies between 1990 and 2015, the average annual rate of diffusion of MCS was approximately 16% (see Table 4.2 in Sect. 4.2), while in upper-middle-income economies, the rate of diffusion was almost twice as high at 30% per annum. Undeniably, this phenomenally rapid spread of this form of communication was—to a large extent—facilitated by the dropping prices of mobile-cellular services (and hence increasing affordability) and growing accessibility of required infrastructure. Even countries where backbone infrastructure was limited and poorly developed, or the national economy was suffering from insufficient financial recourses, gained the huge opportunity of access to this form of communication. Mobile-cellular telephony reached undeserved, geographically isolated and/or rural areas, opening the 'opportunity window' for technologically backward societies. Given the fact that in all examined economies, the growth rates of ICT penetration were extraordinarily high, not surprisingly we have also witnessed falling relative technological inequalities. In addition, despite the fact that absolute digital divides have widened between 1980 and 2015, in fact, all developed economies shifted their *status* from technologically (ICT) poor to technologically (ICT) rich.

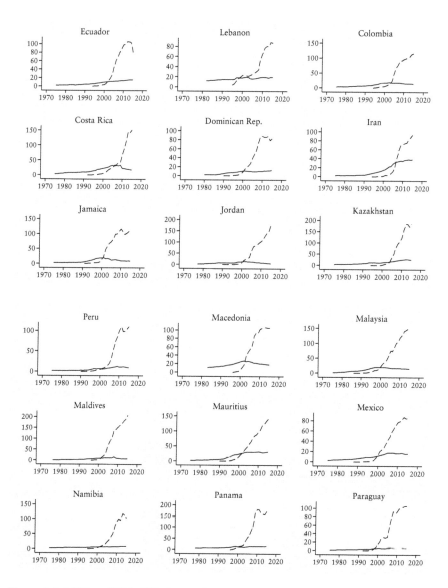

Figure 4.5 MCS and FTL diffusion paths. Country-specific evidence. Upper-middle-income economies. Period 1975–2015

Note: Solid line represents mobile-cellular telephony diffusion path, dash line represents fixed-telephony diffusion line. On the X-axis, we see the time, and on the Y-axis, we see the MCS and FTL penetration rates (expressed in number of subscribers per 1000 inhabitants).

Source: Author's elaboration.

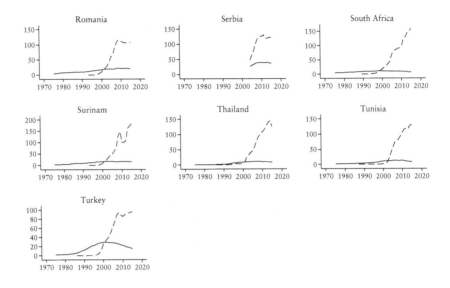

Figure 4.5 (Continued)

First, considering exclusively the evidence on MCS diffusion in high-income economies, the first impressive observation is that across all examined countries, the shift in access to mobile-cellular telephony was disruptive between 1980 and 2015, and each (with only few exceptions) out of 34 analyzed countries achieved the level of MCS saturation far exceeding 100%. The latter denotes that an *average* inhabitant of a high-income country legally owned more than one mobile-cellular subscription. The most prominent examples are the United Arab Emirates, Saudi Arabia and Uruguay, where MCS penetration rates in 2015 were 187.3 per 100 inhabitants, 176.6 per 100 inhabitants and 160.2 per 100 inhabitants, respectively. Note that in 2015, the average MCS penetration rate was at about 129 per inhabitants, and 22 economies were located above the average. In 2015, the three 'bottom' (the worst performing) economies were Canada, Venezuela and Cyprus, where MCS deployment rates were 81.9 100 per inhabitants, 92.9 100 inhabitants and 95.4 per 100 inhabitants, respectively. At the beginning of the period of our analysis in 1980 and then in 1990, when mobile telephony was emerging technology, all economies were equally poor and lacked unlimited access to this form of communication. But luckily, in late 1990s, average prices of access to and use of services of mobile-cellular telephony began to drop gradually, which became an effective driver of growing demand for new technological solutions. When accounting for countries' individual data between 1990 and 2015, the average annual growth rate of the mobile-cellular penetration rate was slightly exceeding 42%, while countries that reached the higher average annual MCS growth rates were the Russian Federation at 90.5% per annum, Slovakia at 72.7% per annum and Poland at 67.7% per annum. The countries where deployment of mobile-cellular telephony was increasing at the slowest pace were, surprisingly, three Nordic countries—namely, Sweden, Norway and Finland, where MCS was increasing at *only* 20% annually. Again, this varies between countries. Although enormously high, it did not impede the process of fast adoption of the newly arisen mode of communication, but, as mentioned before, the bad news is that it generated new forms of divides—digital divides.

Logistic growth estimates, summarized in Table 4.4, unveil other specific characteristics of the process of mobile-cellular telephony diffusion in high-income economies between 1980 and 2015. Notably, with only a few exceptions (Canada, Cyprus and France), the estimated κ parameters, explaining the upper ceiling (saturation, growth limit), are higher than 100, which suggests that the countries in question have achieved 'full' saturation with mobile-cellular telephony. The highest values of κ are reported for Saudi Arabia at $\kappa = 190.7$, Seychelles at $\kappa = 177.1$ and the United Arab Emirates at $\kappa = 169.5$. These three 'best performers' are followed by Oman, Uruguay, Singapore, Italy, Lithuania, Poland, Austria and Finland, for which the estimated κ parameters were insignificantly lower. Taking into account the midpoint—denoted as β, indicating the exact time when the process of diffusion is half-completed (the country reached 0.5κ)—we observer that it spans from 1998 to 2006. This means that within this nine-year period, all of the examined economies reached 50% of their estimated saturation with mobile-cellular telephony. Countries that passed the earliest unique inflection point along MCS diffusion patterns in 1999 were Israel, Ireland, Iceland, Norway, Portugal, Slovenia and Sweden. In contrast, the inflection point (midpoint) was reached the latest, in 2006, in Oman, Saudi Arabia, Seychelles and Uruguay. In this respect, among other examples, the case of Seychelles deserves special attention. It is a country where mobile-cellular telephony was being implemented for the first time (in the high-income group) in 1995. However, with the effective demand growing at 52% per annum, in 2015, it achieved the MCS penetration rate of 158 per 100 inhabitants.

Another estimated parameter is the specific duration, ΔT, which explains the time needed to pass from 10% to 90% of saturation. According to our estimates, it differs hugely among high-income economies. Note that the highest value of ΔT was reported for Japan at 18.3 years. The case of Japan is followed by another three economies with the longest estimated specific duration—namely, Canada (16.9 years), Finland (16.8 years) and Seychelles (16.5 years). The shortest specific duration periods are demonstrated in Slovenia (5.5 years), the Russian Federation and Lithuania (5.7 years for both). In these countries, it took only 5.5 years to pass from 10% to 90% of saturation, which obviously coincides with highest values of estimated α parameters (pace of diffusion[9]), which for Slovenia, the Russian Federation and Lithuania was –0.80, 0.77 and 0.78, respectively.

Table 4.4 MCS logistic growth estimates.[1] High-income and upper-middle-income economies. Period 1980–2015

Country	κ (upper asymptot / ceiling)	β (mid-point)	α (rate of diffusion / curve steepness)	ΔT (specific duration)	R-squared
Upper-middle-income economies					
Algeria	100.8	2,005.7	0.77	5.6	0.98
Angola	63.6	2,007.6	0.63	6.9	0.99
Azerbaijan	114.6	2,007.1	0.57	7.6	0.99
Belarus	120.7	2,006.2	0.61	7.3	0.99
Bosnia and Herzegovina	91.4	2,005.1	0.50	8.8	0.99
Botswana	189.7	2,008.7	0.39	11.1	0.99
Brazil	149.4	2,007.6	0.34	12.9	0.99
Bulgaria	142.2	2,004.2	0.66	6.6	0.99
China	111.3	2,008.8	0.28	15.3	0.99
Colombia	107.6	2,005.5	0.61	7.3	0.99
Costa Rica	234.0 (overestimated)	2,012.0	0.3	14.1	0.98
Dominican Republic	88.8	2,005.3	0.51	8.6	0.98
Ecuador	100.3	2,005.3	0.62	7.1	0.98
Iran	85.4	2,007.2	0.74	5.9	0.99
Jamaica	107.5	2,002.9	0.56	7.8	0.99
Jordan	185.6	2,008.5	0.28	15.4	0.98
Kazakhstan	194.5	2,008.2	0.50	8.9	0.99
Lebanon	173.8	2,013.8	0.17	25.6	0.94
Macedonia	107.4	2,004.8	0.52	8.4	0.99
Malaysia	159.3	2,006.1	0.3	14.6	0.99
Maldives	191.4	2,006.6	0.48	9.2	0.99
Mauritius	150.1	2,007.3	0.3	15.5	0.99
Mexico	89.5	2,005.1	0.36	12.8	0.99
Namibia	115.4	2,008.1	0.53	8.4	0.98
Panama	175.4	2,006.5	0.63	6.9	0.97
Paraguay	110.1	2,005.6	0.40	10.9	0.98
Peru	106.6	2,006.9	0.69	6.4	0.99
Romania	110.7	2,004.5	0.61	7.2	0.99
Serbia	124.2	2,004.8	0.76	5.7	0.96
South Africa	176.8	2,007.8	0.27	16.4	0.98
Suriname	180.1	2,007.7	0.39	13.8	0.92
Thailand	142.9	2,006.6	0.38	11.5	0.99
Tunisia	125.0	2,006.1	0.48	9.1	0.99
Turkey	94.7	2,003.1	0.46	9.5	0.99
High-income economies					
Argentina	155.8	2,005.9	0.54	8.1	0.99
Australia	118.2	2,001.6	0.31	14.2	0.98
Austria	157.1	2,002.1	0.31	13.9	0.98
Belgium	109.1	2,000.5	0.53	8.3	0.99
Brunei Darussalam	117.1	2,003.5	0.33	13.3	0.99
Canada	86.4	2,003.1	0.26	16.9	0.99
Chile	144.7	2,005.7	0.31	14.4	0.99

Table 4.4 (Continued)

Country	κ (upper asymptot / ceiling)	β (mid-point)	α (rate of diffusion / curve steepness)	ΔT (specific duration)	R-squared
Croatia	112.1	2,002.7	0.55	7.9	0.98
Cyprus	98.1	2,002.4	0.46	9.5	0.99
Czech Republic	126.7	2,001.1	0.68	6.4	0.99
Denmark	127.7	2,000.5	0.34	12.8	0.99
Estonia	152.3	2,002.9	0.38	11.4	0.98
Finland	155.8	2,001.4	0.26	16.8	0.97
France	95.8	2,000.5	0.45	9.7	0.99
Germany	117.6	2,001.1	0.46	9.5	0.98
Greece	114.1	2,000.6	0.51	8.7	0.97
Hungary	118.2	2,001.9	0.53	8.0	0.99
Iceland	107.5	1,998.7	0.56	7.8	0.99
Ireland	108.2	1,999.8	0.57	7.6	0.99
Israel	124.9	1,999.5	0.54	8.1	0.99
Italy	157.4	2,001.1	0.39	11.1	0.99
Japan	120.1	2,002.3	0.24	18.3	0.98
Korea (Rep.)	109.9	2,000.8	0.35	12.6	0.98
Latvia	120.9	2,003.5	0.50	8.8	0.99
Lithuania	156.8	2,003.2	0.78	5.7	0.99
Malta	127.3	2,003.4	0.33	13.4	0.96
Netherlands	118.8	2,000.5	0.47	9.4	0.98
New Zealand	114.9	2,001.7	0.35	12.7	0.99
Norway	115.2	1,999.1	0.36	12.2	0.99
Oman	164.2	2,006.2	0.62	7.1	0.99
Poland	148.6	2,004.9	0.41	10.8	0.99
Portugal	116.4	1,999.9	0.58	7.6	0.98
Qatar	147.5	2,004.5	0.36	12.2	0.99
Russian Federation	154.9	2,004.9	0.77	5.7	0.99
Saudi Arabia	190.7	2,006.3	0.62	7.1	0.99
Seychelles	177.1	2,006.4	0.27	16.5	0.98
Singapore	155.4	2,002.3	0.30	14.5	0.98
Slovakia	113.3	2,002.4	0.51	8.6	0.99
Slovenia	102.3	1,999.9	0.80	5.5	0.98
Spain	108.4	2,000.1	0.61	7.2	0.99
Sweden	123.4	1,999.5	0.33	13.6	0.99
Switzerland	135.1	2,001.7	0.32	13.6	0.98
United Arab Emirates	169.5	2,003.3	0.31	13.9	0.98
United Kingdom	124.3	2,000.3	0.47	9.5	0.99
United States	112.7	2,003.2	0.24	7.9	0.99
Uruguay	160.6	2,006.8	0.53	8.4	0.99
Venezuela	103.6	2,004.6	0.46	9.6	0.98

[1] To approximate MCS diffusion trajectories, we use a logistic growth model. For technical details, see Chapter 3.

Note: Estimation method NLS.

Source: Author's estimates.

Generally, the values of parameters α and the number of time periods that account for specific duration are negatively correlated, meaning that the higher pace of diffusion ensures a shorter time to achieve 'full' saturation. It is noteworthy that the pace of diffusion effectively determines the shape of technology diffusion trajectory, mainly because it determines the steepness of the diffusion curve. Consequently, the specific duration, the midpoint and, finally, the value of the ceiling (upper asymptote) is predetermined by the value of α.

Taking a closer look at logistics growth curves, approximating the mobile-cellular telephony development paths (see Figure 4.4) in high-income economies between 1980 and 2015, the first impression is that similarities of all patterns are striking. They unveil beautiful regularities in shape; in the case of each MCS country path, the three characteristic phases of the diffusion process may be easily distinguished. Analyzing MCS country-specific diffusion trajectories, we find that in each country, the initial pre-take-off stage is identifiable, during which the rate of diffusion is low. The length of this pre-take-off stage varies among countries, which predominantly depends on the time that the new technology was first introduced to the national telecommunication market. Next, the sudden take-off emerges, and the country enters the rapid growth stage, during which the saturation with mobile-cellular usually grows at an exponential rate. Finally, as the national telecommunication market approaches 'full' saturation, the diffusion slows down and stabilizes. The most regular, and thus resembling the theoretical S-time trajectory, mobile-cellular telephony diffusion paths are recognized for Belgium, Brunei Darussalam, Denmark, France, Iceland, Norway and the United Kingdom.

Analogous evidence, however, for upper-middle-income economies also contributes significantly to our understanding of the process of mobile-cellular diffusion. Figure 4.5 plots mobile-cellular and fixed-telephony diffusion trajectories between 1986 and 2015. In the group of upper-middle-income economies, data on MCS were first available in 1986, but only for three countries: Malaysia, Thailand and Turkey, while fully balanced time series start from 1998 onward.[10] Table 4.4 additionally summarizes mobile-cellular telephony logistic growth estimates. Having briefly analyzed country-specific mobile-cellular telephony diffusion patterns for all 34 upper-middle-income economies, we find that similarly to what was reported for the high-income country group, this type of technology diffused quickly and broadly enough to be accessed and used by a majority of society members. A great majority of countries, until 2015, reached almost 'full' saturation with mobile-cellular telephony, and none of the countries in our scope remained 'locked' in the early diffusion phase. In 2015, the average[11] MCS penetration rate was higher than 123 per 100 inhabitants. One country, Maldives, until 2015, had achieved even higher MCS penetration rates than the 'top' economy in the high-income group, and it was more than 206 per 100 inhabitants. The other six economies—namely,

Kazakhstan, Surinam, Jordan, Panama, Botswana and South Africa—were performing equally well in terms of adoption of mobile-cellular telephony if compared to the few best high-income economies (United Arab Emirates, Saudi Arabia, Uruguay, Russian Federation, Oman, Seychelles or Austria). Here two examples, Botswana and Maldives, warrant special attention. These are examples of countries where deployment of mobile-cellular telephony boosted enormously in a relatively short time. Note that in Botswana in 1998 the MCS penetration rate was 0.89 per 100 inhabitants, while in 2015, it shifted to 169 per 100 inhabitants, which accounted for the average annual growth rate of 31%. In Maldives, the changes in broad accessibility of mobile-cellular telephony were even more disruptive. In 1996 in Maldives, the MCS penetration rate was 0.007 per 100 inhabitants, while after a 19-year period, in 2015, it grew and reached the level of 206.6 per 100 inhabitants. In Maldives, the average annual pace of mobile-cellular telephony diffusion was at about 54% per annum. What is very characteristic for the diffusion paths of Botswana and Maldives is that the pre-take-off stage was extremely short (see Figure 4.5), and these countries noted the immediate take-off along the MCS diffusion trajectory.

Considering the countrywide mobile-cellular telephony diffusion patters pictured in Figure 4.5, another notable observation arises. All mobile-cellular telephony diffusion paths developed for upper-middle-income economies are quite similar in shape, and they resemble theoretical S-time pattern. Analogous to what was observed in high-income economies along each country-MCS-diffusion path, three characteristic phases are clearly visible— namely, early (pre-take-off) stage, rapid growth stage and stabilization stage. In some economies, such as in Bulgaria, Ecuador, Jamaica, Peru, Panama, Surinam, Thailand or Turkey, we observe slight falls in mobile-cellular telephony penetration rates at the end of the examined time period. However, these drops are not necessarily associated with real decreases in the number of legal mobile-cellular telephony subscribers, but rather with some statistical corrections periodically introduced by national statistical offices. However, if compared to countrywide mobile-cellular telephony diffusion paths developed for high-income economies, the MCS diffusion curves are characterized by a significantly shorter pre-take-off stage and higher steepness in the curve. It suggests that in poorer economies, the process of mobile-cellular telephony diffusion proceeds more abruptly. Note that high-income and upper-middle-income economies in 2015 achieved an almost equal level of MCS penetration rates (see Table 4.2 in Sect. 4.2), but in the poorer income group, mobile-cellular telephony started to diffuse a few years later. The happy irony of this is that relatively poorer countries that initially were lagging behind managed to rapidly catch up with the rich ones, radically lifting the level of access to and use of new communication technologies. *Would the poorer economies take advantage of their relative backwardness as Gerschenkron suggested already in 1962? Probably this is exactly the case that confirms his controversial hypothesis.*

Table 4.4 presents the outcomes of mobile-cellular telephony logistic growth estimates for 34 upper-middle-income economies, which sheds more light on the issues discussed. Country-specific estimates of κ parameter, showing the growth limit of the system, for all countries except Costa Rica where overestimates are returned, are statistically significant and reflect the growth pattern of mobile-cellular telephony in the analyzed economies, suggesting that all countries have reached almost 'full' saturation.

Our estimates also demonstrate that the values of parameter β, denoting the midpoint of the diffusion curve, vary between 2002 and 2013, which means that during this 11-year period, all 34 countries managed to reach the midpoint along the mobile-cellular telephony diffusion trajectory. It was Jamaica where the inflection point was reported the earliest in 2002. Next, in 2003, it was observed in Turkey and then in 2004 in four other countries: Bulgaria, Macedonia, Romania and Serbia. In 2013, the midpoint was observed in Lebanon, whereas only one year earlier in 2012, it was seen in Costa Rica. Respecting the estimated values of ΔT (specific duration) in explaining how long it takes to shift from 10% to 90% of saturation, we see that countries differ in this regard. The highest value of ΔT is reported for Lebanon at 25.6 years, while the lowest is for Algeria at 5.6 years, Serbia at 5.7 years and Iran at 5.9 years. By definition, in the countries where the specific duration is relatively short, the intrinsic rate of diffusion is relatively high. Note that for Algeria, Serbia and Iran the α were 0.77, 0.76 and 0.74, respectively.

The vastly documented description of the diffusion paths of mobile-cellular and fixed (wired) telephony in developed countries raises question concerning two unique processes. First, the empirical evidence (see Figures 4.4 and 4.5) unveiled that in many of the examined economies, we witnessed gradually falling market shares possessed by fixed telephony. This type of old communication is being substituted by mobile-cellular telephony, which rapidly evades the telecommunication markets. Second, in several economies, we identified another very specific process of technological leapfrogging.

The process of '*fixed-to-mobile technological substitution*' demonstrates market competition between old and new technologies. In effect, because of growing demand for new technological solutions, its market shares are increasing, which inevitably leads to gradually diminishing market shares possessed by old technologies. In our case, we claim that mobile-cellular telephony may be labeled the new technology that evades the telecommunication market, while fixed telephony is the old type of technology being gradually substituted by the new one. The process of switching from old to new technologies begins immediately as societies perceive that newly emerging technologies are more advantageous and offer more gains and benefits when compared to the old ones. Undeniably, mobile-cellular telephony is the type of communication technology that offers to each individual a broader array of opportunities and benefits compared to fixed telephony. First, mobile-cellular telephony is quickly installable and diffusible, mainly because it does not require hard infrastructure to be installed. The traditional (fixed) telephony needs a well-developed backbone infrastructure to be installed, which many poorly developed countries lack. Undeserved and geographically isolated regions lack well-developed copper- and/or fiber-based infrastructure, which are necessary to install a fixed-telephony network. For areas that have not been reached by a fixed-telephony network because of a poorly developed infrastructure, countrywide adoption of mobile-cellular telephony appears to be not only the best option, but, above all, the *only* option. Evidently, the process of switching from old to new communication technologies is dramatically faster in relatively poorer economies suffering from unfavorable geographical conditions where the vast majority of the country's population lives in rural areas. Wireless networks offering new ways of communication are far less costly solutions compared to fixed networks and may be installed faster and used at lower prices for individual users. What is also of seminal importance is that the marginal cost of every additional new user of wireless networks is *zero* (sic!), which makes this technology readily available '*for all*', offering inter-personal connectivity and giving rise to new kinds of social and economic networks. It is noteworthy that in some cases, the process of 'fixed-to-mobile' technological substitution is more illusion than fact. In the broad study of Lechman (2015), we find exhaustive evidence on the process of switching from old to new technologies in low-income and lower-middle-income economies between 1980 and 2012. However, Lechman claims that in economically backward economies, this is rather illusive, because in low-income countries, the state of development of backbone infrastructure that would allow for the installation of fixed-telephony is negligible. There are many examples of countries like this, inter alia, Nepal, Rwanda, Myanmar or Niger, where fixed-telephony penetration rates did not exceed even 1 per 100 inhabitants.

Henceforth, because of severe shortages in basic communication infrastructure, such countries immediately started to assimilate mobile-cellular modes of communications, as it was the only available technology allowing people to communicate. Countries with negligibly developed fixed(wired) infrastructure are directly heading towards adopting wireless technologies, simply omitting the '*fixed-infrastructure stage of development*'.

Hence, the process of quitting the 'fixed' and deploying the 'wireless' is not observed. The latter account for the very unique process of '*technological leapfrogging*' that is often reported in countries which do not follow the traditional development path, but rather jump directly to assimilation of more favorable technological solutions. Paradoxically, such countries benefit from their technological backwardness. Steinmueller (2001) defines the '*technological leapfrogging*' as the process of '*bypassing stages in capacity building or investment through which countries were previously required to pass during the process of economic development*'. Some scholars label this process leapfrog-type technological development and argue that it often enforces radical and disruptive changes and fast technological advancements in regions where previously technology was, in fact, nonexistent.[12]

Our empirical results unveiling the process of mobile-cellular telephony and fixed-telephony diffusion process, which are summarized in Figures 4.4–4.5 and Tables 4.3–4.4, additionally allows for the recognition of the 'fixed-to-mobile' technological substitution and technological leapfrogging processes in the examined country income groups. Recognition of the latter contributes significantly to our profound understanding of the phenomenal process of ICT spread and its far-reaching implications, which are predominantly demonstrated through changing structures of telecommunication markets. Having carefully analyzed the countrywide fixed- and mobile-cellular telephony diffusion paths, the first obvious conclusion is that these two types of communication technology were expanding in development simultaneously. After taking a closer look at these diffusion trajectories and the detailed examination of the changing telecommunication market shares possessed by fixed- and mobile-cellular telephony, we conclude that all countries in the scope of our analysis may be classified into *three different categories*. These are as follows:

1. Countries where telecommunication market penetration has been growing until a certain point in time and then started to fall as mobile-cellular telephony was rapidly evading the market. In these countries, the '*fixed-to-mobile' technological substitution is reported*, and the gap between market shares possessed by mobile-cellular telephony is rapidly increasing at the expense of fast-dropping market shares of fixed telephony. In these countries, the gap between market shares possessed by fixed- and mobile-cellular telephony is gradually widening. We may also claim that in these types of economies, the '*fixed-to-mobile' technological substitution is a definite and irreversible process*.

2. Countries where we observe simultaneously growing fixed- and mobile-cellular telephony penetration rates, but the mobile-cellular telephony rate diffusion is significantly higher compared to fixed-telephony. In these countries, the '*fixed-to-mobile' technological substitution is* also *reported*, despite the fact that the gap between market shares possessed by the two types of communication technologies is not necessarily growing but closely related to the difference between fixed- and mobile-cellular telephony deployment growth rates. In these countries, the '*fixed-to-mobile' technological substitution is a hypothetically reversible process*.

3. Countries where fixed-telephony networks have never become broadly available communication technology, mainly because of infrastructural and/or financial shortages and unfavorable geographical conditions. In such countries, the fixed-telephony penetration rates remained indecently low. The process of *fixed-to-mobile' technological substitution is illusive, and these countries demonstrate leapfrog-type technological development paths*.

Table 4.5 'Fixed-to-mobile' technological substitution and leapfrog-type technological development. High-income and upper-middle-income countries categorization. Period 1975–2015

	High-income economies	Upper-middle-income economies
Category (1)	*Argentina*, Australia, Austria, Belgium, Brunei Daruss, Canada, Chile, Croatia, Cyprus, Czech Republic, Denmark, Estonia, Finland, France, Germany, Greece, Hungary, Iceland, Ireland, Israel, Italy, Latvia, Lithuania, Netherlands, Singapore, New Zealand, Norway, Poland, *Qatar*, Russian Federation, Saudi Arabia, Seychelles, Slovak Rep., Slovenia, Spain, Sweden, Switzerland, United Arab Emirates, United Kingdom, United States, *Venezuela*	Bosnia and Herzegovina, Brazil, Bulgaria, China, *Colombia, Peru*, Macedonia, Malaysia, *Maldives, Mexico, Paraguay*, Romania, Serbia, *South Africa, Surinam, Thailand, Thailand*, Turkey
Category (2)	*Argentina*, Japan, Korea (Rep. of), Malta, *Oman*, Portugal, Uruguay, *Venezuela*	Azerbaijan, Belarus, Ecuador, Lebanon, Dominican Republic, Iran, Jamaica, Jordan, Mauritius, Panama
Category (3)	Qatar, Oman	Algeria, Angola, Azerbaijan, Botswana, Colombia, Ecuador, Dominican Republic, Jamaica, Jordan, Peru, Maldives, Mexico, Namibia, Panama, Paraguay, South Africa, Surinam, Thailand, Tunisia

Note: Countries in italics are classified into more than one category.

Source: Author's elaboration.

Table 4.5 summarizes the results of the classification of all 47 high-income and 34 upper-middle-income economies into these three categories. When classifying countries, we tried to avoid rigidly setting the threshold (regarding FTL penetration rates, for instance), which might be misleading; rather, our countries' categorization is based on intuition and economic reasoning.

Among high-income economies, 5 countries were classified into category (2), 38 countries fell into category (1), 2 countries (Argentina and Venezuela) fell into category (1) and (2) simultaneously, 1 country (Qatar) fell into category (1) and (3) simultaneously and 1 country (Oman) fell into category (2) and (3) simultaneously. Not surprisingly, among high-income economies, the most numerous category was the first one encompassing the countries in which fixed-telephony penetration rates were growing until a certain point in time, and then they started to drop radically along with the fast-growing demand for mobile-cellular telephony. An interesting observation is that in a great majority of these economies, the fixed-telephony penetration rates began to fall once the midpoint on the MCS diffusion curve was reached (compare graphs in Figure 4.4). Put differently, once 50% of κ (predicted saturation with MCS) was achieved, the fixed-telephony penetration rates began to decline. In effect, the gap between fixed- and mobile-cellular telephony market shares was widening, indicating the definite and irreversible 'fixed-to-mobile' technological substitution. As 38 (out of 47 examined) countries were classified into category (1), arguably, we may claim that this type of behavior of two competing technologies in the telecommunication market was dominant among high-income economies between 1975 and 2015.

The category (2) grouped only five economies, where fixed- and mobile-cellular telephony penetration rates are increasing contemporaneously, which allows for concluding that the process of 'fixed-to-mobile' technological substitution might be reversible. Surely, the reversibility or, opposing, irreversibility of the 'fixed-to-mobile' technological substitution is exclusively determined by the differences in rates of diffusion of two technologies. *If* mobile-type technologies spread at a slower pace compared to fixed-technologies, the 'fixed-to-mobile' technological substitution could be reversed. However, bearing in mind the permanently growing demand for mobile solutions, such a scenario is hardly possible.

We have also identified two economies which had to be classified into (1) and (2) at the same time. In these countries, Argentina and Venezuela, between 1975 and 2015, we have slight instabilities in fixed-telephony diffusion paths. At the end of the analyzed period, the fixed-telephony penetration rates were increasing and decreasing by rotation; henceforth, we were unable to classify these economies rigidly. One country, Qatar, fell into categories (1) and (3) at the same time, which suggests, first, that the technological leapfrogging has been reported and, second, that initially fixed telephony was gaining in popularity, but since 2003 onward, drops in this regard are observed. Finally, another country, Oman, fell into categories (2) and (3) simultaneously. The latter means that in Oman, the technological leapfrogging has been reported and that fixed-telephony diffusion path unveiled relative instability. We observed ups and downs, which disables the ability to determine the direction of change definitely.

Regarding the upper-middle-income group, we have identified the following: 11 countries fell into category (1), 4 countries fell into category (2), 4 countries fell into category (3), 9 countries fell into categories (1) and (3) simultaneously and 6 countries fell into categories (2) and (3) simultaneously. This classification shows internal heterogeneity of the upper-middle-income country group. This group of economies is much more diversified compared to the high-income one. The first point to note is that only 11 economies are countries where the 'fixed-to-mobile' technological substitution may be recognized as definite and irreversible. Next, in only four countries (Belarus, Iran, Lebanon and Mauritius) the 'fixed-to-mobile' technological substitution is not actually definite, and the fixed-telephony diffusion trajectories demonstrate relative instability with regard to the direction of change. Another four countries (Algeria, Angola, Botswana and Namibia) exemplified the leapfrog-type technology development pattern. All four are African economies, with poorly developed backbone and wired infrastructure, as well as other economic (especially financial), political and institutional constraints, which impeded technological development. Angola is the country where even in 2015 fixed telephony was a luxury and an inaccessible good that less than 1% of the country's society could possess. There, as well as in the remaining three countries, the mobile-cellular telephony is in fact the only option to choose, and thus any type of 'fixed-to-mobile' technological substitution is just an illusion. Still, among upper-middle-income economies, we have found nine countries (Colombia, Peru, Maldives, Mexico, Paraguay, South Africa, Surinam, Thailand and Tunisia) which were classified into categories (1) and (3) at the same time. All these are economies where technological leapfrogging took place, but at the same time, the wired infrastructure was growing until a certain point in time (but still fixed-telephony penetration rates remained low) and then started to fall as mobile technologies were becoming widely available. Finally, we have six countries (Azerbaijan, Dominican Republic, Ecuador, Jamaica, Jordan and Panama) which fell into categories (2) and (3). These are economies which on the one hand demonstrate the leapfrog-type technological development pattern, and on the other hand the fixed infrastructure was diffusing until a certain point in time, but then we observe random ups and downs in this regard.

Internet Network Expansion

Needless to say, the Internet network '*has become the most powerful driver of innovation that the world has ever seen*' (Cairncross, 1997, p. 118). The Internet network changes the way that people communicate, markets work and economies move forward. It creates new forms of networks, thus facilitating global knowledge and information flows; it eases information and knowledge sharing worldwide. The Internet encourages markets and industries to compete, shifts productivity and eradicates information asymmetries, thus making economies work more efficiently. To some extent, the Internet offers societies a different type of network than networks created by electricity, railways or roads. The Internet network has a great ability to expand quickly society-wide; the network usually spreads at a low cost, is easily installable and then assimilated by companies and individuals. The Internet network has proliferated all spheres of life, and thus it enforces the emergence of economies of scale, which are among the prime drivers of economic development. The Internet has reshaped, altered and revolutionized economies, societies and institutions at an astonishing pace. Henceforth, it is worth taking a closer look at this phenomenal process.

In Sect.4.3.2, we address the empirical results explaining the process of growing access to fixed-broadband and mobile-broadband networks, and—what is closely related—the increasing share of individuals having access to the Internet in each country. Figures 4.6 and 4.7 illustrate FBS, AMS and IU countrywide diffusion trajectories, while consecutive Tables 4.5, 4.6 and 4.7 summarize the results of logistic growth estimates in respect to each ICT indicator. To visualize fixed-broadband network diffusion paths in upper-middle- and high-income economies, we have used data for the period of 1998–2015. Statistics for active mobile-broadband are available for the period between 2007 and 2015, while data explaining changes in the share of the population using the Internet (IU) trace back to 1990. Before 1998, individuals could access the Internet network mainly by using fixed-narrowband infrastructure; however, this low-speed solution never became widely available. Individuals and companies rapidly switched from fixed-narrowband to fixed-broadband technology, as the latter offered high-speed connection, making the network more efficiently. These analogue forms of accessing the Internet were substituted by 'fiber optic' high-speed connections, which enabled further facilitation of unrestricted access to Internet network. However, although fixed-broadband networks are relatively advantageous if compared to narrowband technology, still this form of accessing the Internet is a kind of 'luxury' good for huge parts of many societies. Nonetheless, for fixed (wired) networks to be installed, well-developed backbone infrastructure and financial resources are required, which many regions still lack. These fundamental prerequisites constitute a major impediment for broad and unrestricted diffusion of high-speed fixed networks, which disables the ability of disadvantageous regions to forge ahead technologically and then economically. Luckily, in 2007, mobile (wireless)- broadband technology started to spread worldwide and became a new favorable solution for those who wanted access to the World Wide Web. Mobile-broadband technology is designed to overcome 'traditional' geo-physical barriers, and thus become available 'for all'. Since its inception, this communication channel has been highly desirable and thus is extremely successful worldwide. Mobile-broadband technologies reveal a special importance for rural, remote and technologically underserved areas, where huge parts of the population have been deprived of any type of technology that would allow them to connect with the rest of the world. Mobile-broadband is cheaper compared to wired infrastructure and can be installed faster even in unfavorable geographical environments; this technology has redefined Internet access, shifted penetration rates and empowered individuals, offering them multiple transformative opportunities. Notably, since its emergence, reported increases in mobile-broadband technology penetration rates in rural and geographically isolated areas are remarkable. In 2015, its coverage exceeded 30% of the world's rural population.[13] According to ITU estimates, since then, mobile-broadband technology has become the most dynamic telecommunication market segment, and between 2007 and 2015, its average

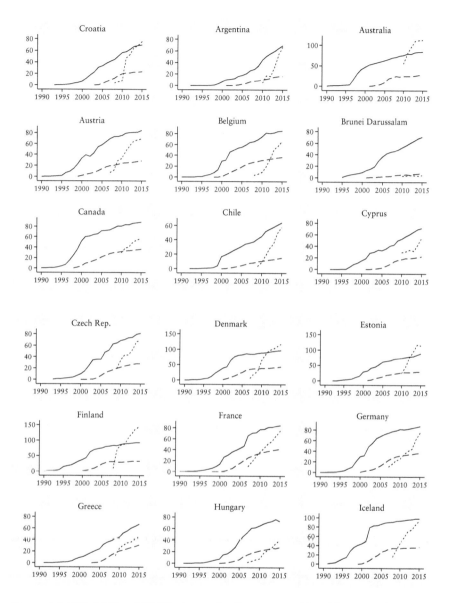

Figure 4.6 FBS, AMS and IU diffusion paths. Country-specific evidence. High-income countries. Period 1990–2015

Note: The solid line represents the IU development path; the long dash line represents the active mobile-broadband diffusion path, and the short dash line represents the fixed-broadband diffusion path. On the X-axis, we see the time, and on the Y-axis, we see the IU, FBS and AMS penetration rates (expressed in number of subscribers per 100 inhabitants).

Source: Author's elaboration.

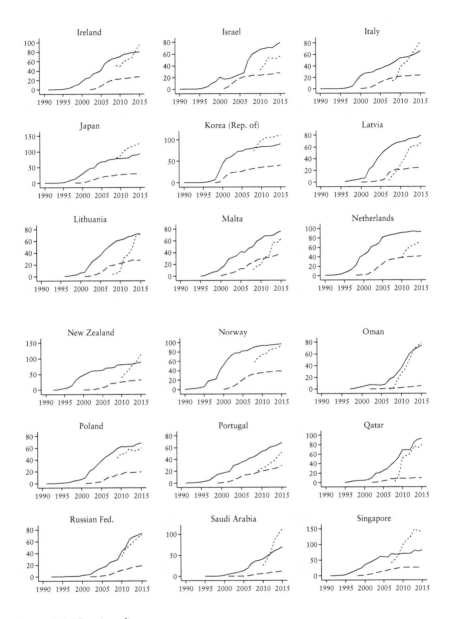

Figure 4.6 (Continued)

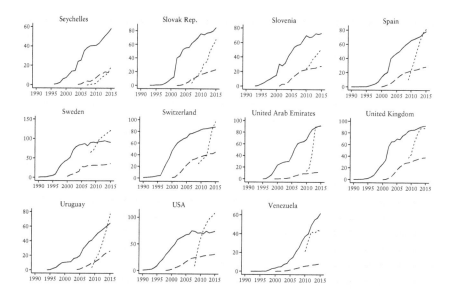

Figure 4.6 (Continued)

worldwide penetration rates grew twelvefold, and it still it continues to increase at a high pace.

Next, we explore major trends in the changing accessibility of the Internet network by examining two core ICT indicators: FBS and AMS. This evidence is confronted with the analysis of growing usage of the Internet (IU). By convention, we develop countrywide FBS, AMS and IU diffusion trajectories, and the time span of the analysis is fully subjected to data availability in respect to each individual country.

Arguably, the key message from our empirical evidence is that all examined countries are paralleling their accelerated access to and use of the Internet. Despite obviously existing cross-country differences with regard to FBS and AMS penetration rates achieved in 2015, all countries are quickly heading towards meaningfully extending their possibilities to access the Internet. Notably, because of rapidly expanding mobile-broadband accessibility, we also observe dramatic shifts in the population's share of using the Internet.

Figure 4.6 illustrates fixed-broadband and mobile-broadband networks diffusion curves in high-income economies between 1998 and 2015. This picture of changing access to these two types of ICT is compared to country-specific paths demonstrating the growing usage of the Internet (IU). First, examining the fixed-broadband diffusion process, we see that its penetration rates growth was relatively moderate. That is not to say that this type of ICT did not reach a significant share of the population, but compared to, for instance, mobile-cellular telephony in 2015, the fixed-broadband penetration rates

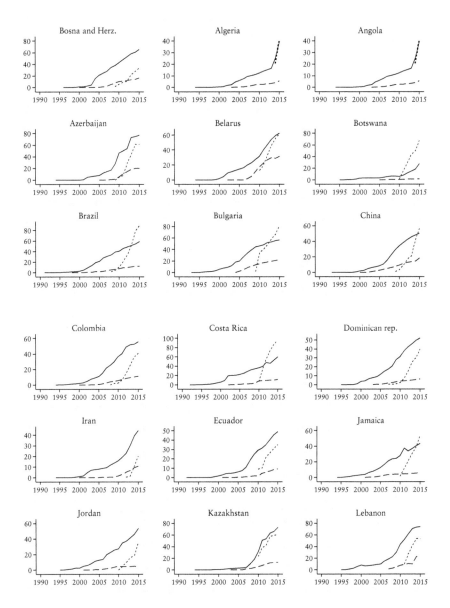

Figure 4.7 FBS, AMS, IU diffusion paths. Country-specific evidence. Upper-middle-income economies. Period 1990–2015

Note: The solid line represents IU's development path; the long dash line represents active mobile-broadband diffusion path, and the short dash line represents the fixed-broadband diffusion path. On the Y-axis, we see the IU, FBS and AMS penetration rates (expressed in number of subscribers per 100 inhabitants).

Source: Author's elaboration.

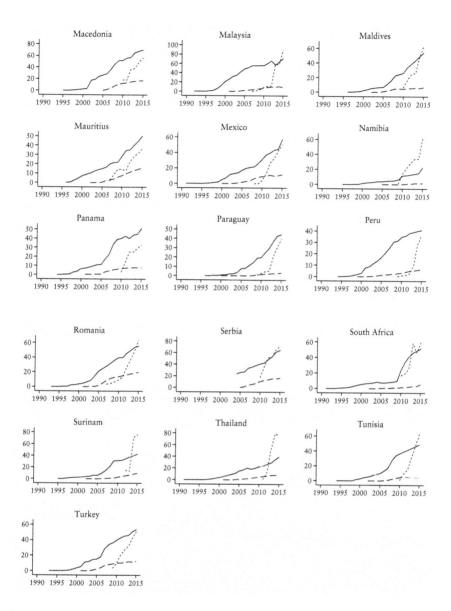

Figure 4.7 (Continued)

Table 4.6 FBS logistic growth estimates. High-income and upper-middle-income economies. Period 1998–2015

Country	κ (upper asymptote / ceiling)	β (midpoint)	α (rate of diffusion / curve steepness)	ΔT (specific duration)	R-squared
Upper-middle-income economies					
Algeria	10.1	2,014.8	0.28	15.4	0.96
Angola	Overest.	2,051	0.4	11.8	0.97
Azerbaijan	20.2	2,010.9	1.2	3.8	0.99
Belarus	30.6	2,009.7	0.9	4.8	0.99
Bosnia and Herzegovina	15.3	2,009.3	0.67	6.6	0.98
Botswana	2.7	2,013	0.3	12.0	0.97
Brazil	13.2	2,009.1	0.4	10.6	0.99
Bulgaria	21.4	2,008.1	0.56	7.8	0.98
China	20.9	2,010.7	0.34	12.8	0.98
Colombia	12.1	2,010.1	0.45	9.7	0.99
Costa Rica	11.1	2,009.3	0.69	6.3	0.97
Dominican Republic	6.5	2,009.4	0.43	10.1	0.98
Ecuador	10.6	2,011.9	0.61	7.2	0.99
Iran	12.9	2,012.7	0.74	5.8	0.99
Jamaica	5.2	2,006.5	0.51	8.5	0.97
Jordan	4.5	2,007.6	1.03	4.2	0.99
Kazakhstan	14.1	2,010.7	0.65	6.7	0.99
Lebanon	Overest.	2,017.3	0.34	12.8	0.91
Macedonia	16.5	2,008.3	0.72	6.1	0.98
Malaysia	10.2	2,008.1	0.54	8.0	0.98
Maldives	5.6	2,006.6	0.9	4.8	0.97
Mauritius	17.4	2,010.5	0.47	9.3	0.99
Mexico	10.8	2,007.5	0.69	6.3	0.99
Namibia	1.8	2,011.4	1.01	4.3	0.99
Panama	7.8	2,006.8	0.81	5.4	0.98
Paraguay	3.1	2,010.6	0.6	7.3	0.95
Peru	7.8	2,010.6	0.32	13.7	0.99
Romania	18.3	2,007.6	0.62	7.1	0.98
Serbia	16.6	2,009.2	0.62	7.1	0.99
South Africa	Overest.	2,064.0	0.26	16.5	0.97
Suriname	11.7	2,012.2	0.52	8.5	0.99
Thailand	9.8	2,010.0	0.45	9.6	0.99
Tunisia	4.8	2,008.1	1.3	3.2	0.99
Turkey	11.6	2,006.8	0.7	6.3	0.99
High-income economies					
Argentina	17.2	2,008.9	0.41	10.7	0.99
Australia	25.7	2,005.7	1.07	4.1	0.98
Austria	27.4	2,005.1	0.43	10.1	0.99
Belgium	35.1	2,004.7	0.46	9.5	0.99
Brunei Darussalam	8.3	2,008.5	0.31	14.1	0.96
Canada	35.1	2,004.1	0.49	10.8	0.99

(Continued)

Table 4.6 (Continued)

Country	κ (upper asymptote / ceiling)	β (midpoint)	α (rate of diffusion / curve steepness)	ΔT (specific duration)	R-squared
Chile	14.8	2,007.3	0.39	11.1	0.99
Croatia	22.9	2,007.7	0.72	6.1	0.99
Cyprus	21.9	2,007.3	0.68	6.4	0.99
Czech Republic	27.3	2,007.2	0.56	7.7	0.99
Denmark	40.1	2,004.1	0.63	6.9	0.99
Estonia	28.3	2,005.2	0.55	8.1	0.99
Finland	30.9	2,003.9	0.89	4.8	0.99
France	39.8	2,006.1	0.52	8.5	0.99
Germany	35.7	2,006.1	0.56	7.8	0.99
Greece	29.2	2,008.6	0.59	7.4	0.99
Hungary	26.4	2,006.8	0.55	8.1	0.99
Iceland	35.4	2,003.7	0.75	5.8	0.99
Ireland	25.6	2,006.1	0.76	5.7	0.98
Israel	25.3	2,003.7	0.79	5.5	0.97
Italy	23.1	2,005.2	0.63	7.0	0.99
Japan	28.8	2,004.1	0.53	8.3	0.98
Korea (Rep.)	37.1	2,002.3	0.46	9.5	0.95
Latvia	23.4	2,006.7	1.2	3.6	0.98
Lithuania	26.7	2,006.6	0.61	7.3	0.98
Malta	36.8	2,006.8	0.43	10.3	0.99
Netherlands	39.9	2,004.3	0.66	6.7	0.99
New Zealand	29.9	2,006.6	0.63	7.0	0.98
Norway	37.5	2,004.7	0.67	6.5	0.99
Oman	7.8	2,012.7	0.37	11.8	0.98
Poland	18.9	2,007.0	0.66	6.7	0.98
Portugal	28.2	2,007.1	0.35	12.5	0.97
Qatar	9.4	2,005.8	0.91	4.8	0.98
Russian Federation	19.2	2,009.6	0.54	8.1	0.99
Saudi Arabia	12.3	2,009.9	0.50	8.7	0.98
Seychelles	15.5	2,009.9	0.48	9.1	0.98
Singapore	27.6	2,004.7	0.48	9.3	0.99
Slovakia	22.6	2,008.1	0.52	8.4	0.98
Slovenia	26.1	2,005.9	0.59	7.3	0.99
Spain	26.8	2,005.7	0.51	8.7	0.99
Sweden	33.4	2,003.6	0.65	6.7	0.97
Switzerland	41.9	2,005.1	0.53	8.3	0.98
United Arab Emirates	11.6	2,006.7	0.56	7.9	0.98
United Kingdom	35.8	2,005.6	0.58	7.6	0.98
United States	30.2	2,004.6	0.48	9.1	0.99
Uruguay	34.0	2,011.7	0.39	11.3	0.99
Venezuela	8.3	2,008.3	0.48	9.2	0.99

Note: Estimation method NLS.

Source: Author's estimates.

Table 4.7 AMS logistic growth estimates. High-income and upper-middle-income economies. Period 2007–2015

Country	κ (upper asymptote / ceiling)	β (midpoint)	α (rate of diffusion / curve steepness)	ΔT (specific duration)	R-squared
Upper-middle-income economies					
Algeria	Only for 2014–2015				
Angola	20.5	2,012.6	1.06	4.2	0.99
Azerbaijan	64	2,012.0	1.34	3.3	0.99
Belarus	68.7	2,012.1	0.78	5.7	0.99
Bosnia and Herzegovina	42.0	2,013.1	0.7	6.1	0.98
Botswana	72.1	2,012.0	0.98	4.4	0.97
Brazil	110.1	2,013.1	0.76	5.7	0.99
Bulgaria	85.1	2,011.5	0.6	7.0	0.91
China	100.8	2,014.6	0.67	6.5	0.98
Colombia	45.6	2,012.7	1.00	4.4	0.99
Costa Rica	95.6	2,011.7	1.08	4.0	0.99
Dominican Republic	43.8	2,012.7	0.87	5.0	0.99
Ecuador	38.4	2,011.9	0.74	5.9	0.99
Iran	21.2	2,013.9	2.7	1.6	0.99
Jamaica	63.7	2,013.2	0.87	5.0	0.98
Jordan	Overest.	2,020.0	0.5	8.7	0.96
Kazakhstan	63.3	2,010.6	0.76	5.7	0.96
Lebanon	55.2	2,012.1	1.4	3.8	0.99
Macedonia	73.8	2,012.6	0.49	8.9	0.95
Malaysia	109.3	2,013.5	0.88	4.9	0.94
Maldives	Overest.	2,016.0	0.5	9.7	0.96
Mauritius	61.1	2,013.7	0.33	13.1	0.95
Mexico	52.1	2,012.3	0.93	4.7	0.98
Namibia	Overest.	2,051.0	0.3	14.7	0.90
Panama	30.1	2,011.1	1.61	2.7	0.96
Paraguay	43.1	2,013.1	1.25	3.5	0.98
Peru	38.7	2,013.6	2.0	2.1	0.99
Romania	99.6	2,013.9	0.54	8.0	0.99
Serbia	73.6	2,011.2	0.78	5.6	0.97
South Africa	63.1	2,011.8	0.81	5.5	0.93
Suriname	11.7	2,012.2	0.52	8.5	0.99
Thailand	78.6	2,012.7	2.67	1.6	0.99
Tunisia	78.5	2,013.5	0.91	4.8	0.99
Turkey	61.7	2,012.6	0.61	7.3	0.98
High-income economies					
Argentina	107.8	2,014.2	0.67	6.6	0.97
Australia	115.7	2,010.1	0.88	4.9	0.99
Austria	71.7	2,010.1	0.67	6.5	0.98
Belgium	71.5	2,012.1	0.86	5.0	0.99
Brunei Darussalam	4.3	2,009.4	1.9	2.3	0.96
Canada	64.1	2,010.3	0.44	9.3	0.98
Chile	69.3	2,012.7	0.68	6.4	0.99

(Continued)

Table 4.7 (Continued)

Country	κ (upper asymptote / ceiling)	β (midpoint)	α (rate of diffusion / curve steepness)	ΔT (specific duration)	R-squared
Croatia	70.1	2,010.8	1.51	2.9	0.96
Cyprus	Overest.	2,109.0	0.13	32.9	0.83
Czech Republic	88.1	2,011.6	0.39	11.2	0.95
Denmark	112.9	2,009.8	0.92	4.8	0.99
Estonia	122.3	2,011.6	0.94	4.7	0.99
Finland	146.6	2,010.0	0.62	7.1	0.91
France	85.6	2,010.9	0.43	10.3	0.98
Germany	Overest.	2,024.0	0.23	19.3	0.98
Greece	44.9	2,010.1	0.65	6.8	0.95
Hungary	47.5	2,012.3	0.57	7.6	0.99
Iceland	35.8	2,003.7	0.75	5.8	0.95
Ireland	Overest.	2,123.0	0.11	38.7	0.95
Israel	55.2	2,009.7	0.97	4.5	0.94
Italy	96.7	2,011.6	0.46	9.5	0.97
Japan	132.6	2,008.2	0.43	10.2	0.99
Korea (Rep.)	108.7	2,006.9	0.72	6.1	0.99
Latvia	67.6	2,010.3	0.78	5.6	0.99
Lithuania	86.2	2,012.3	0.72	6.2	0.97
Malta	76.7	2,011.8	0.51	8.6	0.96
Netherlands	70.9	2,009.8	0.82	5.3	0.99
New Zealand	Over	2,014.0	0.31	14.2	0.99
Norway	97.9	2,006.7	0.33	13.3	0.98
Oman	83.3	2,011.3	0.76	5.8	0.99
Poland	53.1	2,002.1	4.9	0.89	0.98
Portugal	Overest.	2,094.0	0.15	28.2	0.99
Qatar	73.1	2,009.7	1.55	2.8	0.95
Russian Federation	78.9	2,010.4	0.46	11.1	0.98
Saudi Arabia	129.8	2,012.2	0.66	6.6	0.99
Seychelles	32.1	2,014.4	0.56	7.8	0.98
Singapore	152.4	2,009.1	0.56	7.7	0.98
Slovakia	89.7	2,012.6	0.46	9.5	0.99
Slovenia	67.5	2,011.7	0.36	12.2	0.99
Spain	87.4	2,011.5	0.76	5.7	0.99
Sweden	135.9	2,008.5	0.33	13.3	0.99
Switzerland	Overest.	2,017.0	0.3	14.3	0.96
United Arab Emirates	95.4	2,011.9	1.6	2.8	0.97
United Kingdom	93.8	2,009.9	0.68	6.5	0.97
United States	105.6	2,009.8	0.89	4.9	0.98
Uruguay	111.6	2,013.6	0.58	7.6	0.99
Venezuela	43.3	2,010.1	1.4	3.3	0.97

Note: estimation method NLS.

Source: Author's estimates.

Table 4.8 IU logistic growth estimates. High-income and upper-middle-income economies. Period 1990–2015

Country	κ (upper asymptote / ceiling)	β (midpoint)	α (rate of diffusion / curve steepness)	ΔT (specific duration)	R-squared
Upper-middle-income economies					
Algeria	Over	2,080.0	0.2	21.2	0.95
Angola	29.5	2,015.0	0.35	12.4	0.98
Azerbaijan	87.5	2,010.4	.47	9.2	0.99
Belarus	87.3	2,011.6	0.28	15.4	0.99
Bosnia and Herzegovina	66.9	2,008.0	0.37	11.9	0.98
Botswana	Overest.	2,079.0	0.22	19.6	0.96
Brazil	59.1	2,006.9	0.33	13.1	0.99
Bulgaria	57.4	2,006.1	0.39	11.1	0.99
China	54.1	2,008.8	0.41	10.1	0.99
Colombia	62.7	2,009.0	0.36	12.2	0.99
Costa Rica	67.6	2,008.5	0.23	19.4	0.99
Dominican Republic	63.7	2,008.5	0.31	14.3	0.99
Ecuador	55.7	2,010.1	0.37	11.7	0.98
Iran	Overest.	2,078.0	0.19	22.5	0.98
Jamaica	46.9	2,008.1	0.31	14.1	0.99
Jordan	74.2	2,011.7	0.24	18.1	0.99
Kazakhstan	72.1	2,010.8	0.76	5.6	0.99
Lebanon	94.1	2,010.6	0.36	12.3	0.99
Macedonia	71.3	2,006.7	0.35	12.7	0.98
Malaysia	62.6	2,002.2	0.43	10.7	0.98
Maldives	72.1	2,011.3	0.29	14.7	0.99
Mauritius	93.3	2,014.4	0.18	24.2	0.98
Mexico	81.7	2,012.1	0.21	20.7	0.98
Namibia	Overest.	2,023.0	0.18	23.8	0.96
Panama	50.1	2,006.9	0.38	11.5	0.98
Paraguay	64.7	2,012.2	0.31	13.9	0.99
Peru	41.8	2,005.8	0.37	11.6	0.99
Romania	57.7	2,007.3	0.33	13.2	0.99
Serbia	Overest.	2,149.2	0.09	47.1	0.98
South Africa	73.9	2,012.0	0.36	12.2	0.96
Suriname	42.5	2,008.1	0.47	9.3	0.98
Thailand	47.4	2,009.9	0.22	19.8	0.97
Tunisia	49.5	2,007.8	0.44	9.9	0.99
Turkey	78.6	2,013.6	0.91	4.8	0.99
High-income economies					
Argentina	89.9	2,010.3	0.26	16.5	0.99
Australia	76.9	1,999.3	0.50	8.8	0.97
Austria	82.3	2,002.3	0.34	12.8	0.99
Belgium	81.8	2,002.5	0.37	11.9	0.98
Brunei Darussalam	71.7	2,005.7	0.30	14.6	0.98

(Continued)

Table 4.8 (Continued)

Country	κ (upper asymptote / ceiling)	β (midpoint)	α (rate of diffusion / curve steepness)	ΔT (specific duration)	R-squared
Canada	81.3	1,999.6	0.48	8.9	0.98
Chile	67.6	2,006.1	0.25	17.3	0.97
Croatia	71.7	2,005.8	0.32	13.7	0.99
Cyprus	77.9	2,006.3	0.24	18.6	0.99
Czech Republic	80.8	2,004.9	0.35	12.5	0.99
Denmark	91.7	2,000.6	0.55	8.4	0.99
Estonia	81.4	2,002.4	0.38	11.5	0.99
Finland	90.7	2,000.6	0.37	11.8	0.99
France	86.8	2,004.4	0.35	12.6	0.99
Germany	83.5	2,001.6	0.50	9.2	0.99
Greece	74.4	2,007.7	0.26	16.7	0.99
Hungary	74.5	2,004.9	0.43	10.3	0.99
Iceland	96.3	1,999.7	0.42	10.2	0.98
Ireland	81.7	2,004.2	0.35	12.6	0.99
Israel	85.5	2,006.5	0.29	14.7	0.97
Italy	63.5	2,003.9	0.27	15.8	0.97
Japan	85.3	2,001.8	0.39	11.1	0.99
Korea (Rep.)	82.9	2,000.3	0.66	6.6	0.99
Latvia	74.9	2,004.2	0.49	8.8	0.99
Lithuania	70.6	2,004.8	0.43	10.3	0.99
Malta	77.6	2,005.1	0.29	14.8	0.98
Netherlands	92.7	2,000.6	0.4	10.7	0.99
New Zealand	80.7	1,999.8	0.39	11.2	0.97
Norway	93.3	1,999.7	0.47	9.4	0.99
Oman	89.1	2,010.0	0.42	10.5	0.99
Poland	66.1	2,004.3	0.43	10.2	0.99
Portugal	71.4	2,005.4	0.25	17.4	0.99
Qatar	108.5	2,009.1	0.31	14.4	0.99
Russian Federation	92.3	2,010.4	0.34	13.1	0.99
Saudi Arabia	76.6	2,009.1	0.34	12.9	0.99
Seychelles	54.4	2,005.2	0.34	12.7	0.98
Singapore	75.4	2,000.7	0.39	11.1	0.98
Slovakia	77.4	2,003.1	0.48	9.0	0.98
Slovenia	73.7	2,003.4	0.34	12.8	0.99
Spain	73.6	2,003.7	0.39	11.0	0.99
Sweden	91.9	1,999.7	0.47	9.2	0.99
Switzerland	83.9	2,000.1	0.46	9.6	0.99
United Arab Emirates	100.7	2,006.2	0.26	16.7	0.98
United Kingdom	87.3	2,001.6	0.46	9.7	0.99
United States	73.1	1,999.1	0.45	9.8	0.99
Uruguay	74.1	2,007.9	0.26	16.8	0.99
Venezuela	73.7	2,009.9	0.32	13.6	0.99

Note: Estimation method NLS.

Source: Author's estimates.

remained at a significantly lower level. In 2015, the average FBS penetration rate was only 27.3%, while the highest FBS was reported in Switzerland where it reached almost 45 subscriptions per 100 inhabitants, and in next 4 countries (Denmark, Netherlands, France and Korea (Rep. of)), the FBS slightly exceeded 40 subscriptions per 100 inhabitants. The lowest fixed-broadband penetration rate was observed in Oman, where it was only 5 subscriptions per 100 inhabitants. In other countries, fixed-broadband network diffusion was also very low; for instance, in Brunei Darussalam, Venezuela and Qatar, FBS reached only 8.0, 8.2 and 10.1 subscriptions per 100 inhabitants, respectively. When analyzing the countrywide FBS diffusion curves, the principal observation is that most of them resemble the S-time pattern, despite the fact that in any of examined economies, the 'full' (100%) saturation rate is reported. According to FBS logistic growth estimates summarized in Table 4.6, we see that the return value of the upper ceiling (upper asymptote) varies from 7.8 in Oman to slightly above 40 in Switzerland and Denmark (the maximum values among high-income economies), which suggests that these two countries have already passed the full development path in respect to fixed-broadband network deployment. The latter also allows us to conclude that no further significant shifts in this regard can be projected. The estimated midpoints indicting the year when the FBS diffusion has been 'halfway' vary between 2002 in Korea (Rep. of) and 2012 in Oman, and thus it encompass a ten-year period. As indicated, the earliest midpoint was achieved in Korea (Rep. of); in 2003, it was reported in another four countries (Finland, Iceland, Israel and Sweden). The specific duration (ΔT) denoting the time needed to pass from 10% to 90% of saturation ranged from 3.6 years in Latvia, 4.1 in Argentina and 4.8 in Qatar, to 14.1 years in Brunei Darussalam, 12.5 in Portugal and almost 12 in Oman.

Relatively poor development of fixed-broadband networks in high-income economies is, however, nothing surprising after taking a look at the process of spreading mobile broadband (AMS). Since 2007, the individual demand for this newly emerged type of ICT service boosted and rapidly gained the telecommunication market.

According to our estimates, in 2007, the average AMS penetration rate was only 8.2 subscriptions per 100 inhabitants.[14] Two years later in 2009, it grew to almost 30, and, finally, in 2015, it reached 79 subscriptions per 100 inhabitants. In 2015, the 'top-five' countries in respect to mobile-broadband penetration rates were Finland (144 subscriptions per 100 inhabitants), Singapore (142 subscriptions per 100 inhabitants), Japan (126 subscriptions per 100 inhabitants), Sweden (122 subscriptions per 100 inhabitants) and Denmark (116.8 subscriptions per 100 inhabitants). Unfortunately, still in 2015, there were a few countries which were lagging behind in this respect; these were Brunei Darussalam (the worst performing country) with only 4.5 subscriptions per 100 inhabitants and Seychelles with 19 subscriptions per 100 inhabitants These basic data suggest that among high-income countries, there emerged a huge gap in respect to access to mobile-broadband network.

In absolute terms, it was more than 139 %pp., indicating the difference in AMS penetration rates between 'top' and 'bottom' country. These enormous cross-country disparities indicate that even among the richest countries, there still exist significant differences regarding access to ICT. High average annual growth rates achieved in this regard are promising; however, it might be a bit misleading when trying to draw conclusions. The enormously high growth pace was determined by in a few countries forging ahead, while there remained regions lacking this form of ICT.

Plotted in Figure 4.6, country-specific mobile-broadband diffusion trajectories unveil several interesting features. First, in a great majority of cases, the mobile-broadband diffusion does not follow the sigmoid-type trajectory. In terms of share, they significantly differ from development paths showing the spread of fixed-broadband or mobile-cellular telephony. Second, we can distinguish the pre-take-off stage in only a few cases. The early diffusion phase may be exclusively observed in Croatia, Hungary, Lithuania, Seychelles and Switzerland. Still in the aforementioned countries, the pre-take-off stage is extremely short, lasting just three to four years. In the remaining 42 high-income countries, actually no early diffusion phase is observed, but the mobile-broadband diffusion patterns 'begin' in the high growth stage. This is very unique for the technology diffusion, because it indicates that immediately after the introduction of this technology to the national telecommunication markets, effective demand was boosted. Another interesting observation is that in a great majority of economies, the shape of the mobile-broadband diffusion trajectories does not suggest heading towards the saturation phase. Only in the cases of Australia, Austria, Estonia, Korea (Rep. of), Norway, Qatar, Singapore and United Kingdom did the mobile-broadband market reach the stabilization stage in 2015. The remaining 39 high-income economies, in 2015, were still located in the exponential growth phase along the S-shaped diffusion trajectory and were heading towards achieving 'full' saturation.

When jointly analyzing fixed-broadband and mobile-broadband network diffusion trajectories in each consecutive country, another impressive observation arose. Assume that in a given country the process of diffusion of network technology enabling access to Internet might be decomposed into sub-processes. Put differently, we might claim that the diffusion process of network technology is transformable into a two-growth 'pulses' process, where the first 'pulse' is the growth of the fixed-broadband network, while the second 'pulse' is the growth of the mobile-broadband network. In such a case, the *'component logistic curve'* is generated with two clearly distinguishable growth phases: in our case, the fixed-broadband growth impulse and mobile-broadband growth impulse. Then the 'new' diffusion curve is observed that would be the approximated sum of two discrete wavelets (growth impulses). Among high-income economies, the phenomenon of the two-growth 'pulses' process is unveiled in the cases of Croatia, Argentina, Austria, Canada, Chile, Czech Republic, Estonia, Denmark, Finland, France,

Greece, Iceland, Italy, Latvia, Lithuania, Malta, Netherlands, New Zealand, Oman, Portugal, Qatar, Saudi Arabia (with disruption), Singapore (with disruption), Slovak Rep., Slovenia, Spain, Switzerland, United Arab Emirates, United Kingdom, Uruguay and United States. In each of the aforementioned countries, we observe that the emergence of mobile-broadband technology, actually impedes further expansion of fixed broadband and the first boosts off rapidly gaining the telecommunication market, while the growth of fixed networks significantly slows down.

Table 4.7 summarizes active mobile-broadband logistic growth model estimates for high-income economies. Estimated levels of the upper asymptote (system limit), κ, vary extensively among countries. The value of parameter κ ranges from 4.3 in Brunei Darussalam to 152.4 in Singapore (sic!); however, in another few economies, such as Finland ($\kappa = 146.6$), Japan ($\kappa = 132.6$), Saudi Arabia ($\kappa = 129.8$) or Estonia ($\kappa = 122.3$), the return from the model upper asymptotes are very high and indicate that in some high-income economies, in 2015, societies were already 'fully' saturated with mobile-broadband technology. Interestingly, when taking a closer look at the mobile-broadband diffusion curves in countries, where estimated κ exceeds 100, we may have an impression that despite already achieved 'full' saturation, these countries are still located in exponential growth phase. The shape of mobile-broadband diffusion trajectory does not suggest that the stabilization phase has been reached, but, reversely, mobile-broadband penetration rates are still growing at a high pace. On the other hand, in the group of high-income economies, we witness economies where the mobile-broadband networks have been limited so far. For instance, in Brunei Darussalam, in 2015, the mobile-broadband penetration rate was slightly above 4 per 100 inhabitants, while in Seychelles, it was 19.1 per 100 inhabitants. In another few economies, for instance, Hungary, Greece, Canada or Portugal, in 2015, the mobile-broadband penetration rates were 39.8, 45.6, 56.3 and 52.0, respectively, and these countries were relatively lagging behind in terms of the adoption of this type of technology.

Estimated values of midpoints demonstrate that 50% of κ was reached within a 12-year time span, and thus high-income countries vary significantly in this respect. The midpoint was achieved the earliest in 2002 in Poland and in 2003 in Iceland, while the latest was achieved in 2013 in Argentina and Uruguay, and in 2014 in Seychelles. In effect, the specific duration (ΔT) differs hugely across high-income economies. The shortest specific duration was reported for Poland, where the intrinsic growth rate (α) was at 4.9 (the highest in the group), and thus it took only 0.89 years to pass from 10% to 90% of mobile-broadband saturation. In Brunei Darussalam, the estimated specific duration was only 2.3 years (with the intrinsic growth rate at $\alpha = 1.9$), in Qatar in was 2.8 years (with the intrinsic growth rate at $\alpha = 1.55$), in Croatia it was 2.9 years (with the intrinsic growth rate at $\alpha = 1.51$) and in Venezuela it was 3.3 years (with the intrinsic growth rate at $\alpha = 1.4$). However, among high-income economies, there were also countries where the reported specific duration was significantly longer. The longest specific duration was observed in Norway and Sweden where ΔT = 13.3 years for both (with the intrinsic growth rate α = 0.33), Slovenia where ΔT = 12.2 (with the intrinsic growth rate α = 0.36) and Czech Rep. and the Russian Federation where countrywide specific durations were almost equal and reached 11.2 and 11.1 years, respectively.

Such enormous differences among high-income countries unveil an internal heterogeneity of this income group. However, it should be born in mind that these differences may account for a relatively short time span during which we can examine the process of diffusion of mobile-broadband networks, and thus—to some extent—the results of our estimates may be biased. Undeniably, mobile-broadband technologies have been rapidly evading the telecommunication markets from its inception. Needless to say, they are the 'better option' of accessing the Internet network compared to fixed (wired)- broadband solutions, which spread even across high-income economies have not as fast and overwhelming as recognized in the case of mobile-broadband technologies.

The overall landscape regarding the process of fixed-broadband and mobile-broadband network diffusion in upper-middle-income economies also unveils several unique characteristics worth paying attention to. The country-specific, fixed-broadband and mobile-broadband diffusion patterns are plotted in Figure 4.7, while respective logistic growth estimates are summarized in Tables 4.6 and 4.7. The first data on fixed-broadband technology trace back to 1998 (in Brazil) and on mobile-broadband to 2007 (in Dominican Republic, Malaysia, Mauritius and Romania).

As for the spread of fixed-broadband networks, the fundamental observation is that in upper-middle-income economies, the FBS penetration rates remained very low during the whole analyzed period. In 2010, the average fixed-broadband penetration rate was at about 6 per 100 inhabitants, and until 2015, it grew only until 11 per 100 inhabitants. Despite the fact that in 2015 there were few countries where FBS penetration rates exceeded the group average, in 20 countries (out of 34 examined), the fixed-broadband deployment remained below average. The worst performing country was Angola, where in 2015, the FBS = 0.67 per 100 inhabitants. In the other 8 countries (Namibia, Botswana, Paraguay, Jordan, Tunisia, South Africa, Algeria and Jamaica), the FBS penetration rates were below or equal to 5 per 100 inhabitants. Conversely, the three best performing countries with regard to fixed-broadband development were Belarus, Lebanon and Bulgaria, where FBS achieved at 31.3, 22.7 and 22.4 per 100 inhabitants, respectively. Since quite a share of upper-middle-income economies failed in the economy-wide adoption of the fixed-broadband networks, by definition, their growth in FBS penetration rates were negligible between 1998 and 2015. This spasmodically proceeding process of spreading fixed-broadband network is visualized in Figure 4.7, which plots country-specific FBS diffusion trajectories. The first striking observation is that the full-length FBS diffusion curve is not demonstrated in any of the examined countries. In a few countries, we observe the '*quasi-take-off*', which means that a country has left the pre-take-off diffusion stage, and it seems that the diffusion curve take offs and enters the exponential growth phase. In fact, even if some countries have undeniably left the early diffusion stage, it did not enforce the real take-off into exponential growth. Still, after passing this '*quasi-critical point*' along the FBS diffusion curve, the pace of adoption by new users of the fixed-broadband network remained relatively low, or even the process of further expansion of this type of technology has been impeded. This specific '*quasi-take-off*' can be distinguished in Bosnia and Herzegovina, Azerbaijan, Belarus, Bulgaria, China, Colombia, Iran, Ecuador, Kazakhstan, Lebanon, Macedonia, Mauritius, Romania, Serbia and Turkey (in total, 15 out of 34 countries examined). For instance, in Turkey, the 'critical year' could be hypothetically identified in 2007, as 2006 and 2007 FBS penetration rates grew at 2.8 %pp. However, during the consecutive years, the fixed-broadband deployment was increasing at barely 1%pp per year, which shows that this growth was stable but not exponential. In the remaining countries mentioned earlier, the in-time behavior of fixed-broadband diffusion was analogous. In the case of the other 19 upper-middle-income economies, the developed country-specific FBS diffusion lines indicate that these economies, in 2015, were still located in the early diffusion stage and did not manage to take off (see Figure 4.7). In fact, all of these 19 economies were virtually 'locked' in a low-diffusion trap, and for the whole analyzed period, their level of assimilation of wired-broadband technologies remained indecently low. The prominent examples of the latter are five African countries—namely, Angola, Botswana, Namibia, Tunisia and South Africa; one Latin American country, Paraguay; and, finally, the last one in East Asia, Jordan. In Algeria, Jamaica and Peru, the state of adoption of fixed broadband has been just slightly higher, but still all these economies permanently suffer from a heavy shortage of wired infrastructure disabling the installation of novel technological solutions. FBS logistic growth estimates for each single upper-middle-income economies, displayed in Table 4.6, are *false-optimistic* and might be a bit misleading. On the one hand, the reported intrinsic growth rates are fairly high. See, for instance, Tunisia ($\alpha = 1.3$), Azerbaijan ($\alpha = 1.2$), Jordan ($\alpha = 1.03$) or Namibia ($\alpha = 1.01$). This in turn generates a relatively short specific duration period. For Tunisia, Azerbaijan, Jordan and Namibia, the returned ΔT are 3.2 years, 3.8 years, 4.2 years and 4.3 years, respectively. Note that comparatively short specific duration times are also reported for Belarus, Iran, Mexico, Panama and Turkey, just to cite few. Such results might lead to the conclusion that the process of fixed-broadband expansion is dynamic, and these economies quickly head towards 'full' saturation. However, the estimated values of upper ceilings (κ) show that the process of diffusion of fixed-broadband networks is not that dynamic as it would seem at first sign, but rather it is hindered by some external factors. Note that the highest value of κ is found for Belarus, and it is only

30.6 per 100 inhabitants. Next, we have reported $\kappa = 20.2$ for Azerbaijan, $\kappa = 21.4$ for Bulgaria and $\kappa = 20.9$ for China. For another 30 economies, the values of the upper asymptote indicates the system limit is far below 20. These results show that in the group of upper-middle-income economies, the average deployment of wired-broadband network was extremely limited, and the vast majority of these countries were—and still are—deprived from unlimited access to this type of ICT.

Our findings on fixed-broadband technology diffusion in upper-middle-income economies significantly contrast with the empirical results explaining rapid expansion of mobile-broadband networks. The evidence on active mobile-broadband development covers the period between 2007 and 2015 and draws an optimistic scenario for the future of growing connectivity and accessibility of new technologies. Compared to the slow deployment rates of fixed networks, mobile-broadband solutions induce revolutionary changes, unleash new potential to connect people and rapidly evade telecommunication markets in this country group. During the period of 2007–2015, advancements in the deployment of mobile-broadband networks are astonishing. In 2009, the average AMS penetration rate was barely 2.7 per 100 inhabitants. In 2010, it reached 8.6 per 100 inhabitants, and, finally, in 2015, there was observed an abrupt upswing to almost 55 per 100 inhabitants. In 2015, the most proliferated country was Costa Rica, where the AMS penetration rate was higher than 95 per 100 inhabitants. Bearing in mind the fact that in Costa Rica in 2010 the AMS penetration rate was 7.2 per 100 inhabitants, between 2010 and 2015, it was growing with the average annual speed of 52% (sic!). Next, the three top countries were Malaysia, Brazil and Bulgaria, with deployment rates exceeding 80 per 100 inhabitants in 2015. These economies are quickly catching up and diminishing their technological backwardness. Unfortunately, several countries remained relatively stagnant in mobile-broadband deployment rates. For instance, in Angola, Iran, Panama and Bosnia and Herzegovina, in 2015, the AMS penetration rates were, respectively, 19.3, 20.0, 32.6 and 33.5 per 100 inhabitants.

Figure 4.7 plots country-specific mobile-broadband diffusion curves for upper-middle-income countries. Similarly to what was observed in respect to analogous trajectories for high-income economies (to compare, see Figure 4.6), in this case, we recognize their very specific shape. Detailed research unveils that exclusively in eight economies—namely, Bosnia and Herzegovina, Colombia, Dominican Republic, Iran, Malaysia, Mexico, Peru, Romania—the early diffusion stage may be distinguished. However, in these countries, the pre-take-off phase is extremely short, and the AMS diffusion curve abruptly upswings shortly after the mobile-broadband technology is introduced to the society. In the remaining 29 countries, all pictured AMS diffusion paths are also very unique in shape; in fact, they only exhibit the exponential growth phase, while neither early nor saturation phases are encountered.

Likewise, in high-income economies, when analyzing jointly fixed-broadband and mobile-broadband network diffusion trajectories in country, there emerges another remarkable observation. Both fixed-broadband and mobile-broadband diffusion curves create a '*component logistic curve*' with two easily identifiable growth impulses (wavelets), fixed-broadband growth impulses and mobile-broadband growth impulses. In the group of upper-middle-income economies, we can identify '*component logistic curve*' in all 34 countries, although in Algeria, Angola, Ecuador, Kazakhstan, Serbia, South Africa and Surinam, we find discontinuities along countrywide '*component logistic curve*'. Each of the '*component logistic curves*' encompass an early stage of diffusion during which we observe fixed-broadband deployment and exponential growth phase during which the mobile-broadband networks expand rapidly. One more issue worth noting is that until 2015, the saturation (stabilization) stage of diffusion did not appear in any of the examined economies, which inevitably leads to the conclusion that until then, no signals of slowing down were reported.

Table 4.7 displays the results of active mobile-broadband logistic growth estimates in each of examined upper-middle-income countries. This evidence confirms our previous findings on the extraordinarily high speed of diffusion of mobile broadband across the examined 34 upper-middle-income economies. The estimated values of intrinsic growth rates α are significantly higher compared to those estimated for high-income economies. To give an example, in Iran, $\alpha = 2.7$; in Thailand, $\alpha = 2.67$; in Peru, $\alpha = 2.0$; and in Panama, $\alpha = 1.6$, which in turn determines very short specific durations (ΔT). In Iran, Thailand, Peru and Panama, the estimated values of ΔT were, respectively, 1.6 years, 1.6 years, 2.1 years and 2.7 years. For instance, if we consider the case of Iran, the value of $\Delta T = 1.6$ years indicates the time needed to pass from 10% to 90% of the estimated κ. For countries which achieved high saturation with mobile-broadband technology, the values of the specific durations are usually higher compared to China (6.5 years), Brazil (5.7 years), Malaysia (4.9 years) and Romania (8.0 years). The estimated time period when country-specific midpoints were achieved ranged from 2010 in Kazakhstan to 2014 in China; henceforth, each of the analyzed countries reached its unique midpoint within the five-year time span.

Putting together the empirical evidence on mobile- and wired-broadband networks development patterns in both income groups, there arises a fundamental conclusion that mobile-broadband technologies are well ahead of fixed ones. In previous paragraphs, we systematically outlined that mobile-broadband solutions expand faster and, in 2015, achieved significantly higher penetration rates compared to fixed-broadband technologies, despite the fact that enormous cross-country diversity is observed in this regard. Rapidly boosting the demand for wireless telecommunication services, similar to the case of mobile-cellular telephony, enforced the emergence of a unique '*fixed-to-mobile technological substitution*' process. Here the '*fixed-to-mobile technological substitution*' explicitly concerns the process of gradual switching from fixed (wired)- broadband to mobile (wireless)- broadband technologies enabling access to the Internet network.

Since an outstanding feature of wireless technologies is their ability to be deployed fast and at low-cost, mobile-broadband networks are evading the national telecommunication market, while fixed-broadband networks' market shares are diminishing in time. Mobile-broadband networks, analogous to mobile-cellular communication technologies, in poorly developed and geographically isolated regions are not only the best, but, first of all, they are the *only* option to get access to the outside world. But negligible access to fixed-infrastructure, which drives societies to assimilate directly and put into usage wireless solution, enforces the emergence of another unique process: technological leapfrogging. In this case, the technological leapfrogging consists in omitting the *'fixed-infrastructure stage of development'* and moving directly to the *'mobile-infrastructure stage'*. Both processes, *'fixed-to-mobile technological substitution'* and technological leapfrogging, generate profound and usually persistent structural shifts in national telecommunication markets. The market shares possessed by mobile technologies are systematically increasing at the expense of diminishing demand for fixed-infrastructure solutions.

In Figures 4.6 and 4.7, we have demonstrated country-specific fixed-broadband and mobile-broadband diffusion curves in high-income and upper-middle-income economies between 1998 and 2015. Generally speaking, we have identified three major tendencies in this respect. First, the process of spreading fixed-broadband networks has been far less dynamic compared to the mobile-broadband deployment pace. Second, in 2015, the average fixed-broadband penetration rates were significantly lower compared to the average level of mobile-broadband adoption. Third, during the examined time period, telecommunication market shares possessed by mobile-broadband technologies have been rapidly shifting, while the wired networks have been losing their market position.

The general scheme of the process of *'fixed-to-mobile technological substitution'* is very similar across all countries in the scope of our analysis. Since 1998 onwards, the fixed-broadband networks have been deployed; however, the process of diffusion of this type of technology was rather slow. The average penetration rates were systematically growing, but this kind of technology has never become widespread (note that, in 2015, the highest FBS penetration rate was reported in Argentina, and it was 44 per 100 inhabitants, while the lowest was in Angola, where it was barely 0.6 per 100 inhabitants). To some extent, access to fixed networks has always been impeded by infrastructural, geographical and financial constraints, and, in fact, it has always been a kind of luxury good that not everyone could afford. In both country income groups, during the period 1998 and 2005, the state of development of fixed-broadband networks in many economies was still negligible, but to some extent, this type of telecommunication infrastructure was evading the markets. Next, the period between 2005 and 2010 is marked by the relatively highest shifts in FBS penetration rates. In high-income countries, the average change in absolute FBS penetration rate was

5.4 per 100 inhabitants, while the analogous average in high-income economies reached the value of 11.2 per 100 inhabitants.[15] The most dynamic growth was reported in Germany and Greece, where the change in the absolute FBS penetration rate exceeded 18 per 100 inhabitants; next, we have Belarus, Malta and New Zealand, with the absolute change at about 14 per 100 inhabitants, Since 2007 onwards, mobile-broadband technology began to evade the telecommunication markets and rapidly growing demand for this type of ICT, enforcing radical drops in dynamics of diffusion of wired telecommunication networks. Reported shifts in FBS penetration rates unveil that the process of deployment of fixed networks has significantly slowed down. Between 2010 and 2015, the average change in FBS penetration rates, in high-income economies, dropped until 5.1 per inhabitants, while, in parallel, mobile-broadband penetration rates grew enormously (for countrywide calculations, see Appendix 1 and 2). The latter suggests gradual switching from fixed- to mobile-broadband networks, and thus the '*fixed-to-mobile technological substitution*' may be identified. This unique process of '*fixed-to-mobile technological substitution*' is graphically visualized in Figures 4.6 and 4.7, where we observe that fixed-broadband and mobile-broadband diffusion paths have diverged since the mobile networks were first introduced to national telecommunication markets. To some extent, the process differs slightly from what was demonstrated in the case of substituting landline telephony with a mobile-cellular one, where we have observed falling fixed-telephony penetration rates. Here falls in FBS deployment are not reported in countrywide statistics, but rather we observe a significant slowdown in the growth of adoption of wired-broadband networks, and at the same time, mobile networks penetration rates were raising fast.

Figure 4.8 graphically portrays country-specific absolute changes in FBS penetration rates during the period of 2010–2015, which are confronted with analogous values for mobile-broadband technology. Next, according to the value of absolute change in FBS penetration rates between 2010 and 2015, we have classified countries into three categories (see Table 4.9). Such classification seems to be very instructive to seeing and understanding the unique character of the process of '*fixed-to-mobile technological substitution*' unveiled across the examined countries.

In the first category, we have classified those countries in which, between 2010 and 2015, the absolute change in FBS penetration rates was below 5%pp, and we have labeled them 'slow FBS growth countries'. Among high-income economies, we have identified 28 (out of 47) where absolute change in FBS penetration rates was below 5%pp, and another 18 upper-middle-income economies. In these economies, the emergence of mobile broadband has effectively enforced the slowdown in further growth of deployment of wired-broadband technology, while, on the other hand, mobile-broadband services have been rapidly gaining in the market. Arguably, in countries falling into the first category, the '*fixed-to-mobile technological substitution*' is evident, and its irreversibility is highly probable.

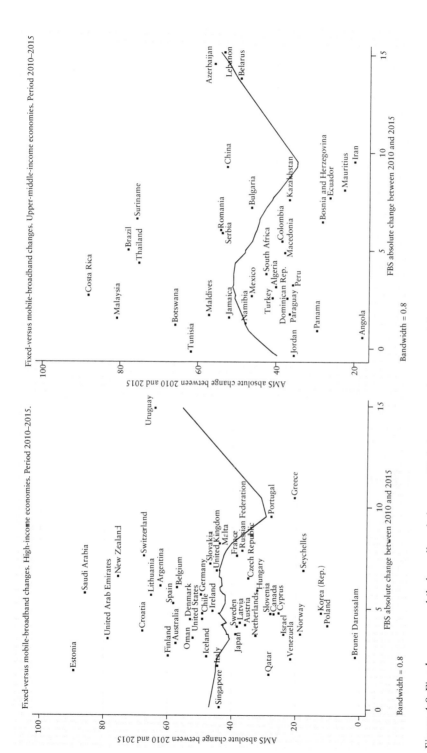

Figure 4.8 Fixed- versus mobile-broadband changes. High-income and upper-middle-income economies. Period 2010–2015

Note: On the X-axis, we see the absolute change in FBS penetration rates between 2010 and 2015 (raw values), and on the Y-axis, we see the absolute change in AMS penetration rates between 2010 and 2015 (raw values). For country-specific data, see Appendix 2.

Source: Author's elaboration.

Table 4.9 Fixed-broadband penetration rates absolute changes. High-income and upper-middle-income economies. Period 2010–2015

	Slow FBS growth countries (FBS change < 5%pp.)	Moderate FBS growth countries (FBS change ∈ (5%pp.-10%pp.))	Fast FBS growth countries (FBS change > 10%pp.)
High-income economies	Ireland, Korea (Rep. of), Cyprus, Chile, Slovenia, Canada, United States, Denmark, Latvia, Austria, Poland, Sweden, Croatia, Japan, Norway, Israel, Netherlands, Oman, United Arab Emirates, Australia, Finland, Iceland, Brunei Darussalam, Venezuela, Italy, Estonia, Qatar, Singapore	Portugal, Malta, Russian Federation, France, Switzerland, Slovakia, United Kingdom, Seychelles, New Zealand, Czech Rep., Argentina, Belgium, Hungary, Saudi Arabia, Germany, Lithuania, Spain	Uruguay, Greece
Upper-middle-income economies	Macedonia, Thailand, South Africa, Peru, Algeria, Costa Rica, Mexico, Turkey, Dominican Republic, Paraguay, Maldives, Jamaica, Malaysia, Namibia, Botswana, Panama, Angola, Tunisia (negative value), Jordan (negative value)	Iran, China, Mauritius, Ecuador, Kazakhstan, Bulgaria, Surinam, Bosnia and Herzegovina, Romania, Serbia, Colombia, Brazil	Lebanon, Azerbaijan, Belarus

Note: For country-specific values, see Appendix 2.

Source: Author's elaboration.

Next, in the second category, we have classified those economies where, during the period of 2010 and 2015, the absolute change in FBS penetration rates ranged from 5%pp to 10%pp, and we have labeled them as 'moderate FBS growth countries'. Seventeen (out of 47) high-income and another 12 upper-middle-income economies fell into the second category, and these are countries where rapid growth of mobile-broadband solutions did not cause considerable slowdown in diffusion of fixed networks. Finally, in the third category, we classified those countries in which, between 2010 and 2015, the absolute change in FBS penetration rates exceeded 10%pp, and we have labeled them 'fast FBS growth countries'. Among high-income economies, two countries were exclusively classified in the third category: Greece (with the FBS penetration rate grew at 10.4%pp) and Uruguay (with the FBS penetration rate grew at 14.9%pp), while among the upper-middle-income group, three countries were placed in the third category: Azerbaijan (with the FBS penetration rate grew at 14.5%pp), Belarus (with the FBS penetration rate grew at 13.7%pp) and Lebanon (with the FBS penetration rate grew at 15.1%pp).

Furthermore, our empirical research helped to identify in several countries the specific technological leapfrogging effect. Our findings demonstrate that in some of examined economies, during the whole period of the analysis, the state of development of fixed-broadband network was indecently low, and countries did not make any significant achievements in this field. To give an example, in Angola, in 2015, the FBS penetration rate was 0.67 per 100 inhabitants. In another countries such as Namibia, Paraguay and Jordan, the FBS deployment reached 1.7, 3.1 and 4.1 per 100 inhabitants, respectively. In total, in 18 upper-middle-income economies, the wired-broadband infrastructure deployment rate did not exceed 10 per 100 inhabitants, while in another seven, it was below 15 per 100 inhabitants. These unfavorable conditions have, paradoxically, generated a solid background for the emergence of the leapfrog-type technological development path. Countries in which the fixed-broadband technology diffusion was hindered 'jumped' directly to the more advanced wireless-broadband solutions. They have simply taken advantage of their profound technological backwardness and omitted the *'fixed-infrastructure'* stage of development, heading directly towards society-wide assimilation of wireless solutions.

Our evidence on the process of diffusion of fixed- and mobile-broadband networks allows us to conclude that accessibility of ICT has been continuously shifting between 1998 and 2015. Multiple countries have made huge efforts towards broader assimilation of new technologies into societies and changed their telecommunication market structures, giving more space for wireless technological solutions. The great merit of this abrupt upswing in ICT adoption is that it creates solid fundaments for broader usage of the Internet network and creates new opportunities for societies living in relative technological backwardness. It might give the impression that increasing accessibility of ICT infrastructure allowing for Internet connection has rapidly enforced the increasing usage of various digital technologies. Technically speaking, ensuring physical access to computers might be a touchstone in creating technological opportunities, and it should inevitably lead to higher Internet usage rates among individuals. The results of our research on changes in Internet penetration rates (IU) suggest that its development follows the familiar S-shape pattern in a great majority of both high-income and upper-middle-income countries. Available statistics unequivocally suggest that between 1990 and 2015, Internet penetration rates have grown enormously, and this explosive growth in Internet use fuels optimistic expectations for increasing connectivity, offering prospects for the future to eradicate huge existing cross-country inequalities in this regard. In 2015, the average Internet penetration rate was at about 80% in high-income economies; henceforth, we may agree that societies in these countries can enjoy unbounded access to Internet networks and effectively take advantage of it. Upper-middle-income economies did slightly worse in terms of Internet penetration rates. In 2015, the average IU was just 52%, but nonetheless, all these economies made impressive progress towards improving deployment of ICT infrastructure between 1990 and 2015. Notwithstanding, our findings undeniably show rapid increases in Internet usage. Still, there are some economies that relatively lag behind. Significant rates of increases in Internet assimilation rates are critical, especially in countries technologically and economically backward, as newly deployed ICT infrastructure creates new types of communication networks leading to economic and social life improvements. Unquestionably, wider connectivity improves overall quality of socio-economic life.

Internet network is undeniably the most important new technology that has diffused worldwide. However, despite its indisputable success, differences in access to and use of new ICT between rural and urban areas are still significant. Rural, remote and underserved regions permanently suffer from technological isolation, insufficiently developed backbone infrastructure, limited access to information and slow rates of adoption of technological innovations. These shortages generate rural-urban type differences in people. Across high-income economies, the rural-urban type inequalities are usually far less striking compared to those reported in upper-middle-income countries. According to ITU 2016 statistics,[16] for instance, in Brazil, in urban areas, 59% of individuals use the Internet, while only 29% of those living in rural locations use it. In Iran, the rate is 36% for urban and only 12% for rural regions. The rural-urban digital divide is, however, similarly huge in multiple countries. The differences in access to and use of digital technologies are not exclusively exhibited through rural-urban gaps, but notable inequalities in the usage of ICT are even more evident when accounting for level of education. Not surprisingly, people who have completed only primary and/or secondary lower educational levels are far more deprived from access to and use of the Internet network, which is hugely determined by their low-income status, and they are more often living in rural areas. Conversely, people who have completed the tertiary level of education generally are much better 'equipped' with digital infrastructure. In some countries, the digital gaps between poorly and well-educated groups are striking. For instance, in Jamaica, only 16.3% of people who have completed primary and/or secondary lower educational levels use the Internet,[17] while 89% of those who have completed the tertiary educational level use the Internet. In Kazakhstan, this gap is even wider and accounts for 95% pp. In countries such as Mexico, Panama, Paraguay and the United States, this type of digital gap is at about 50%–60% pp. However, observing the dynamic expansion of low-cost wireless broadband technologies offering Internet connections, the prospects for the future are optimistic and raise hope for closing these—still existing—enormous cross- and within-country disparities.

A Final Note

In this section, we have extensively explored how ICT expanded across the developed world for the last few decades. Undoubtedly, regardless of cross-country differences in terms of speed of diffusion of ICT diffusion time path shape, new technologies have quickly spread in all economies regardless of their economic performance, institutional framework or dominant religion or social norms. We have witnessed the enormous ability of societies to assimilate and adopt new technologies, which, undeniably, shall have far-reaching economic and social implications in the future. Giving people the tool that allows them to 'stay connected with the outside world' is revolutionary. Not only because it intensifies and multiplies peoples' contacts but also because it forces the emergence of totally new forms of networks—networks which inevitably will impact the way that people live and the ways that economies function. Nonetheless, the mobile technologies have been gaining in popularity at different paces in different countries; it may be recognized as extremely successful technology that profoundly affected telecommunication markets, generating radical transformations in its structure and changing the way that people communicate and thus enforcing enormous social changes.

Our empirical results bring us to the few very important observations on the nature of the process of diffusion of new technologies. The deployment rates of mobile (wireless) technologies have been astonishingly high, both in high-income and upper-middle-income economies. This brings to mind the idea that the diffusion of new ICT is endogenous in its nature, and once the specific critical mass of new users (innovators) is reached, it proceeds at an exponential rate. Moreover, the diffusion of new mobile technologies speaks in support of the hypothesis on network effects (network externalities), which are recognized as one of the prime drivers of new technologies society-wide dissemination. From an economic and social point of view, worldwide diffusion of wireless solutions is essential for physically isolated, underserved and infrastructural backward regions. Diffusion of mobile solutions offers to people living in remote areas the opportunity to get connected. Many argue that mobile technology is the first and, probably, the only way people in backward regions access the Internet.

The phenomenally rapid shifts in adoption of mobile-cellular telephony and mobile-broadband networks gave rise to the unique process of '*fixed to-mobile technological substitution*'. We have unveiled that this specific process of switching from the old-type technology (wired solutions) to the new-type technology (mobile solutions) may be recognized in all of the examined economies. It basically consists of radical structural changes of national telecommunication markets; once mobile technologies are pervasively evading the markets, the role of wired technology quickly diminishes. Additionally, in several economies, we have identified the technological leapfrogging effects, which are revealed when countries do not follow the 'traditional' development path but rather they omit some development stages. Countries that permanently suffer from negligibly growing backbone (fixed) infrastructure take advantage of their relative technological backwardness and head directly towards the adoption of more advanced—in our case, mobile—technological solutions. The leapfrog-type development paths are characteristic of those countries where fixed infrastructure is virtually nonexistent, and thus assimilation of wireless technologies is for them the only and best option to catch up with technologically from more advanced economies.

Notes

1. See www.itu.int/en/ITU-D/Statistics/Pages/publications/wtid.aspx (accessed December 2016)
2. The exception is Serbia, which became an independent country in 2006.
3. Note: In this section, the empirical evidence reflects exclusively changes in averages.
4. Coefficient of variations is a classical/standard measure of dispersion, usually defined as the ratio of standard deviation to mean value in sample. The coefficient demonstrates the extent of variability in relation to the mean in the analytical sample. The higher value of the coefficient of variation of values of given variables in the empirical sample (see, for instance, Atkinson (1970), Shorrocks (1980)).
5. Best performing economy.
6. Worst performing economy.
7. For conceptualization, see, for instance, works of Compaine (2001), DiMaggio and Hargittai (2001), James (2001), Norris (2001), Rogers (2001), Mossberger et al. (2003), Van Dijk and Hacker (2003), Vehovar et al. (2006), Servon (2008), Ragnedda and Muschert (2013).
8. More evidence on conceptualization and empirics of fixed-to-mobile telephony substitution may be traced in works of, inter alia, Gruber (2001), Sung and Lee (2002), Banerjee and Ros (2004), Garbacz and Thompson (2005 and 2007), Gunasekaran and Harmantzis (2007), Narayana (2010), Briglauer et al. (2011), Grzybowski (2011), Ward and Zheng (2012), Srinuan et al. (2012) or Wulf et al. (2013).
9. The α parameter in logistic growth function denotes the rate of diffusion that is reported for the inflection point. It is also labeled intrinsic growth rate.
10. Except Serbia, for which data on MCS starts in 2004 when Serbia emerged as an independent country.
11. Refers to unweighted average.
12. For more literature on 'technological leapfrogging', see works of Antonelli (1991), Alzouma (2005), Galperin (2005) or James (2009, 2012, 2014).
13. See ITU 2016 statistics.
14. Because of limited data availability, calculations are for only ten countries.
15. To compare country-specific changes in FBS penetration rates between 2005 and 2010, see Appendix 1.
16. ITU World Telecommunication/ICT Indicators database 2016.
17. See ITU World Telecommunication/ICT Indicators database 2016.

References

Alzouma, G. (2005). Myths of digital technology in Africa: Leapfrogging development? *Global Media and Communication*, *1*(3), 339–356.
Antonelli, C. (1991). The diffusion of advanced telecommunications in developing countries. Paris: OECD.

Atkinson, A. B. (1970). On the measurement of inequality. *Journal of Economic Theory, 2*(3), 244–263.

Banerjee, A., & Ros, A. J. (2004). Patterns in global fixed and mobile telecommunications development: A cluster analysis. *Telecommunications Policy, 28*(2), 107–132.

Briglauer, W., Schwarz, A., & Zulehner, C. (2011). Is fixed-mobile substitution strong enough to de-regulate fixed voice telephony? Evidence from the Austrian markets. *Journal of Regulatory Economics, 39*(1), 50–67.

Cairncross, F. (1997). *The death of distance*. London: Orion.

Compaine, B. M. (2001). The digital divide: Facing a crisis or creating a myth? Cambridge, MA: MIT Press.

DiMaggio, P., & Hargittai, E. (2001). From the 'digital divide' to 'digital inequality': Studying Internet use as penetration increases. *Princeton: Center for Arts and Cultural Policy Studies, Woodrow Wilson School, Princeton University, 4*(1), 4–2.

Galperin, H. (2005). Wireless networks and rural development: Opportunities for Latin America. *Information Technologies and International Development, 2*(3), 47–56.

Garbacz, C., & Thompson, H. G. Jr. (2005). Universal telecommunication service: A world perspective. *Information Economics and Policy, 17*(4), 495–512.

Garbacz, C., & Thompson, H. G. Jr. (2007). Demand for telecommunication services in developing countries. *Telecommunications Policy, 31*(5), 276–289.

Gerschenkron, A. (1962). *Economic backwardness in historical perspective: A book of essays*. Cambridge, MA: Belknap Press of Harvard University Press.

Gruber, H. (2001). Competition and innovation: The diffusion of mobile telecommunications in Central and Eastern Europe. *Information Economics and Policy, 13*(1), 19–34.

Grzybowski, L. (2011). *Fixed-to-mobile substitution in the European Union*. Working Paper, University of Cape Town, South Africa.

Gunasekaran, V., & Harmantzis, F. C. (2007). Emerging wireless technologies for developing countries. *Technology in Society, 29*(1), 23–42.

ITU. (2015). *The world in 2015. ICT facts and figures*. International Telecommunication Union.

James, J. (2001). Bridging the digital divide with low-cost information technologies. *Journal of Information Science, 27*(4), 211–217.

James, J. (2009). Leapfrogging in mobile telephony: A measure for comparing country performance. *Technological Forecasting and Social Change, 76*(7), 991–998.

James, J. (2012). The distributional effects of leapfrogging in mobile phones. *Telematics and Informatics, 29*(3), 294–301.

James, J. (2014). Relative and absolute components of leapfrogging in mobile phones by developing countries. *Telematics and Informatics, 31*(1), 52–61.

Lechman, E. (2015). ICT diffusion in developing countries: Towards a new concept of technological takeoff. Springer.

Linstone, H. A. (1991). Multiple perspectives on technological diffusion: Insights and lessons. In N. Nakicenovic & A. Grübler (Eds.), *Diffusion of technologies and social behavior* (pp. 53–92). Berlin and Heidelberg: Springer.

Mokyr, J. (2001). The Industrial Revolution and the economic history of technology: Lessons from the British experience, 1760–1850. *The Quarterly Review of Economics and Finance, 41*(3), 295–311.

Mossberger, K., Tolbert, C. J., & Stansbury, M. (2003). *Virtual inequality: Beyond the digital divide*. Georgetown University Press.

Narayana, M. R. (2010). Substitutability between mobile and fixed telephones: Evidence and implications for India. *Review of Urban & Regional Development Studies*, 22(1), 1–21.

Norris, P. (2001). Digital divide: Civic engagement, information poverty, and the internet worldwide. Cambridge: Cambridge University Press.

Ragnedda, M., & Muschert, G. W. (2013). The digital divide: The internet and social inequality in international perspective (Vol. 73). Routledge.

Rogers, E. M. (2001). The digital divide. *Convergence*, 7(4), 96–111.

Servon, L. J. (2008). Bridging the digital divide: Technology, community and public policy. John Wiley & Sons.

Shorrocks, A. F. (1980). The class of additively decomposable inequality measures. *Econometrica: Journal of the Econometric Society*, 48(3), 613–625.

Srinuan, P., Srinuan, C., & Bohlin, E. (2012). Fixed and mobile broadband substitution in Sweden. *Telecommunications Policy*, 36(3), 237–251.

Steinmueller, W. E. (2001). ICTs and the possibilities for leapfrogging by developing countries. *International Labour Review*, 140(2), 193–210.

Sung, N., & Lee, Y. H. (2002). Substitution between mobile and fixed telephones in Korea. *Review of Industrial Organization*, 20(4), 367–374.

Van Dijk, J., & Hacker, K. (2003). The digital divide as a complex and dynamic phenomenon. *The Information Society*, 19(4), 315–326.

Vehovar, V., Sicherl, P., Hüsing, T., & Dolnicar, V. (2006). Methodological challenges of digital divide measurements. *The Information Society*, 22(5), 279–290.

Ward, M. R., & Zheng, S. (2012). Mobile and fixed substitution for telephone service in China. *Telecommunications Policy*, 36(4), 301–310.

Warschauer, M. (2004). Technology and social inclusion: Rethinking the digital divide. Cambridge, MA: MIT Press.

Wulf, J., Zelt, S., & Brenner, W. (2013, January). Fixed and mobile broadband substitution in the OECD countries—A quantitative analysis of competitive effects. In S. Kaisler, F. Armour, J. A. Espinosa, & W. Money (Eds.), *46th Hawaii International Conference on System Sciences (HICSS)* (pp. 1454–1463). IEEE.

5 Technological Take-Offs
Country Perspective

Data Explanation

By convention, the remainder of Chapter 5 is divided into 2 separate parts: Sect.5.2 is designed to challenge the isolation of the country-specific critical mass and technological take-offs, as well as to answer the question under which conditions countries leave the pre-take-off stage and break out into exponential growth along ICT diffusion trajectories, while Sect.5.3 discusses the results of more 'conventional' analysis of ICT diffusion determinants.

To meet the major targets of Sect.5.2, we have selected a wide array of factors, which potentially may affect the process of achievement of the critical mass and the technological take-off that follows after regarding the diffusion of mobile-cellular telephony and growth of Internet penetration rates. Our defined dataset includes five 'shared' factors (variables) which are used to explain the diffusion of mobile-cellular telephony and to examine the prerequisites of increasing Internet penetration rates. These are as follows:

- gross domestic product per capita
- economic freedom Index
- investment freedom index
- country freedom status
- telecommunication market competition

In our study, we use data on gross domestic product per capita expressed in constant 2010 US$, and these statistics are derived from the World Development Indicators 2016 database. Next, we apply the economic freedom index and one of its sub-indices: the investment freedom index. Economic freedom index data starts in 1995 and are published annually by the Heritage Foundation[1] for 186 world countries. The economic freedom index measures countries' freedoms in four basic areas: rule of law, government size, regulatory efficiency and market openness, and it is widely used to demonstrate countries' progress towards improving their economic performance, which is seen not only through the lens of incomes but also 'goes beyond' that. The value of the economic freedom index ranges from 0 to 100, where 100 indicates fully free country, with no binding constraints to economic prosperity. The investment freedom index is one its sub-indexes, and it shows to what extent flows of capital are constrained (or, reversely, freed) by a regulatory framework. Again, the ideally free country would receive a score of 100. In our study, we also hypothesize that a country's political regime might be a decisive factor for the technology diffusion; hence, we propose to use the country freedom status variable, which allows discriminating by 'free', 'partly free' and 'not free' countries. The country freedom status explains a country's freedom status in respect to political rights (consider the freedom of the electoral process, political pluralism and participation, as well as functioning of government) and civil liberties (consider the freedom of belief and expression, association and organizational rights, rule of law, personal autonomy and individual rights). It has been published since 1973 by the Freedom House,[2] although the availability of data for selected countries may differ for different years for 195 world territories, and it allows tracking changes in broadly defined personal and political freedoms of individuals. Each year, world countries are rated according to their accomplishments of political rights and civil liberties, which determines countries' status: free, if rated from 1.0 to 2.5; partly free, if rated from 3.0 to 5.0; and not free, if rated from 5.5 to 7.0. Finally, we believe that free and unbounded spread of new technologies may be effectively enhanced or constrained by the type of telecommunication market competition. In our work, using the International Telecommunication Union Regulatory Framework[3] categorization, we classify national telecommunication markets, into three types: monopoly, when services are provided exclusively by one operator; partial competition, when services are provided by a limited number of licensed companies; and full competition, when the number of issued licenses to operators is not arbitrary limited by national authorities. Additionally, we use the database on the level of competition in Internet services (data from 2000 to 2010) and the level of competition in mobile services (data from 2000 to 2010) provided by the United Nation agency Integrated Implementation Framework.[4]

Additionally, to explain the country-specific prerequisites for the emergence of technological take-off, we use data on

- fixed-telephony penetration rate for mobile-cellular telephony;
- price of a one-minute call (peak, on net) for mobile-cellular telephony;
- prices of one SMS (peak, on net) for mobile-cellular telephony;
- fixed-broadband penetration rate for the Internet penetration rate;
- active mobile-broadband penetration rate for the Internet penetration rate; and
- fixed-broadband monthly subscription charge for the Internet penetration rate.

The price of a one-minute call (peak, on net) indicates the prices of a one-minute local call on a prepaid tariff made to the same mobile-cellular network during the peak time. Prices of one SMS (peak, on net) refers to the prices of one SMS sent on a prepaid tariff to the same mobile-cellular network during the peak time. Both the price of a call and the price of SMS are expressed in US dollars, and all data are derived from ITU World Telecommunication/ICT Indicators (edition 2016). The fixed-broadband monthly subscription charge refers to a monthly charge for fixed (wired)-broadband Internet service. Basically, it shows the price of Internet connection of downstream speed equal to, or greater than, 256 kbits/s. These data are also extracted from ITU World Telecommunication/ICT Indicators (edition 2016).

Finally, the fixed-telephony penetration rate, fixed-broadband penetration rate and active mobile-broadband penetration rate variables have been already explained in Sect. 4.1. in Chapter 4, and thus we will not repeat it here.

Sect. 5.3 presents results of additional analysis of new technology diffusion determinants across examined economies. To this aim, we use analogous explanatory indicators as in Sect.5.2, including two more variables: population density and urbanization rate. By definition, population density expresses the number of people per square kilometer of land area, while urbanization rate expresses the proportion of a country's total population living in urban areas. All data on population density and urbanization are derived from World Development Indicators 2016 database.

Technological Take-Offs—Paths and Pre-conditions

As presented in Chapter 4, almost all of the examined economies, between the period of 1990 and 2015, made huge progress towards increasing their mobile-cellular telephony and Internet penetration rates. Developed country-specific diffusion paths that visualize the process of gradually increasing access to and use of mobile-cellular telephony and Internet network resemble the theoretical S-shaped time diffusion trajectory. In fact, in a great majority of the countries, the characteristic phases of the process of ICT diffusion may be easily distinguished, meaning that initially, the process of ICT deployment is slow (pre-take-off phase), and then in a specific moment in time it abruptly takes off in exponential growth and finally stabilizes, reaching the maturity stage. In contrast, developed diffusion paths graphically presenting the process of spreading fixed-broadband inevitably lead to the conclusion that this type of technology did not spread economy-wide across countries in the scope of our analysis. Many countries remained 'locked' in the early diffusion phase, unable to take-off into self-sustaining growth.[5] Their progress in the deployment of fixed-broadband networks remained negligible, and this form of ICT did not become widely available for all society members, especially in upper-middle-income economies. As we have also identified, the process of diffusion of mobile-broadband networks is a totally different case. Conversely to what was observed in respect to fixed-broadband networks, this type of technology has diffused across countries at an astonishingly high pace in a very short time. It took just few years to reach mobile-broadband penetration rates exceeding 100% in many of the examined countries.[6] As already argued, the mobile-broadband networks diffusion patterns are very characteristic; it seems that countries have simply 'omitted' the initial diffusion phase and headed immediately towards the exponential growth stage (see countrywide diffusion curves in Chapter 4).

Our detailed analysis of country-specific ICT diffusion trajectories leads to the conclusion that exclusively in respect to mobile-cellular telephony and Internet penetration rates, we are able to identify the critical mass (critical penetration rate), technological take-off and length of the pre-take-off phase. Henceforth, the following Sect.5.2 summarizes and discusses the results of our analysis designed to challenge the identification of the country-specific critical mass (or, critical penetration rate), the critical year technological take-off that follows right after and the length of the pre-take-off stage along ICT diffusion patterns. To this aim, we use the methodological approach explained earlier in Chapter 3. By definition, our research on the critical mass and technological take-off centers on 47 high-income and 34 upper-middle-income countries between 1990 and 2015. Additionally, this section aims to trace the bundle of the country-specific condition during the critical years in each analyzed country. We wish to answer the question of whether achievements of critical mass that enhance entering the exponential growth phase are determined by some specific conditions, or if the process of diffusion of newly emerged technologies is highly endogenous, enforced by the network effects (externalities) and to some extent driven by itself. Put differently, we aim to understand the major driving forces and/or impediments that enable/disable the technological take-off. This is a challenging task that requires country-specific and contextual thinking; however, it broadens our knowledge on the main prerequisites of diffusion of new ICT.

To meet the main targets of this analysis, first we designate the ICT marginal growths and ICT replication coefficients,[7] allowing for the denotation of the critical penetration rate and the critical year. Figures summarized in Appendix 5 graphically display country-specific patterns of ICT marginal growths and ICT replication coefficients for mobile-cellular telephony in high-income economies, mobile-cellular telephony in upper-middle-income economies, IU in high-income economies and IU in upper-middle-income economies, respectively. Displayed ICT marginal growths and ICT replication coefficient patterns allow for the identification of these countries where the critical mass was reached, and thus they managed to take-off along the technology diffusion paths.[8] Detailed calculations of ICT marginal growths and ICT replication coefficients for each of examined economies are summarized in Appendix 3 and 4. Although in respective countries, the calculated values of ICT marginal growths and ICT replication coefficients vary substantially, all of the ICT marginal growths and ICT replication coefficient patterns are very different (no regularities in their shape may be identified); we may claim that in each of analyzed countries (only with the except of Serbia), the critical mass was reached, and it was followed by the specific technological take-off, giving rise to exponential growth in ICT deployment. More detailed analysis of our results reveals several interesting aspects of the process of mobile-cellular telephony diffusion and growing usage of the Internet network. Not surprisingly, the rates of diffusion of new technologies differ significantly across countries (compare results of logistic growth estimates summarized in Sect.4.3), implying different dynamics of this process, which, in turn, results in different levels of critical penetration rates, lengths of pre-take-off diffusion stage and, finally, various technological take-off periods.

Let us first concentrate on the mobile-cellular telephony diffusion process. Figures in Appendix 5 visualize country-specific MCS marginal growth and MCS replication coefficient patterns[9] for both country income groups, while Table 5.1 summarizes the results of MCS critical mass[10] calculations and identifies the MCS critical years,[11] lengths of the MCS pre-take-off stage[12] and MCS technological take-off[13] periods (intervals). A closer look at country-specific MCS marginal growth and MCS replication coefficient patterns reveals several striking observations. First, we observe that during the initial diffusion phase, the value of the MCS replication coefficient is higher than MCS marginal growth. Obviously, the absolute difference (gap) between these two values differs among countries; however, as diffusion proceeds and more new users enter the national telecommunication market, the value of the MCS replication coefficient gradually decreases, and at the time, the MCS marginal growth was growing over time. The changing relationships between MCS replications coefficients and MCS marginal growth values supports the hypothesis on the emerging network effects, which enforces rapid diffusion of new technology and substantial increases in the number of users. Finally, if the process of diffusion of mobile-cellular telephony is strong enough, the MCS marginal growth and MCS replication coefficient patterns converge (intersect), and so in a specific moment of time, the values of MCS marginal growth and MCS replication coefficients are equalized. More specifically, we label this unique moment in time the MCS critical year and the specific penetration rate during it is labelled the MCS critical mass (MCS critical penetration rate). Right after the MCS critical mass is achieved, the value of MCS marginal growth is abruptly shifted. The value in Figures 5.1 and 5.2 is visualized as a rapid upswing of the MCS marginal growth patterns. At the same time, the values of MCS replication coefficients fall, and this changing relationship is graphically displayed as a growing gap between the MCS marginal growth and MCS replication coefficient patterns. The abrupt upswing of the MCS marginal growth pattern reflects the emergence of the MCS technological take-off that follows right after the MCS critical mass is reached, suggesting that countries enter the exponential growth phase along the MCS diffusion curve and significant shifts in numbers of users of this kind of ICT are reported.As telecommunication markets head

Table 5.1 Technological take-off, country-specific conditions. Mobile-cellular telephony. High-income and upper-middle-income economies

Country	Critical year	Critical mass (mobile telephony penetration rate)	Takeoff period	Length of the pre-take-off stage (in years)	Fixed telephony penetration rate	Price of one-minute call (peak. on net)	Price of on SMS (peak. on net)	Telecommunication market competition	Economic freedom index	Investment freedom index	Country freedom status	GDP per capita
Upper-middle-income economies												
Algeria	2004	14.6	2005–2006	14	7.4	0.07	0.06	FC	58.1	70.0	Not free	4093
Angola	2004	4.6	2005–2006	11	0.6	0.04	0.08	PC	n.a.	n.a.	Not free	2260
Azerbaijan	2003	12.6	2004–2006	9	11.2	0.09	0.06	FC	54.1	30.0	Not free	2158
Belarus	2003	11.4	2004–2005	10	31.4	0.05	0.05	PC	39.7	30.0	Not free	3253
Bosnia and Herzegovina	2001	11.4	2002–2003	6	21.8	0.2	0.05 (2003)	PC	36.6	30.0	n.a.	3107
Botswana	2000	12.6	2001–2002	2	7.7	0.36	0.04 (2003)	FC	65.8	50.0	Free	4931
Brazil	1998	4.3	1999–2000	8	11.8	0.32	0.13 (2005)	duopoly	52.3	50.0	Partly free	8604
Bulgaria	2000	9.2	2001–2002	7	36.0	0.56	0.08 (2002)	FC	47.3	70.0	Free	3958
China	2000	6.6	2001–2002	12	11.3	0.04	0.01 (2003)	PC	56.4	50.0	Not free	1761
Colombia	2001	8.1	2002–2003	7	18.2	0.14	0.09	PC	65.6	70.0	Partly free	4775
Costa Rica	2000	5.3	2001–2002	8	22.3	0.11	0.003 (2003)	M	68.4	70.0	Free	6040
Dominican Rep.	1999	4.9	2000–2001	9	9.7	0.12	0.02 (2003)	FC	58.1	50.0	Free	3757
Ecuador	2001	6.7	2002–2003	7	10.5	0.5	0.13 (2003)	PC	55.1	70.0	Partly free	3760
Iran	2003	5.1	2004–2005	9	22.4	0.22	0.02 (2006)	M	43.2	30.0	Not free	4947
Jamaica	1999	5.6	2000–2001	8	19.0	0.09	0.06 (2002)	FC	64.7	70.0	Free	4753
Jordan	2000	8.1	2001–2002	10	13.0	0.21	0.04 (2002)	PC	67.5	70.0	Partly free	3006
Kazakhstan	2002	7.1	2003–2004	8	14.2	0.22	0.06	duopoly	52.4	30.0	Not free	5607
Lebanon	2004	22.9	2005–2006	9	16.3	0.56	0.28	n.a./ in 2008 monopoly	56.9	50.0	Not free	6632
Macedonia	2000	5.6	2001–2002	4	24.7	0.31	0.09 (2003)	M	n.a.	n.a.	Partly free	3488
Malaysia	1999	13.1	2000–2001	13	19.4	0.07	0.03 (2003)	PC	68.9	50.0	Partly free	6520
Maldives	2001	6.8	2002–2003	5	9.8	0.18	0.07	M	n.a	n.a.	Not free	4198
Mauritius	1998	5.2	1999–2000	8	21.0	0.04	0.02 (2002)	duopoly	n.a.	n.a.	Free	5169
Mexico	1999	7.6	2000–2001	11	10.7	0.27	0.07 (2002)	PC	58.5	70.0	Partly free	8261
Namibia	2002	7.6	2003–2004	7	6.2	0.21	0.09	M	65.1	70.0	Free	3854
Panama	1999	7.8	2000–2001	3	15.4	0.4	0.15 (2003)	duopoly	72.6	70.0	Free	5255
Paraguay	1998	4.5	1999–2000	6	5.1	0.28	0.01 (2003)	FC	65.2	90.0	Partly free	2912
Peru	2001	6.8	2002–2003	11	5.9	0.6	0.07	FC	69.6	70.0	Partly free	3307

Romania	1999	6.1	2000–2001	6	16.6	0.1	0.1 (2002)	FC	50.1	70.0	Free	4780
Serbia — not identifiable												
South Africa	1997	4.3	1998–1999	9	10.8	0.31	0.07 (2002)	FC	63.2	70.0	Free	6085
Suriname	2000	8.8	2001–2002	7	16.1	0.20	0.04 (2002)	PC	45.8	50.0	Partly free (1999)	5587
Thailand	2001	11.9	2002–2003	15	9.6	0.06	0.07	FC	68.9	70.0	Free	3551
Tunisia	2002	5.9	2003–2004	15	10.3	0.17	0.04	PC	60.2	70.0	Not free	3144
Turkey	1998	5.7	1999–2000	12	27.4	0.19	0.09 (2001)	FC	60.9	70.0	Partly free	7902
High-income economies												
Argentina	2003	20.6	2004–2005	14	22.7	0.12	0.03	FC	56.3	50.0	Free	7357
Australia	1994	6.8	1995–1996	7	49.4	0.30	n.a.	FC [1997]	n.a.	n.a.	Free	37063
Austria	1996	7.5	1997–1998	11	48.7	0.50	n.a.	FC	68.9	70.0	Free	37253
Belgium	1996	4.7	1997–1998	10	45.4	0.58	n.a.	n.a.	66.0	70.0	Free	35784
Brunei Darussalam	1994	5.5	1995–1996	6	21.4	n.a.	n.a.	M [2012]	n.a.	n.a.	n.a.	33675
Canada	1994	6.4	1995–1996	9	59.5	0.29	n.a.	n.a.	n.a.	n.a.	Free	36893
Chile	1998	6.4	1999–2000	9	20.2	0.29	n.a.	FC [2012]	74.9	70.0	Free	9727
Croatia	1999	6.5	2000–2001	9	36.2	0.22	n.a.	n.a.	53.1	50.0	Partly free	9903
Cyprus	1995	5.2	1996–1997	7	40.7	0.13	n.a.	FC	n.a.	n.a.	Free	23839
Czech Republic	1997	5.1	1998–1999	6	31.8	0.23	n.a.	PC	68.8	70.0	Free	13936
Denmark	1993	6.9	1994–1995	11	58.9	0.43	n.a.	PC [2012]	n.a.	n.a.	Free	45595
Estonia	1996	4.9	1997–1998	5	36.1	0.38	n.a.	FC [2001]	65.4	90.0	Free	7804
Finland	1992	7.7	1993–1994	12	54.5	0.38	n.a.	n.a.	n.a.	n.a.	Free	30150
France	1996	4.2	1997–1998	10	56.5	0.93	n.a.	FC [1998]	63.7	50.0	Free	34499
Germany	1996	4.5	1997–1998	11	52.9	0.85	n.a.	FC	69.1	70.0	Free	34968
Greece	1996	4.9	1997–1998	3	49.5	0.58 (1998)	n.a.	PC [2001]	60.5	70.0	Free	20391
Hungary	1996	4.6	1997–1998	6	26.7	0.32	n.a.	n.a.	56.8	70.0	Free	8909
Iceland	1994	8.2	1995–1996	8	55.9	0.25	n.a.	FC [1998]	n.a.	n.a.	Free	29777
Ireland	1995	4.4	1996–1997	10	36.3	0.39	n.a.	FC [1998]	68.5	70.0	Free	28084
Israel	1995	8.3	1996–1997	5	43.2	0.21	n.a.	n.a.	61.5	90.0	Free	23604
Italy	1995	6.8	1996–1997	10	43.9	1.1	n.a.	n.a.	61.2	70.0	Free	32832
Japan	1995	9.5	1996–1997	14	50.1	0.7	n.a.	n.a.	75.0	50.0	Free	38945
Korea (Rep.)	1996	7.7	1997–1998	10	43.6	0.24	n.a.	PC [2012]	73.0	50.0	n.a.	12978
Latvia	1998	6.9	1999–2000	6	30.8	0.14	n.a.	PC [2012]	63.4	70.0	Free	6283

(Continued)

Table 5.1 (Continued)

Country	Critical year	Critical mass (mobile telephony penetration rate)	Takeoff period	Length of the pre-take-off stage (in years)	Fixed telephony penetration rate	Price of one-minute call (peak. on net)	Price of on SMS (peak. on net)	Telecommunication market competition	Economic freedom index	Investment freedom index	Country freedom status	GDP per capita
Lithuania	1998	7.5	1999–2000	6	31.3	0.32	n.a.	FC [2012]	59.4	70.0	Free	6662
Malta	1999	9.2	2000–2001	8	32.6	0.43	n.a.	FC [2000]	59.3	70.0	n.a.	17170
Netherlands	1996	6.5	1997–1998	11	54.3	0.47	n.a.	FC [1997]	n.a.	n.a.	Free	39629
New Zealand	1994	6.6	1995–1996	7	45.8	0.43	n.a.	FC [1990]	n.a.	n.a.	Free	26162
Norway	1993	8.6	1994–1995	12	54.2	0.49	n.a.	n.a.	n.a.	n.a.	Free	65115
Oman	1998	4.5	1999–2000	13	10.1	0.06	n.a.	PC [2012]	64.9	50.0	Not free	18106
Poland	1998	5.1	1999–2000	6	22.9	0.71	n.a.	PC [2012]	59.2	70.0	Free	7804
Portugal	1996	6.5	1997–1998	7	37.7	0.44	n.a.	n.a.	64.5	70.0	Free	18644
Qatar	1996	5.6	1997–1998	6	26.1	0.16	n.a.	PC [2012]	n.a.	n.a.	Not free	n.a.
Russian Federation	2001	5.3	2002–2003	10	22.7	0.12 (2003)	0.06 (2003)	FC	49.8	50.0	Partly free	6851
Saudi Arabia	2000	6.8	2001–2002	10	14.7	0.32	0.08 (2001)	M	66.5	30.0	Not free	14980
Seychelles	1998	6.6	1999–2000	3	24.1	0.30	n.a.	PC [2012]	n.a.	n.a.	Partly free	9741
Singapore	1993	5.4	1994–1995	5	37.8	0.12	n.a.	FC [2000]	n.a.	n.a.	n.a.	25990
Slovakia	1998	8.6	1999–2000	7	28.6	0.16	n.a.	n.a.	57.5	50.0	Free	10192
Slovenia	1997	4.7		6	35.7	0.37	n.a.	FC [2004]	55.6	50.0	Free	16423
Spain	1996	7.6	1997–1998	10	39.0	0.47	n.a.	n.a.	59.6	70.0	Free	24473
Sweden	1993	8.8	1994–1995	12	67.3	0.55	n.a.	n.a.	n.a.	n.a.	Free	35239
Switzerland	1995	6.4	1996–1997	8	63.8	0.67	n.a.	FC [1998]	n.a.	n.a.	Free	61330
United Arab Emirates	1995	5.5	1996–1997	13	28.6	0.24	n.a.	PC [2012]	n.a.	n.a.	Not free	63561
United Kingdom	1994	6.8	1995–1996	9	27.6	0.45	n.a.	n.a.	n.a.	n.a.	Free	29527
United States	1993	6.1	1994–1995	8	56.5	0.65	n.a.	n.a.	n.a.	n.a.	Free	37078
Uruguay	1998	4.6	1999–2000	6	24.1	0.6	n.a.	FC [2002]	68.6	70.0	Free	9439
Venezuela	1997	4.7	1998–1999	9	12.2	0.40	n.a.	FC [2000]	52.8	50.0	Partly free (1999)	12808

Note: All data are for the country-specific critical year (reported if otherwise); if data are not available for the critical year, then data for the nearest year are used. Data on the price of one SMS (peak, on net) are available since 2000 onwards. Most of high-income economies are not reported for the critical year. FC, full competition; PC, partial competition; M, monopoly. GDP per capita are in constant 2010 US$.

towards 'full' saturation with mobile-cellular telephony, we observe drops in value of MCS marginal growth, while the value of MCS replication coefficients remain equally low as before.

Analysis of countrywide MCS marginal growth and MCS replication coefficient patterns shows that in respective economies, the values of both MCS marginal growth and MCS replication coefficients vary substantially, which, consequently, generates differences with regard to the year designated as the critical year, the level of the critical penetration rate and the length of the pre-take-off phase. In Appendix 3, we have summarized country-specific calculations in this respect. In upper-middle-income countries, the MCS critical mass was reached the earliest in South Africa in 1997. Next, it was observed in Brazil, Mauritius, Paraguay and Turkey in 1998, and one year later in another six countries (see Appendix 3), while the MCS critical year was noted the latest in Algeria and Angola in 2004, which are recognized as relatively lagging behind in this respect among upper-middle-income countries. According to our calculations, in the upper-middle-income group, the 'average' MCS critical year was 2000. In contrast, the 'average' MCS critical year in high-income economies is denoted as 1996, which suggests that, on average, high-income economies reached the critical penetration rates four year earlier compared to upper-middle-income ones. Among high-income economies, Finland was the first country to achieve the MCS critical mass in 1992. Finland was then followed by another five economies, which reached the MCS critical penetration rates during the following year in 1993. In only three economies—namely, Argentina, Russian Federation and Saudi Arabia—the MCS critical mass was reported in or after the year 2000.

When comparing the average level of MCS critical mass[14] in both country income groups, we see that in high-income economies, it was at about 6.64 per 100 inhabitants, while in upper-middle-income, it was about 8.14 per 100 inhabitants. If, for instance, across high-income economies, the average level of MCS critical mass is reported as 6.64 per 100 inhabitants, it suggests that within this income group, the MCS technological take-off emerged once the mobile-cellular telephony penetration rates of 6.64 per 100 inhabitants were achieved in an 'average country'. Analogously, in upper-middle-income economies, the MCS technological take-off was reported right after achieving the mobile-cellular telephony penetration rates of 8.14 per 100 inhabitants. Obviously, when taking a closer look at specific countries, we observe that the difference in respect to the level of the MCS critical mass may be substantial. For instance, the highest levels of MCS critical penetration rates are reported for Lebanon, Argentina, Algeria or Malaysia, where it was 22.9, 20.6, 14.6 and 13.1, respectively. In these countries, the MCS technological take-off emerged at relatively high MCS critical penetration rates. But on the other hand, among countries in the scope of our analysis, we find countries such as France, Germany, Belgium, Ireland, Hungary, Uruguay, Venezuela, Brazil or South Africa, where the level of MCS critical mass is slightly above 4.00, indicating that they reached the level of about 4.00 per 100 inhabitants with regard to the mobile-cellular telephony penetration rate was enough to give rise to the MCS technological take-off.

In fact, the absolute difference in average MCS critical penetration rates between two examined country income groups is relatively small at 1.5 per 100 inhabitants, and such negligible difference speaks in support of the hypothesis that the technological take-off giving rise to exponential growth is achieved at certain specific technology penetration rates, and it gives strong impulse for further increases in the number of new users of that technology. The latter may additionally support our supposition that the process of technology diffusion is highly endogenous, and once the critical mass is achieved, the further spread of technology becomes a self-sustaining (self-perpetuating) process, regardless of the country-specific conditions.

When examining the country-specific lengths of the MCS pre-take-off stages, we observe that economies differ in this regard. The length of the MCS pre-take-off phase is determined by the rate of diffusion during initial years as well as by the strength of the network externalities that drive the spread of new technology, thus allowing for the number of new users to grow in time. In some economies, we see that the MCS pre-take-off stage was quite long, such as in Thailand and Tunisia (15 years in both countries); Algeria, Argentina and Japan (14 years in each); and Oman, United Arab Emirates and Malaysia (13 years in each). These countries took a relatively long to take-off into self-sustaining growth; they were 'locked' in the initial diffusion stage, unable to boost deployment of mobile-cellular telephony. But, reversely, in a few economies, the MCS pre-take-off phase was extremely short; see Botswana (two years), Panama, Greece or Seychelles (three years in both countries), where the MCS technological take-off occurred immediately after introduction to the market mobile-cellular telephony. However, regardless of the existing difference in the length of the pre-take-off stage in different countries, it is noteworthy to state that in both country income groups, the average length of the pre-take-off stage[15] is almost the same: It is 8.53 years and 8.66 years in high-income and upper-middle-income economies, respectively. This surprising observation again supports our supposition that technology diffusion is endogenously driven and enhanced by strong network effects, which enforce the 'multiplication' of new users.

Next, we briefly discuss the evidence regarding the identification of the critical mass in respect to Internet penetration rates (approximated by IU indicators). Figures in Appendix 5 visualize country-specific IU marginal growth and IU replication coefficient patterns[16] for both country income groups, while respective tables in Appendix 4 summarize the results of IU critical mass[17] calculations and identifies the IU critical years,[18] lengths of the IU pre-take-off stage[19] and IU technological take-off[20] periods (intervals). Analogously, as it was reported in the case of mobile-cellular telephony diffusion, taking a closer look at IU marginal growth and IU replication coefficient patterns, we note that in each case, during the very initial stage of diffusion, the level of country-specific IU replication coefficients are much higher compared to IU marginal growth. This gap is especially huge, for instance, in Argentina, Belgium, Hungary, Poland, Azerbaijan, Costa Rica, Malaysia and Thailand. However, as new individuals start using the Internet network, IU marginal growth and IU replication coefficient patterns are gradually converging and finally intersecting. The 'intersection time' indicates the achievement of the IU critical mass (IU critical penetration rate), which enforces leaving the early diffusion phase (pre-take-off stage) and entering the exponential growth stage along the IU diffusion curve. This specific time period when the IU critical mass is reached, by convention, we label as the IU critical year, and the two-year time period that follows right after it is labeled the IU technological take-off interval. Once the country reaches the IU critical mass, the number of users of Internet network boosts and starts increasing at an exponential rate. During this exponential growth stage, the IU marginal growth and IU replication coefficient patterns are initially diverging, but afterwards, as the telecommunication market inevitably heads towards 'full' saturation, they tend to converge again. Once the country is leaving the exponential growth phase, and the IU marginal growth and IU replication coefficient patterns are again converging (as is recognized during the initial diffusion phase), it suggests that the process of growth of new Internet network users slows down, and the system stabilizes.

The results of our research summarized in the table in Appendix 4, show, inter alia, country-specific IU critical years, level of IU critical penetration rates and IU length of the pre-take-off stage. Regarding upper-middle-income economies, the countrywide IU critical years are reported between 1998 and 2012. In 1998, the earliest the IU critical mass was reached in Malaysia, while the latest, in 2012, was reached in Angola. In high-income country groups, the IU critical years span from 1994 in Finland and the United States, to 2006 in Oman. Similarly, as in the case of mobile-cellular telephony diffusion, here we note that the countrywide critical years occur a few years earlier in high-income economies compared to upper-middle-income economies. Across upper-middle-income economies, country-specific IU critical penetration rates (IU critical mass) reported for the IU critical years range[21] from 4.3% in Belarus to 17.3% reported for Macedonia and Panama. In other six countries—namely, Algeria, Brazil, China, Colombia, Jordan and Mauritius—the level of IU critical mass is just slightly higher—but still below 5%—than in Belarus. The 'average'[22] level of IU critical mass in upper-middle-income economies is at about 8.3% (if Serbia is excluded), while in high-income economies, it is 6.85%. Interestingly, across high-income economies, country-specific IU critical penetration rates vary from 4.1% in Ireland, Poland and United Kingdom, to 16.6% in Chile, which is analogous to what was observed in the case of the upper-middle-income group. The 'average' IU critical penetration rate in high-income economies is 6.85%, which implies that 'an average high-income country' leaves the initial diffusion stage once the IU penetration rate reaches 6.85% and then enters the exponential growth phase along the diffusion curve.

Put differently, until the IU penetration rate is below 6.85%, the country is still located in the pre-take-off phase, but only after this critical threshold is passed does the country take off and the number of users of the Internet network grow at an exponential rate.

The results of our research on countrywide achievements of MCS and IU critical mass and technological take-off allow for the drawing of several impressive conclusions. First, between 1980 and 2015, in of all of the examined economies, the MCS critical mass was identified. The latter implies that none of the analyzed countries remained 'locked' in the initial diffusion stage, and in each country, the MCS technological take-off was observed. Moreover, in a great majority of economies, we have additionally noticed that their telecommunication markets achieved almost 'full' saturation with mobile-cellular telephony. Second, between 1990 and 2015, in each country in the scope of this research, the IU critical mass was reached, suggesting that all countries managed to leave the early diffusion stage and take off along the IU diffusion pattern. Third, the 'average' MCS and IU critical penetration rates are nearly the same in the group of high-income countries at 6.64 per 100 inhabitants and 6.85%, respectively. Fourth, the 'average' MCS and IU critical penetration rates, again, are practically the same in upper-middle-income economies at 8.14 per 100 inhabitants and 8.3%, respectively. The last two conclusions are of seminal importance, as they support the hypothesis that the process of new technology diffusion is endogenous, strongly subjected to the emerging network externalities, and once the specific technology penetration rate—threshold—is reached, the diffusion curve steeps and further growth of new users of a given technology increases at an exponential rate. The process of technology diffusion may be thus regarded as self-perpetuating.

Next in this section, we target the answer to the question, under what specific conditions does technological take-off emerge across countries in the scope of our research? Put differently, we wish to identify whether there exist any 'necessary' preconditions that enable the break out of technological stagnation into exponential growth along the diffusion curve. To meet this aim, we have arbitrary selected a bundle of factors,[23] which hypothetically may enforce, or reversely impede, the emergence of MCS and IU technological take-offs in each of the high-income and upper-middle-income economies. By convention, we have tested the emergence of technological take-off exclusively for two ICT indicators—namely, MCS and Internet penetration rates (IU)—in the case of the two indices of 'full-time' diffusion trajectory, which were observed with clearly distinguishable characteristic phases: pre-take-off stage (early diffusion phase), exponential growth phased and, finally, stabilization (maturity) phase. In the case of other two ICT indicators analyzed here—namely, fixed-broadband networks and mobile-broadband networks—the shape of the diffusion curve did not actually allow for incontestable identification of the critical mass and the technological take-off which follows right after. As already noted, in the case of fixed-broadband networks, a huge majority of countries seemed to be 'locked' in the early dif-fusion phase, unable to take off, while in the case of active mobile-broadband network, the technological take-off was 'immediate', thus no 'standard' pre-take-off stage was reported.

Luckily, in each of the 47 high-income and 34 upper-middle-income econ-omies, we have identified the MCS and IU critical mass, which gave the positive impulse to the emergence of technological take-offs in these coun-tries. The good news is that none of the examined economies remained vir-tually 'stuck' in the early diffusion phase, but most of those quickly headed towards 'full' saturation with new information and communication tech-nology. And despite the fact that the critical years were reported in different time periods, the level of the critical mass varied across countries as well as the length of the pre-take-off stage, with all these economies breaking out into self-sustaining growth of ICT. However, as we have observed, in the case of the mobile-cellular telephony, the 'average' length of the pre-take-off stage both in the high-income and in upper-middle-income groups differs insignificantly: It is 8.53 years and 8.66 years, respectively. The 'aver-age' level of the MCS critical mass was very similar as well: 6.64 and 8.14 per 100 inhabitants in high-income and upper-middle-income economies, respectively. Analogous similarities have been reported in the case of Inter-net penetration rates. In in this case, we have also demonstrated that the 'average' lengths of the pre-take-off stage do not vary significantly, nor do the 'average' levels of the IU critical mass. These facts may speak in sup-port of our initial supposition that the emergence technological take-off is facilitated by the 'bundle' of necessary initial (critical) socio-economic and institutional prerequisites, which *must* occur to enforce rapid spread of new technology and growth of its new users. The remainder of this section is fully devoted to verify this supposition.

Consecutive Tables 5.1 and 5.2 summarize our findings regarding country-specific conditions (prerequisites) *observed during the MCS and IU critical years*.[24] Such an approach first allows for the recognition of the unique conditions of the countries during the technological take-off and second, it makes it possible to assess whether these conditions were similar in each of the examined economies or if they differed significantly.

When intending to identify the country-specific conditions during the technological take-off, we should bear in mind the fact that economies in the scope of our analysis vary hugely in multiple aspects. Although, according to the World Bank statistics, they are classified only in two income groups, their potential homogeneity is spurious. These countries differ greatly in terms of *per capita* income; note that, for instance in China, the GDP *per capita* is effectively lower compared to, for instance, oil-rich economies such as Norway, Saudi Arabia and Qatar. These differences in monetary wealth matter, mainly in terms of countries' ability to the finance adoption of new technologies. However, these economies are different in more dimensions. They differ in terms of economic freedoms, dominant religion, socially accepted norms and attitudes towards adoption and usage of technological novelties. These aspects are seminal when new technology is introduced to national markets and tries to invade it and gain new users. Peoples' attitudes towards new technology are decisive, as they precondition the emergence of the network effects which enforce the fast spread of new technology over social and economic actors. These economies have different geographical locations and conditions; we find landlocked countries where physical conditions may be unfavorable for deployment of backbone (hard) infra-structure. The developments of basic infrastructure is often recognized as one of the main enablers of spreading new technology. Countries examined in our study function under different political regimes; we have countries classified as 'free' where people enjoy political freedoms, but we also have 13 economies which are only 'partly free' and another 14 countries that are 'not free' where people's civil and political rights are constrained. Finally, in these countries we observe different telecommunication market compe-tition types. A vast majority were recognized as full competition, and thus no limits of telecommunication markets are legally imposed,[25] but we also identified economies where telecommunication markets were monopolized, or just partly free in terms of competition.

Let us first consider the country-unique conditions reported during the critical years regarding the *mobile-cellular telephony diffusion* process (for these, compare data summarized in Table 5.1). As reported in Table 5.1, the MCS critical years were observed between 1997 and 2004 in upper-middle-income economies and between 1992 and 2003 in the high-income group, and for these time spans, we have collected country-specific information on fixed-telephony penetration rates, prices of a one-minute call (peak, on net) and one SMS, telecommunication market competition type, economic and investment freedom, country freedom status and gross domestic product *per capita*.[26] We consider the aforementioned direct stimuli of the emergence of the MCS critical mass and MCS technological take-off.

Careful examination of country-specific structural conditions during the MCS allows for the drawing of several impressive conclusions. The first factor, which potentially may enforce rapid diffusion of mobile-cellular telephony, is low accessibility to wired-telephony infrastructure. Negligible fixed-telephony penetration rates may constitute a strong stimulus for rapid deployment of mobile-cellular services, as the latter are hence recognized as the only solution for people who wish to communicate with others. Hence-forth, we hypothesize that in countries where fixed-telephony network was poorly developed, mobile-cellular solution should be deployed faster. The respective fixed-telephony penetration rates vary significantly, especially across upper-middle-income economies where the fixed-telephony pene-tration (FTL) ranges from 0.6 in Angola to 31.4 per 100 inhabitants in Belarus. Interestingly, in these two countries, the length of the pre-take-off stage is almost the same: 11 and 10 years in Angola and Belarus, respectively. We find also that in Peru the pre-take-off phase was as long as in Angola

(11 years), while the FTL penetration rate during the MCS critical year was 5.9 per 100 inhabitants. Next, for instance, in Macedonia, the initial diffusion phase lasted for four years and in Maldives for five years, while the FTL penetration rates were 24.7 and 9.8 per 100 inhabitants, respectively. In Turkey, the initial phase was 12-year long, and the FTL penetration rate was 27.4 per 100 inhabitants When looking at analogous relationships, however, in high-income economies, in this country income group, we observe huge disparities, and as a first sign we do not observe any correlation between the lengths of the MCS pre-take-off phases and the FTL penetration rates during the MCS critical year. Notably, as in the case of upper-middle-income economies, the fixed-telephony density varies among economies. The best performing country in this respect was Sweden, where the FTL penetration rate was 67.3 per 100 inhabitants during the years 1993 (the MCS critical year) and the initial MCS diffusion phases lasted 12 years. However, interestingly, in Argentina, the initial diffusion phase was reported as 14 years, while the FTL penetration rate was just 22.7 per 100 inhabitants. Next, in Oman, where it took 13 years to take off, the FTL penetration rate was 10.1 per 100 inhabitants. Analogously, among high-income economies, we find countries with FTL penetration rates similar to what was observed in Argentina with significantly different lengths of the pre-take-off stages; these are, inter alia, Brunei Darussalam (six years), Chile (nine years), Poland (six years), Qatar (six years) and Seychelles (only three years; sic!). This brief analysis leads to the conclusion that state of development of wired telephony infrastructure does not actually correlate with the length of the MCS initial diffusion stage, and the latter is not determined by the FTL penetration rates. The latter may also suggest that regardless of the availability of the 'old' communication technology, the newly emerged mobile-cellular networks are highly advantageous compared to fixed-telephony, and people's demand for this type of technology is high regardless of whether wired telephony is widely available or not. Notably, these findings that *infrastructural* shortages do not impede the spread of mobile-cellular telephony are valid both for high-income and upper-middle-income economies.

Next, we aim to examine whether broadly defined income conditions determine the emergence of the MCS critical mass and thus MCS technological take-off, both in high-income and upper-middle-income economies. To this aim, we use three variables, which we believe are decisive for the affordability of mobile-cellular telephony services and thus fundamental for the MCS uptake. These are gross domestic product *per capita*, prices of a one-minute call (peak, on net) and prices of one SMS (peak, on net).[27] Let us first consider the *per capita* incomes reported for respective economies. When taking into account the GDP per capita average values calculated for country-specific MCS critical years in high-income economies, it was 25,155 US$ *per capita*, while in upper-middle-income economies it was 4,588 US$ *per capita*.[28] Henceforth, we see that, on average, in the high-income group, the MCS technological take-off emerged at around five times higher per capita income compared to upper-middle-income economies. At first sign, this would yield the conclusion that the low level of GDP per capita, de facto, does not impede the achievement of the MCS critical mass and break out into self-perpetuating growth of new users of mobile-cellular telephony. Intuitively, we also conclude that the level of GDP per capita reported for the MCS critical year does not directly correlate with the length of the pre-take-off stage, meaning that regardless of the material wealth of society, the mobile-cellular telephony diffusion proceeds; it takes off at a certain point in time and starts to spread at an exponential rate. In China, during the MCS critical year, the GDP *per capita* was the lowest among upper-middle-income economies, and it was reported at 1,761 US$ *per capita*, while the MCS initial diffusion phase lasted 12 years. However, in Mexico (the second-richest country during the MCS critical year among the upper-middle-income group), the pre-take-off stage ended after 11 years, while in Turkey (the third-richest country) I ended after 12 years, analogously to China. Regarding high-income countries, we also discovered striking disparities in this respect. Note that during the MCS critical year, the economically wealthiest country was Norway, with GDP *per capita* 65,115 US$, while Argentina was one of the poorest at 7,357 US$ *per capita*. Interestingly, the calculated length of the MCS pre-take-off phase was 12 and 14 years, respectively. Next, in another two countries with a comparable level of *per capita* income during the MCS critical—namely, Brunei Darussalam and Germany (33,675 US$ and 34,968 US$, respectively)—the lengths of the initial MCS diffusion phase are crucially different. In Brunei Darussalam, it took 6 years to take-off into self-sustaining growth, while in Germany, it took almost twice that long at 11 years. When looking more closely at the GDP per capita variability noted for high-income economies during their MCS critical years, another striking observation arose. Countries which were relatively poor during their MCS technological take-off, meaning they were lagging behind economically in terms of per capita income level within the high-income group, had relatively fast taken-off, technologically. That was, for instance, the case with Estonia, Hungary, Latvia, Lithuania, Poland, Seychelles and Uruguay. In these countries, the GDP *per capita* was far below the group average, while, surprisingly, the reported lengths of their MCS pre-take-off stages were also below the group average (8.53 years). The shortest MCS pre-take-off phase was identified in Seychelles, where it took only three years to break out into an exponential growth phase along the mobile-cellular telephony diffusion trajectory. Next, in Estonia, it took slightly longer: five years, while in Latvia, Lithuania, Hungary, Uruguay and Poland it took six years.

Considering the prices of basic services of mobile-cellular telephony—namely, prices of a one-minute call and one SMS sent on peak on net—we may argue that they approximate affordability to buy basic mobile-cellular telephony services. The general observation is that the average prices of a one-minute call reported for the MCS critical year is twice as high in high-income economies compared to the upper-middle-income group. In the high-income group, it was at about 0.41 US dollars, while in the upper-middle-income group, it was 0.22 US dollars.[29] This surprising observation is probably because in upper-middle-income economies, the MCS technological take-offs emerged a few years later, which is crucial, as world telecommunication market prices for access to and use of mobile-cellular telephony are rapidly dropping. The following are a few examples for upper-middle-income economies. Relatively, the highest prices of a one-minute call during the MCS critical year were detected in Bulgaria and Lebanon (0.56 US dollars) and Peru (0.60 US dollars), where the MCS pre-take-off stage lasted 7 years, 10 years, 11 years, respectively. However, equally long, or even longer, were MCS pre-take-off phases reported in China at 12 years and the one-minute call price at 0.04 US dollars; in Algeria, the pre-take-off phase was 14 years and the one-minute call price was 0.07 US dollars, and in Angola, the pre-take-off phase was 11 years and the one-minute call price was 0.04 US dollars. Next, in Botswana and Panama where the initial MCS diffusion phase lasted just two years and three years, repectively, the prices of a one-minute call was relatively high at 0.36 US dollars in Botswana and 0.4 US dollars in Panama. The other two examples of countries where the MCS initial diffusion stage was equally long at 15 years are Thailand and Tunisia. However, in Tunisia, the price of a one-minute call was almost three times higher compared to Thailand. Similar 'contradictions' are encountered among high-income economies. In Argentina and Japan, the MCS initial diffusion stage lasted 14 years, but in Argentina, during the MCS critical year, the price of a one-minute call was 0.12 US dollars, while in Japan it was approximately five times higher. In Oman, it took 13 years for take-off, while the costs of access to mobile-cellular telephony were comparably low at only 0.06 US dollars for a one-minute call, while in Greece it took just 3 years for take-off and the price of a one-minute call was almost 0.6 US dollars. What we see here is that prices of both a one-minute call and SMS varied extensively among analyzed countries during their specific MCS critical years. Surprisingly, even under relatively unfavorable conditions in countries where the price for access and use of mobile-cellular network were high compared to other countries, it did not impede the emergence of the MCS technological take-off, nor did it prolong the MCS pre-take-off stage in these countries. Falling prices of calls and SMSs seem to be fundamental conditions for the growth of deployment of mobile-cellular services. The cost of access to this type of technology seems to be especially important in relatively poorer economies, which are generally worse off compared to better-performing economies. Hypothetically, high prices of access to and use of mobile-cellular telephony network should effectively impede the emergence of MCS technological take-off because of the limited amount people can pay to use this type of technology. However, our evidence, to some extent, is at odds with basic intuition and proves that relatively high costs of access to mobile-cellular network do not hinder reaching the MCS critical mass and thus the take-off is enabled. This surprising observation may suggest that people's propensity to gain access to this type of ICT is extremely high and is not impeded even by relatively high costs. This again supports our supposition that new ICT are highly advantageous compared to 'old' ones, as they pave roads to gaining new opportunities, allow people to stay in touch and build new social and economic networks. These findings perfectly coincide with those reported in the work of Lechman (2015); however, for low-income and lower-middle-income economies, where we found that even in very poor countries where the relative cost of getting access to mobile network was high, the spread of ICT was not stopped and proceeded at an exponential rate.

Finally, we address selected institutional and political factors, such as types of telecommunication market competition, economic and investment freedom and country freedom status. Although none of these factors can be called *direct* determinants of the ICT diffusion, undeniably, they shape a country's legal and institutional frameworks, which may potentially have far-reaching implications for the process of spreading a mobile-cellular telephony network. We argue that regardless of the country's political regimes and economic freedoms it enjoys or lacks, the seminal aspect of free and unbound diffusion of ICT is the type of telecommunication market competition. Following the International Telecommunication Union classification, we distinguish three basic types of competition and claim that national telecommunication markets may be fully competitive, partially competitive or monopolized. Needless to say, full competition makes telecommunication markets work more effectively; it creates pressure for price drops and increases in the quality of products and services. More balanced and 'consumer friendly' tariffs make ICT services more affordable for societies, even in countries which economically lag behind, and hence enforce the emergence of the network effects and thus growth of new users of a given technology. State policy makers usually face the problem of setting to what extent telecommunication markets may be exclusively driven by market forces, or, reversely, regulated. Effective competition drives economic effectiveness, and that is what usually determines decisions made by national regulatory bodies in respect to telecommunication markets. Fortunately, since late '80s of the 20th century, especially in developed countries, followed by rapidly proceeding technological advances, lots of national telecommunication markets have become more liberalized and pro-competitive. These advantageous changes provided solid fundaments for significant falls in prices of telecommunication services, allowing for the unveiling the positive network effects and growth of new technological solutions deployment. Growth of telecommunication markets completion as well as gradual drops in costs of access to and use of ICT was additionally enforced by the fact that because of fast technological progress, infrastructural requirements and investments have been reduced. Traditional copper wires are no longer needed to provide telecommunication services; rather, mobile wireless solutions are broadly offered to individuals. Importantly, the fixed costs of providing wireless services to customers are significantly lower compared to fully wired (fixed) networks, and this, inter alia, enhanced price drops. Needless to say, those mobile wireless solutions may be offered to people in underserved and infrastructural underdeveloped areas, and thus the effective demand for this type of technology increases regardless of a country's population density or physical conditions.

The results of our analysis show that during the MCS critical year in the high-income group, 17 national telecommunication markets were fully liberalized (fully competitive, compare Table 5.1), in another 10 countries there was partial competition and in 2 countries they were monopolized (Brunei Darussalam and Saudi Arabia). For the remaining 18 countries, because of a lack of data, we could not identify the type of telecommunication market competition. However, bearing in mind the fact that these were high-income economies, we may suppose that these markets were fully, or at least partially, liberalized during the MCS critical year. Regarding the group of upper-middle-income economies, we have found that during the country-specific MCS critical years, only 12 (out of 34) were fully liberalized. In another 11 countries, we identified partial competition; in 5 countries (Costa Rica, Iran, Macedonia, Maldives and Namibia), we identified a monopoly, and in 4 (Brazil, Kazakhstan, Mauritius and Panama), we identified a duopoly. The latter inevitably may lead to the conclusion that even when the domestic telecommunication market is monopolized and legal regulations impose high entry barriers to it, the MCS technological take-off may emerge. Put differently, our results suggest that the existence of monopoles on telecommunication markets does not constitute an obstacle impeding the achievement of MCS critical mass and MCS technological take-off. Evidently, even under such unfavorable conditions, rapid growth of mobile-cellular telephony deployment is possible. Regarding upper-middle-income economies, another surprising observation is that, conversely to what might be expected, the prices of a one-minute call (peak, on net) reported in countries with monopolized telecommunication markets were below the group average (0.22 US dollars). For instance, in Costa Rica, it was just 0.11 US dollars, and in Maldives, it was 0.21 US dollars. Notably, even countries where a 'full monopoly' was observed during the MCS technological take-off did not remain virtually 'locked' in during the early diffusion phases, but rather entering the exponential growth phase was enabled. For instance, in Maldives, the mobile-cellular penetration rates grew until 206 per 100 inhabitants (sic!) in 2015, which made Maldives the best-performing country in this regard among upper-middle-income economies. In Costa Rica, the analogous value was at about slightly higher than 150 per 100 inhabitants in 2015, while, for instance, in Turkey, with a fully competitive telecommunication market, the MCS in 2015 was just 96 per 100 inhabitants, and in Dominican Republic, it was 82.5 per 100 inhabitants.

Regarding our results on country political freedom status, the evidence is rather mixed (see Table 5.1) and does not allow for concluding any kind of regularities in this respect. Our countries' classification was based on data provided by Freedom House (different editions), and thus we have identified three class of countries, which are 'free', 'partly free' and 'not free'. Countries falling into the first class are those in which civil liberties and political rights are not restricted, and thus people enjoy political empowerment, can freely vote and actively participate in the country's political life. Countries which are recognized as being 'partly free' or 'not free' enjoy fewer political rights and civil liberties. Those societies usually do not fully enjoy the rule of law, freedom of expression, Internet and religion freedoms or unrestricted access to political elections. Potentially, countries with limited civil liberties could suffer from state-restricted access to and use of new technologies. However, this supposition is not confirmed by the results of our research. We have identified 14 countries as being 'not free' during the MCS critical year and another 15 as 'partly free' among the two income groups. Not only did these economies manage to take-off along the MCS diffusion patterns but also the length of the pre-take-off stage was relatively short in some of them—for instance, Qatar (six years) and Maldives (five years). Again, our empirical results are at odds with the elementary logic that the process of diffusion of new technologies is possible *only* under favorable conditions. We have seen that, in fact, regardless of the economic and legal environment, a mobile-cellular telephony network demonstrates the unique ability to spread fast among social actors. We did not identify any factor that would effectively impede the emergence of MCS technological take-off.

The remainder of Sect.5.2 is dedicated entirely to the explanation of the critical conditions under which countries in the scope of our analysis break out into exponential growth along the diffusion curve, demonstrating changes in Internet penetration rate. Here we should underline that in our study of the critical mass and technological take-off, we intentionally consider the IU diffusion curves instead of fixed or mobile networks. The ICT indicator, IU, perfectly reflects real access to and use of Internet networks by individuals in a given society. Note that the effective number of users of the Internet network significantly exceeds the number of legal subscribers to fixed and/ or mobile networks. This was not actually the case with mobile-cellular telephony, where legal subscriptions reflected the number of its individual users relatively well. In the case of the Internet network, it is quite different. People usually have institutional access at work place, schools, universities, or simply provided for free by the state; henceforth, the actual penetration rates of fixed and/or mobile network do not tell us about the share of the population that can use the Internet. Arguably, at least to some extent, access to and use of the Internet have become universal, meaning that even societies living in underserved and remote regions have been reached by new technologies. The latter is a 'great promise' to eliminate the digital divide in accessibility both across and within the country level. The Internet is often perceived as an empowerment tool and as a vital enabler of productivity shifts, as well as offering new education and professional opportunities. Henceforth, state policies are becoming more and more ICT oriented, providing solid fundaments for broad Internet network dissemination.

Table 5.2 comprehensively describes country-specific conditions that were identified during the IU critical years and summarizes the results of our calculations regarding the IU critical year, IU critical mass, length of IU pre-take-off stage and IU technological take-off intervals. In this case, the IU critical years were observed between 1998 and 2012 in upper-middle-income economies and between 1994 and 2006 in high-income ones. As already noted, similar to mobile-cellular telephony diffusion, each of the examined economies managed to achieve the IU critical mass (IU critical penetration rate), which gave the strong impulse to fast growth of individuals who use the Internet network. Put differently, none of the analyzed countries remained 'locked' in the early diffusion phase, but each of them, once the IU critical penetration rate was reached, left the IU pre-take-off phase and took-off into the exponential growth stage. By the end of 2015, many national telecommunication markets in developed countries were almost 'fully' saturated in regard to Internet penetration rates, which undeniably had the positive effect of rapidly diffusing mobile-broadband networks. A vast majority of countries that we have examined also reached the stabilization phase by the year 2015 or even earlier. It shows that between 1990 and 2015, both fixed and mobile (wireless) Internet network penetration rates were high enough to ensure widespread usage of this type of ICT.

In what follows, we briefly discuss the results of our analysis with regard to the country-specific conditions, which is analogous to what was demonstrated in respect to mobile-cellular telephony. We examine unique country-by-country infrastructural, economic and institutional conditions that were reported during the IU critical years for respective economies. As noted earlier, in the upper-middle-income countries, the IU critical years are reported between 1998 and 2012 and, by definition, the IU critical mass is reached in these time periods. In high-income economies, it was reported between 1994 and 2006. The calculated 'average' value of the IU critical mass is 9.03%, which is very close to the 'average'[30] value of MCS critical mass at 8.14 per 100 inhabitants. Still, for upper-middle-income countries, the 'average' length of the IU pre-take-off stage is 9.7 years and, again, well coincides with the 'average' length of the MCS initial diffusion phase at 8.7 years. In the group of high-income economies, the difference in the 'average' IU and MCS values of critical mass are negligible; for IU, it is 6.85%, while for MCS it is 6.7 per 100 inhabitants. The difference between 'average' lengths of pre-take-off phases is higher at 2.4 years, but this 'gap' is still small when considering the dynamics of technology diffusion. These elementary calculations, demonstrating striking similarities in the process of diffusion of two kinds of ICT in two distinct country groups, again support our hypothesis that diffusion of new technology is a strongly endogenous

Table 5.2 Technological take-off, country-specific conditions. Internet penetration rates. High-income and upper-middle-income economies

Country	Critical year	Critical mass	Takeoff	Length of pre-takeoff stage	Fixed-broadband penetration rate	Active mobile-broadband penetration rate	Fixed-broadband monthly subscription charge	Telecommunication market competition	Economic Freedom Index	Investment Freedom Index	Country status freedom	GDP per capita
Upper-middle-income countries												
Algeria	2004	4.6	2005–2006	10	0.1	n.a.	17.1	FC	58.1	70.0	Not free	4093
Angola	2012	6.5	2013–2014	6	0.2	2.02	52.2 (2012)	FC	n.a	n.a.	Not free	3973
Azerbaijan	2006	11.9	2007–2008	12	0.04	0.21 (2009)	85.2	FC	53.2	30.0	Not free	3924
Belarus	2001	4.3	2002–2003	7	0.0001	n.a.	7.1 (2009)	n.a.	38.0	30.0	Not free	2855
Bosnia and Herzegovina	2004	15.4	2005–2006	8	0.2	n.a.	14.2	FC	44.7	30.0	n.a.	3586
Botswana	2011	8.0	2012–2013	16	9.1	1.5 (2010)/42.5 (2013)	57.3 (2011)	FC	68.8	75.0	Free	6489
Brazil	2001	4.5	2002–2003	10	0.18	n.a.	42.7	PC	61.9	50.0	Partly free	8744
Bulgaria	2000	5.4	2001–2002	13	0.08 (2004)	n.a.	14.9	FC	47.3	70.0	Free	3958
China	2002	4.6	2003–2004	9	0.25	n.a.	18.7	PC (only in 2002) /FC	58.2	30.0	Not free	2052
Colombia	2002	4.6	2003–2004	8	0.08	n.a.	33.9	FC	64.2	70.0	Partly free	4826
Costa Rica	2000	5.8	2001–2002	8	0.21 (2002)	n.a.	21.5	M	68.4	70.0	Free	6040
Dominican Rep.	2005	11.5	2006–2007	10	0.65	n.a.	34.8	FC	55.1	50.0	Free	4308
Ecuador	2006	7.2	2007–2008	14	0.32	n.a.	39.9 (2009)	FC	54.6	30.0	Partly free	4401
Iran	2008	12.2	2009–2010	14	0.41	0.00	42.3	PC	45.0	10.0	Not free	5915
Jamaica	2002	6.1	2003–2004	8	0.34	n.a.	48.2	FC	61.7	90.0	Free	4878
Jordan	2001	4.7	2002–2003	6	0.008	n.a.	33.3	FC	68.3	70.0	Partly free	3111
Kazakhstan	2008	11.0	2009–2010	14	2.2	23.3 (2010)	31.1	FC	61.1	30.0	Not free	8698
Lebanon	2005	10.1	2006–2007	10	1.2 (2007)	n.a.	23.2	FC	57.2	30.0	Not free	6600
Macedonia	2002	17.3	2003–2004	7	0.6 (2005)	n.a.	14.6	FC	58.0	50.0	Partly free	3403
Malaysia	1998	6.7	1999–2000	6	0.02 (2001)	n.a.	5.3 (2005)	FC	68.2	50.0	Partly free	6291
Maldives	2006	11.0	2007–2008	10	2.1	n.a.	9.3	M	n.a.	n.a.	Not free	5592
Mauritius	1999	4.6	2000 - 2001	3	0.02 (2002)	n.a.	89.3 (1999)	M	68.5	50.0	Free	5237
Mexico	2000	5.1	2001–2002	9	0.02	n.a.	54.9 (2000)	FC	59.3	70.0	Partly free	8568
Namibia	2010	11.6	2011–2012	15	0.4	14.3	102.3 (2010)	FC	62.2	50.0	Free	5143
Panama	2006	17.3	2007–2008	12	3.3	n.a.	14.9	FC	65.6	70.0	Free	6359

Country											
Paraguay	2007	11.2	2008–2009	11	0.2	3.2 (2010)	38.1	FC	58.3	50.0	Partly free	2906
Peru	2001	7.6	2002–2003	7	0.1	n.a.	38.5 (2006)	FC	69.6	70.0	Partly free	3307
Romania	2002	6.6	2003–2004	9	0.07	n.a.	9.9	FC	48.7	50.0	Free	5621
Serbia	2007	33.1	2008–2009	3	4.1	17.9 (2010)	29.6	FC			Free	5206
South Africa	2009	10.0	2010–2011	18	0.95	16.9 (2010)	23.5 (2009)	FC	68.1	70.0	Free	7282
Suriname	2006	9.5	2007–2008	11	0.53	n.a.	55.3 (2005)	PC	55.1	30.0	Free	7428
Thailand	2001	5.6	2002–2003	10	0.002	n.a.	17.7	FC	68.9	70.0	Free	3551
Tunisia	2003	6.5	2004–2005	9	0.002	n.a.	12.1	FC	58.1	50.0	Not free	3261
Turkey	2001	5.2	2002–2003	8	0.02	n.a.	32.5 (2005)	M (only in 2001) / FC	60.6	70.0	Partly free	7349
High-income countries												
Argentina	2001	16.1	2002–2003	12	0.25 (2001)	n.a.	37.8	FC	68.6	70.0	Free	7756
Australia	1997	16.3	1998–1999	7	0.63 (1999)	n.a.	50.3	FC	75.5	70.0	Free	40114
Austria	1996	6.9	1997–1998	6	0.63 (1999)	n.a.	25.7 (2005)	FC [1998]	68.9	70.0	Free	37253
Belgium	1997	4.7	1998–1999	7	0.1	n.a.	49.7 (2005)	FC [2012]	64.6	70.0	Free	37022
Brunei Darussalam	1997	4.8	1998–1999	2	0.56 (2001)	n.a.	61.6 (2006)	PC [2012]	n.a.	n.a.	n.a.	33093
Canada	1995	4.2	1996–1997	5	0.5 (1998)	n.a.	21.2	FC [1998]	69.4	90.0	Free	37568
Chile	2000	16.6	2001–2002	8	0.04	n.a.	47.8	n.a.	74.7	70.0	n.a.	9833
Croatia	2000	6.6	2001–2002	7	0.07 (2003)	n.a.	16.9 (2006)	n.a.	53.6	50.0	Free	10573
Cyprus	1998	8.9	1999–2000	6	0.26 (2001)	n.a.	41.7	FC [2012]	68.2	70.0	Free	24989
Czech Republic	1999	6.8	2000–2001	7	0.02 (2000)	n.a.	25.0 (2005)	FC [2012]	69.7	70.0	Free	14119
Denmark	1996	5.7	1997–1998	6	1.3 (2000)	n.a.	29.3	n.a.	67.3	70.0	Free	50305
Estonia	1997	5.7	1998–1999	5	1.3 (2001)	n.a.	23.5 (2005)	FC [2001]	69.1	90.0	Free	8824
Finland	1994	4.9	1995–1996	4	0.67 (2000)	n.a.	36.5	n.a.	n.a.	n.a.	Free	30824
France	1997	4.3	1998–1999	7	0.03	n.a.	36.5	FC [1998]	59.1	50.0	Free	35181
Germany	1997	6.7	1998–1999	7	0.32 (2000)	n.a.	36.6	FC [1996]	67.5	70.0	Free	35562
Greece	1999	6.8	2000–2001	8	0.09 (2003)	n.a.	24.5	FC [1994]	61.0	70.0	Free	22491
Hungary	1999	5.8	2000–2001	8	0.03	n.a.	23.1	FC [1992]	59.6	70.0	Free	9985
Iceland	1995	6.8	1996–1997	4	0.02 (1999)	n.a.	63.3 2005	FC [1998]	n.a.	n.a.	Free	29650
Ireland	1997	4.1	1998–1999	6	0.23 (2002)	n.a.	36.6	FC [1998]	72.6	70.0	Free	33510
Israel	1997	4.4	1998–1999	7	0.71 (2001)	n.a.	6.3 (2009)	FC [1998]	62.7	90.0	Free	24780
Italy	1998	4.6	1999–2000	8	0.2	n.a.	44.5 (2003)	FC [1995]	51.9	70.0	Free	34374

(Continued)

Table 5.2 (Continued)

Country	Critical year	Critical mass	Takeoff	Length of pre-takeoff stage	Fixed-broadband penetration rate	Active mobile-broadband penetration rate	Fixed-broadband monthly subscription charge	Telecommunication market competition	Economic Freedom Index	Investment Freedom Index	Country status freedom	GDP per capita
Japan	1996	4.4	1997–1998	6	0.03	n.a.	32.6	n.a.	72.6	50.0	Free	39860
Korea (Rep.)	1998	6.8	1999–2000	8	0.03	n.a.	18.2	FC [1994]	73.3	70.0	n.a.	12729
Latvia	2000	6.3	2001–2002	4	0.01	n.a.	24.7	FC	63.4	70.0	Free	6918
Lithuania	2000	6.4	2001–2002	4	0.07	n.a.	15.3	FC	61.9	70.0	Free	6936
Malta	1998	6.5	1999–2000	3	0.4 (2000)	n.a.	20.3	FC [2005]	61.2	70.0	n.a.	16476
Netherlands	1995	6.5	1996–1997	5	0.5 (1998)	n.a.	36.6	FC [1997]	n.a.	n.a.	Free	38441
New Zealand	1995	4.9	1996–1997	3	0.12 (2000)	n.a.	28.1	FC [1990]	n.a.	n.a.	Free	26965
Norway	1995	6.4	1996–1997	5	0.51 (2000)	n.a.	53.0	n.a.	n.a.	n.a.	Free	70477
Oman	2006	8.3	2007–2008	9	0.78	0.99	31.2 (2006)	M	63.7	50.0	Not free	18273
Poland	1998	4.1	1999–2000	7	0.03 (2001)	n.a.	38.8 (2005)	n.a.	59.2	70.0	Free	7804
Portugal	1997	4.9	1998–1999	6	0.003 (1999)	n.a.	24.5 (2005)	FC	63.6	70.0	Free	19382
Qatar	2001	6.2	2002–2003	6	0.04	n.a.	54.9	M	60.0	50.0	Not free	61020
Russian Federation	2003	8.3	2004–2005	12	0.23	n.a.	13.4	n.a.	50.8	50.0	Partly free	7770
Saudi Arabia	2001	4.7	2002–2003	6	0.07	n.a.	39.7	FC	62.2	30.0	Not free	14640
Seychelles	2001	11.1	2002–2003	5	0.4 (2004)	n.a.	45.5 (2005)	PC	n.a.	n.a.	Partly free	9560
Singapore	1996	8.4	1997–1998	5	0.27	n.a.	73.2 (2005)	FC [2000]	86.5	90.0	n.a.	29951
Slovakia	1999	5.5	2000–2001	6	0.07 (2002)	n.a.	27.8	n.a.	54.2	50	Free	10161
Slovenia	1996	6.1	1997–1998	3	0.27 (2001)	n.a.	42.5	FC [2004]	50.4	30.0	Free	15603
Spain	1998	4.4	1999–2000	8	0.2 (2000)	n.a.	16.3 (2004)	n.a.	62.6	70.0	Free	26307
Sweden	1995	5.1	1996–1997	5	2.8 (2000)	n.a.	30.2	n.a.	61.4	70.0	Free	37687
Switzerland	1997	15.1	1998–1999	7	0.78 (2000)	n.a.	36.3 (2003)	FC [1998]	78.6	70.0	Free	62695
United Arab Emirates	1998	6.9	1999–2000	3	0.01	n.a.	40.6	PC [2012]	72.2	30.0	Not free	62729
United Kingdom	1996	4.1	1997–1998	6	0.23 (1998)	n.a.	35.3 (2004)	n.a.	76.4	70.0	Free	30918
United States	1994	4.9	1995–1996	4	0.25 (1998)	n.a.	15.0	n.a.	n.a.	n.a.	Free	38105
Uruguay	1998	6.9	1999–2000	4	0.8 (2004)	n.a.	24.5 (2006)	PC [2002]	68.6	70.0	Free	9439
Venezuela	2003	7.5	2004–2005	12	0.45	n.a.	47.7	FC [2000]	54.8	50.0	Partly free	9729

Note: All data are for the country-specific critical year (reported if otherwise). Fixed-broadband monthly subscription charge data for 2008 (reported if otherwise), active mobile-broadband penetration rates data starting in 2007, Internet freedom data starting in 2009 (the earliest). FC, full competition; PC, partial competition; M, monopoly. GDP per capita are in constant 2010 US$.

Source: Author's elaboration.

process, and regardless of the type of technology, its in-time dynamics and patterns are homogenous.

When looking at country-specific infrastructural conditions—state of development of fixed-broadband and mobile-broadband solutions, and enabling access to and use of Internet network during the IU critical years—the conclusions we draw are rather surprising for both country income groups. In high-income economies, the average FBS rate was only 0.36 per 100 inhabitants, and in upper-middle-income economies, it was 0.82 per 100 inhabitants. Regarding the average penetration rates, however, for mobile-broadband infrastructure, it was 0.99 per 100 inhabitants and 9.72 per 100 inhabitants for high-income and upper-middle income, respectively. Surprisingly, the average penetration rates are higher in upper-middle-income economies compared to high-income ones. However, it should be born in mind that the IU critical years were achieved *later* in the poorer country groups, and hence, by definition, the penetration rates there were slightly higher. Regarding the group of upper-middle-income economies, it is hard to identify any regularities or correlations between the IU length of the pre-take-off stage and the state of development of fixed-broadband network. The first fundamental observation is that in each of the examined countries, the fixed-broadband penetration rates were negligible and this type of technology was in fact nonexistent. The highest fixed-telephony penetration rate was observed in Botswana, and it was 9.1 per 100 inhabitants, where, at the same time, the IU pre-take-off stage lasted 16 years (sic!). In South Africa, the IU initial diffusion phase was also very long at 18 years, but during the IU critical year, the fixed-broadband penetration rate was just 0.95 per 100 inhabitants. On the other hand, in Mauritius, the IU critical mass was achieved at a fixed-broadband penetration rate of 0.02, and the IU pre-take-off stage lasted just three years. Similarly, we found strange results for high-income countries. The IU technological take-off emerged faster, with the 'average' length of the IU pre-take-off phase, and at an even lower state of development of fixed-broadband networks; note that during the IU critical years, the average fixed-broadband penetration rate was 0.36 per 100 inhabitants. This phenomenon, at least to some extent, may be explained by the fact that in developed countries, prior to fixed- and/or mobile-broadband networks, the fixed-narrowband technology was being deployed. In our study we, however, do not concentrate on this type of 'old' ICT, as these narrowband networks have been fast substituted by broadband ones, but still during the IU critical year, access to fixed-narrowband solutions has been much more popular compared to fixed-broadband ones. Henceforth, it is very possible that the developed countries reached the IU critical penetration rates (IU critical mass) mainly thanks to access to fixed-narrowband networks and the possibility of accessing the Internet network at the workplace or other institutions. More sophisticated technologies, such as fixed- and mobile-broadband solutions, have been introduced to national telecommunication markets and provided another strong impulse for further growth of Internet penetration rates across the examined developed countries. Additionally, as we reported in Chapter 4, the dynamics of diffusion of fixed-broadband networks significantly dropped once mobile-broadband technology started to evade the telecommunication markets. We have observed the emergence of the unusual process *of 'fixed-to-mobile technological substitution'*, indicating gradual switching from fixed-broadband to mobile(wireless)-broadband. However, bearing in mind the fact that prior to fixed-broadband networks, countries were deploying wired networks, thus enabling broader usage of the Internet. Thus, we discovered a kind of two-stage *'fixed-to-mobile technological substitution'* process: first, fixed narrowband were being substituted by fixed broadband and, second, fixed broadband were being substituted by mobile broadband. Notably, in many countries, even in those classified as high- or upper-middle-income ones, the fixed networks, neither the narrowband nor broadband type, have diffused relatively poorly, but they gave the positive impulse for growing usage of the Internet and allowed for reaching the IU critical mass. Next, the exponential growth of new users of the Internet was facilitated by quickly expanding mobile-broadband solutions, which, similarly, to mobile-cellular telephony are technologies with great ability to spread worldwide at a high pace.

When looking at the economic prerequisites, approximated by fixed-broadband monthly subscription charges and gross domestic product *per capita*, of the emergence of IU technological take-off across high-income and upper-middle-income economies, we recognized more odd results. At first sign, we concluded that in each examined economy, the IU critical mass was achieved under highly unfavorable economic conditions, which vary hugely among the countries. Interestingly, the average level of the FBS charge in both income groups was at about 34 US dollars; however, in this regard, enormous disparities among countries were reported. Low costs of access to ICT should effectively drive its rapid deployment by individuals and enforce the emergence of the network effect that, in turn, would provoke exponential growth of new users of this type of technology. Led by general intuition, we would expect that the low cost of acquiring access to a fixed network potentially reduces the length of the IU initial diffusion phase. Moreover, countries which are relatively better off in terms of *per capita* income and thus perform well economically have greater possibilities to finance broad society-wide deployment of Internet network infrastructure. Henceforth, we would expect to find a negative relationship between the length of the IU pre-take-off stage and GDP per capita reported for the IU critical year. However, curiously, we did not recognize such regularities either among high-income or upper-middle-income countries. Consider, for instance, several countries where IU initial diffusion phase lasted only three years. These are as follows: Mauritius, Serbia, Malta or Slovenia, where the FBS charge was 89.3 US dollars, 17.9 US dollars, 20.3 US dollars and 42.5 US dollars, respectively. On the other hand, for example, in Azerbaijan where the cost of accessing fixed-broadband network was equally high as in Mauritius (see Table 5.2), the IU pre-take-off phase was nine years longer. In the Russian

Federation, where the IU initial phase was equally as long as in Azerbaijan, the cost of access to fixed broadband was just 13.4 US dollars. Similarly, paradoxically, are relationships we find in respect to *per capita* incomes. Relatively poorer countries have managed to take-off relatively fast, see, for instance, case of Latvia, Lithuania, Poland, Kazakhstan, Mexico or Jordan (compare data in Table 5.2). But surprisingly, in many relatively rich countries, the IU pre-take-off phase was equally short, such as in Norway, Switzerland and the United Arab Emirates. Despite relatively little difference in the 'average' length of the IU early diffusion phase between the high-income and upper-middle-income groups, which was below 3 years, still, the difference in average GDP per capita reported for the country-specific IU critical years is vast at 21 629 US dollars.[31] Finally, considering the institutional factors, such as telecommunication market competition type and country freedom status, our findings again coincide with those reported in the case of mobile-cellular telephony diffusion. In a great majority of countries (51 out of total 81), we have discovered that national telecommunication markets were fully competitive. In another eight countries, we found that the national telecommunication markets were just partially competitive, while in six (Costa Rica, Maldives, Mauritius, Turkey, Oman and Qatar), they were monopolized. In respect to country freedom status, we have found the following: 48 countries were classified as 'free', 13 as 'partly free' and the last 14 as 'not free'. The latter suggests that that in 27 of the 81 examined economies, civil and political rights and freedoms were too restricted; even so, it did not hinder the emergence of the IU technological take-off.

These findings concerning identification of the country-specific structural conditions, which were reported for the IU critical years, allow for the analogous qualitative conclusions that we have demonstrated in respect to mobile-cellular telephony. Also, in this case, we did not identify any 'common' prerequisites which would be necessary to satisfy to leave the initial diffusion phase and enter exponential growth stage and then head towards 'full' market saturation. It should be emphasized that regardless of country-specific condition, in respect to infrastructural development, economic performance, telecommunication market competition type and political freedom status, none of the examined economies remained virtually 'locked' in the early diffusion phase and unable to take-off. Conversely, in each country, the unveiled network externalities emerging once the new advantageous technology evades the national market were sufficiently strong to ensure rapid diffusion of new ICT. This again speaks in support of the hypothesis that society- and economy-wide ICT diffusion is an endogenously driven process for which the economic, social and institutional or geographical factors play a marginal and, to a large extent, insignificant role.

ICT Diffusion Determinants—A Panel Approach

Intentionally, the last part of Chapter 5 is entirely dedicated to a brief presentation of the additional evidence on ICT diffusion determinants in 47 high-income and 34 upper-middle-income economies. With this aim, we wish to enrich the picture drawn in the previous parts of this chapter and provide a more extensive view of potential factors that impede or hinder the process of spreading new ICT. Similarly to Sect. 5.2, the following evidence is restricted exclusively to two ICT indicators—namely, mobile-cellular telephony and Internet penetration rates. Here, by definition, we do not intend to examine the determinants of deployment of either fixed-broadband networks or mobile-broadband solutions, because we believe that these two should be treated as determinants of the number of people using the Internet network. Traditionally, the time span of our analysis covers the period between 1990 and 2015. To verify what factors might have potentially affected the process of mobile-cellular telephony diffusion, we have selected the following: prices of a one-minute call (peak, on net; negative relationship is expected), fixed-telephony penetration rate (negative relationship is expected), gross domestic product *per capita* (positive relationship is expected), population density (positive relationship is expected) and urbanization rate (positive relationship is expected). In the case of potential IU determinants, we have decided to choose the following factors: fixed-broadband monthly subscription charge (negative relationship is expected), FBS (positive relationship is expected), gross domestic product *per capita* (positive relationship is expected), population density (positive relationship is expected) and urbanization rate (positive relationship is expected). Intentionally, we have not selected the mobile-broadband penetration rates as a factor that might have explained the changes in the number of individuals using the Internet network, as the data on wireless networks are available from 2007 onwards, and hence we believe its explanatory power would be rather weak. The explanation of all the aforementioned variables, as well as data sources, can be found in Sect. 5.1 of this chapter.

Moreover, to enrich the picture, we have selected another six variables approximating costs of access to and use of new ICT, for which we demonstrated in time changes (trends). These are the price of a one-minute call (peak, off net), price of one SMS (peak, on net), price of one SMS (peak, off net), price of buying mobile-broadband plan (1 GB, postpaid),[32] price of buying mobile-broadband plan (1 GB, prepaid)[33] and price of mobile-cellular monthly charge.[34] All aforementioned data are extracted from ITU World Telecommunication/ICT Indicators (edition 2016); however, availability of selected variables varies significantly across time.

In what follows, we present the results of our research regarding the ICT diffusion determinants. However, before discussing these results, we wish to emphasize that all analysis should be very carefully interpreted. One shall bear in mind that the bundle of ICT diffusion determinants have been fully subject to our subjective view and led by general logic and economic intuition. We are fully aware that, first, the statistical correlations we report next may be spurious, and, second, that new technologies adoption is a complex process driven by factors which are hard to quantify or even capture.

Moreover, it was not our intention to say that ICT diffusion is led exclusively by elements mentioned in the following study; however, we wished to contribute to the broad discussion on what factors foster or, reversely, hinder the process of spreading technological innovations. By convention, all selected variables are labeled 'determinants' of ICT diffusion; however, in fact, we exclusively detect the statistical relationships (correlations mainly), which do not necessary imply the existence of the causality between variables, and this shall be born in mind when interpreting results and drawing conclusions.

Figures 5.1 and 5.2 graphically present changing costs of access to and use of mobile-cellular telephony and Internet penetration rates. Consecutive Figures 5.3 and 5.4 explain the statistical relationships between changing mobile-cellular telephony and Internet penetration rates *versus* their selected determinants in all examined high-income and upper-middle-income economies over the period of 1990–2015. Additionally, in Appendix 6, we have summarized the panel regression analysis results concerning the identifications of the 'strength of impact' of selected determinants on the process

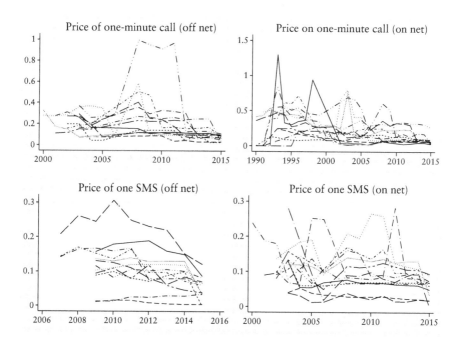

Figure 5.1 Changes in prices in usage of mobile-cellular telephony in selected high-income and upper-middle-income economies. Period 1990–2015

Note: On the Y-axis, the prices are in US dollars; time series vary because of data availability.

Source: Author's elaboration.

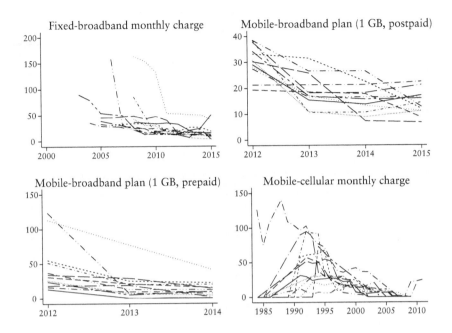

Figure 5.2 Changes in prices in access to Internet network in selected high-income and upper-middle-income economies. Period 1990–2015

Note: On the Y-axis, the prices are in US dollars; time series vary because of data availability.

Source: Author's elaboration.

of growing access to and use of mobile-cellular telephony and the Internet network.

Visual inspection of development of prices of accessing mobile-cellular telephony network (see Figure 5.1) clearly demonstrated that between 1990 and 2015 in both country income groups, drops in respective prices are significant. The longest time series (from 1990 to 2015) are available for the price of a one-minute call (peak, on net), and despite visible cross-country variability in this respect, we show the general downward trend. During the initial years of our research, the average prices of one-minute calls (peak, on net) were relatively high (see, for instance, Belarus, Romania, Italy, Japan or Latvia, where the prices were nearly 1.5 US dollars), but then in all countries, they were radically falling. Similar tendencies are observable in the case of the price of a one-minute call off net. Changes in prices of one SMS, both on net and off net are analogous to those observed for prices of calls. Figure 5.1 displays downward trends in this respect, exhibiting unquestionable falls in costs of buying elementary mobile-cellular services. When looking at Figure 5.2, similar regularities as in previous cases are exemplified. Between

1985 and 2015, we discovered radical decreases in charges that needed to be paid for monthly access to mobile-cellular services.[35] Here, however, an interesting observation arose. During the initial years, between 1985 and 1995, surprisingly, prices of monthly mobile-cellular services were actually increasing, and it was only after the 1995 that they started to drop fast. This initial growth of costs of using mobile-cellular telephony network was probably generated by fast-growing demand for this new type of technological tool offering wireless communication possibilities. Note that initially, the cost of buying a mobile phone was also extremely high—for instance, in the early '80s of the 20th century, the first mobile phones were sold for at about 4,000 US dollars each (sic!), and even such high prices did not restrict growing demand for this revolutionary technology. Similarly, massive drops in costs for usage of mobile-broadband 1GB post- and prepaid plans in respect to fixed-broadband monthly charge are easily detectable. Needless to say, the low cost of access to and use of ICT constitutes a fundamental prerequisite for its broad adoption and usage. Many claim that costs and economic affordability of ICT remain the only and the decisive factors for its society-wide uptake. In some countries, there remains the relatively high price of using ICT, which may constitute a significant barrier of its broad implementation and thus impede worldwide ICT convergence. Because of limited price drops, some countries face the danger of being left behind, and thus the digital divide may be persistent. Legal regulations provided by national authorities are critical for price policies introduced by telecommunication companies. However, luckily, in a great majority of countries (especially developed ones), the national policies are ICT oriented and promote broad implementation of new technologies, mainly by ensuring market liberalization, competition and privatization of state-owned telecommunication companies. Legal frameworks, which do not impose significant constraints on the functioning of national telecommunication markets, may effectively leverage the emergence of the network effects and thus allow for unbounded growth of new users of new technological solutions. Undeniably, connecting the unconnected should not be an issues of price. But if it is, the economically vulnerable groups, unskilled and/or poor people will be simply omitted by the digital transformation; hence, their social and economic exclusion will be even more severe in forthcoming years.

Since 2008 onward, International Telecommunication Union has collected data on ICT Price Baskets.[36] The ICT Price Basket comprehensively measures people's affordability in accessing and using various forms of ICT. It is calculated for three price sets referred to as sub-baskets: fixed-telephone, mobile-cellular and fixed-broadband sub-baskets (Measuring Information Society 2015). The respective sub-baskets refer to average prices of acquiring a standard bundle of services of fixed and mobile telephony and fixed-broadband networks, and their costs are expressed as a percentage of gross national income per capita. The ICT Price Basket value is the average of these three sub-baskets; thus, its higher value shows smaller affordability

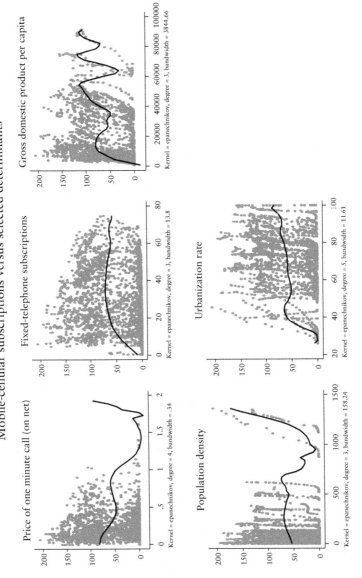

Figure 5.3 Mobile-cellular telephony penetration rates versus its selected determinants

Note: On the Y-axis, there are mobile-cellular telephony penetration rates (raw values) and on the X-axis, there are raw values of selected mobile-cellular telephony determinants. Singapore has been excluded.

Source: Author's elaboration.

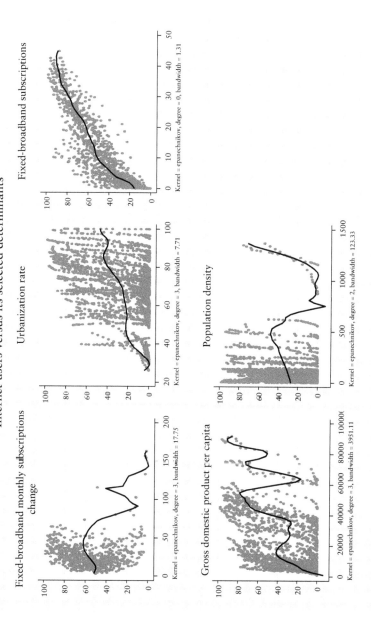

Figure 5.4 Internet penetration rates versus selected determinants

Note: On the Y-axis, there are Internet penetration rates (raw values); on the X-axis, there are raw values of selected Internet penetration rates determinants. Singapore is excluded.

Source: Author's elaboration.

of ICT in a given country. When comparing values of ICT Price Baskets in developed countries between 2008 and 2015, we identified increasing affordability; however, notably, these changes were more visible in relatively poorer countries. For instance, in South Africa in 2008, the ICT Price Basket was 4.2 and in 2015, it dropped to 2.3, suggesting that affordability of ICT had 'doubled'. In Brazil, it decreased from 7.7 in 2008 to 1.8 in 2015; in Peru, it decreased from 6.9 in 2008 to 2.9 in 2015. Interestingly, in the wealthiest countries, between 2008 and 2015, the values of ICT Price Baskets did not changed significantly, or in some countries, the values did not change at all. A few examples include Singapore and Luxembourg, while in Norway, Sweden and the United States, these changes were negligible. The latter suggests, however, first, dynamically growing personal incomes and, second, that in 2008, standard prices of basic ICT services were already relatively low compared to other less-developed economies.

The aforementioned numbers, as well as the graphical evidence displayed in Figures 5.1 and 5.2, allow for the conclusion that during the past decades, rapid and radical drops in cost of access to and use of ICT have possibly been one of the factors enforcing the spread of new technologies. As demonstrated in Chapter 4, in 2015, most of the telecommunication markets in the developed world were heading towards 'full' saturation, suggesting the prices were no longer a barrier in its wide deployment.

Next, Figures 5.3 and 5.4 visualize the relationship between mobile-cellular telephony and Internet penetration rates *versus* their selected determinants over the period of 1990–2015. This picture is enriched by the panel regression estimates,[37] the results of which are summarized in the tables in Appendix 6, offering a quantitative explanation of which factors might have contributed most to growth of deployment of ICT both in high-income as well as upper-middle-income countries.

Visual inspection of consecutive graphs presented in Figure 5.3 allow for the examination of whether any regularities between mobile-cellular telephony penetration rates and selected determinants may be traced in developed countries between 1990 and 2015. Led by general intuition, we would expect that prices of one-minute calls and the fixed-telephony penetration rate *versus* mobile-cellular telephony should be rather negatively correlated. As already argued, decreases in costs of buying mobile-cellular telephony enhanced growth of demand for this type of technology. We also believe that rapid diffusion of mobile-cellular telephony provokes falling demand for landline telephony, and thus the economic role of the latter should be gradually diminishing. Next, we claim that gross domestic product *per capita*, population density and urbanization rate should be positively correlated with mobile-cellular telephony penetration rates. Economic wealth allows for access and use of new technologies, and to some extent, it is should be recognized as a fundamental condition to ensure technology diffusion. Arguably, the level of *per capita* income plays an analogous role in fostering technology spread as low costs of access to and use of it. Considering the fact that technology diffusion it heavily preconditioned by the emergence of network effects demonstrating the strength of random interpersonal contacts in spreading new ideas and innovations, we suppose that both population density and urbanization rate are critical determinants of mobile-cellular telephony dissemination. Mobile-cellular networks hypothetically should spread faster in densely populated regions and highly urbanized areas, as these two factors facilitate inter-personal contacts and thus growth of the number of new users of new technology. However, taking a closer look at Figure 5.3, we concluded that our hypothesized relationships were hardly confirmable. Visual inspection does not actually allow for concluding the negative relationship between prices of one-minute calls and mobile-cellular telephony penetration rates or the negative relationship between fixed- and mobile telephony deployment. Despite the fact that visually the first relationship seems to be negative, the correlations coefficient between these two variables is (–0.08),[38] which would suggest that across high-income and upper-middle-income economies, during the period of 1990–2015, no specific regularity in this respect may be defined. Note that a huge majority of observation is located for prices ranging from almost zero to 0.5 US dollars per one-minute call (peak, on net), and within this price interval, we identify mobile-cellular telephony penetration rates varying from very low to almost 200 per 100 inhabitants. The number of observations falling in the consecutive price interval between 0.5 to 1 US dollar per a one-minute call (peak, one net) is significantly lower; then between 1 and 2 US dollar per a one-minute call (peak, one net), it is negligible. It would suggest that regardless of the prices of access to basic mobile services, mobile-cellular telephony spreads across societies. Regarding the interrelatedness of fixed and mobile telephony, again, we cannot actually identify are strict relationship. The calculated correlation coefficient between these two variables[39] is just 0.12. In this case, however, the lack of expected negative relationship may be determined by two facts: first, in quite a number of the examined countries, the state of development of landline telephony was low during the initial years of analysis and remained as such for the whole period of 1990–2015, and, second, in many other countries, the fixed telephony was gradually losing its role in the telecommunication market, but the pace of dropping penetration rates in this regard was significantly slower compared to extremely fast diffusion of mobile telephony. Concerning the other remaining factors—*per capita* gross domestic product, population density and urbanization rate—we detect a relatively strong relationship for the first variable and mobile-cellular penetration rate. Not surprisingly, we recognize the positive relationship between *per capita* income and growth of users of mobile telephony. Surprisingly, we do not find any 'satisfactory' correlation between either population density or urbanization rate *versus* mobile-cellular telephony. To some extent, we might claim that this graphical evidence demonstrated in Figure 5.3 is inconclusive and generally contradicts with our preliminary expectations. Although we have intended to unveil certain regularities, it seems that the variables we have selected have little explanatory power in respect to changes in mobile-cellular telephony penetration rates. Table AP(6)-1 in Appendix 6 summarizes panel regression results, reporting on the mobile-cellular telephony diffusion selected determinants. There are only two explanatory variables—gross domestic product *per capita* and urbanization rate—that reveal persistence in explaining changes in mobile-cellular telephony penetration rates across examined developed countries during the period of 1990–2015. Both variables enter the regressions with an expected sign (positive) and are statistically significant at 5% level of significance. Panel specifications FE(1) and FE(3) demonstrate a higher r-square—0.55 and 0.54, respectively—thus demonstrating the relatively best fit to the empirical data. However, it should be emphasized that despite the fact that gross domestic product *per capita* results are statistically significant, the β coefficients explaining its explanatory power are close to zero in all panel specifications. The latter might suggest that although economic wealth potentially matters for technology diffusion, in fact, its role as an enhancing factor of mobile-cellular telephony diffusion was actually negligible. This conclusion is consistent with our previous findings— see results presented in Sect. 5.2 in this chapter—as well as the graphical evidence in Figure 5.3 concerning how the urbanization rate also enters all regressions with the expected (positive) sign and is statistically significant. Note that, according to the respective regression coefficients, the impact of urbanization on mobile-cellular telephony diffusion is significantly stronger compared to the influence of *per capita* incomes. The latter may be relatively easy to explain, as in highly urbanized regions, the network effects might be stronger and thus give the positive impulse for new technology dissemination through the 'word-of-mouth' effect. Next, two variables—fixed-telephony penetration rates and prices of one-minute calls (peak, on net)—turned out to be statistically insignificant in all specifications. Note that for regressions FE(2), FE(4) and FE(5), we report r-squares equal zero, thus these models do not demonstrate any explanatory power in respect to growing deployment of mobile-cellular telephony. These results again coincide with our previous results on the relationship between landline telephony deployment and costs of access to and use of mobile-cellular services in developed countries between 1990 and 2015. Moreover, these findings speak in support of our initial hypothesis that the process of ICT diffusion is strongly endogenous, and thus, to a large extent, driven by the strength of the network effects, while other multiple (external) factors seem to play insignificant roles in this process.

Finally, we briefly discuss the results of our analysis of determinants of the changing number of individuals using the Internet network. Figure 5.4 graphically displays the relationships between IU (Internet penetration rates) *versus* fixed-broadband monthly subscription charge (expected negative relationship), fixed-broadband network penetration rates (expected positive relationship), gross domestic product *per capita* (expected positive relationship), urbanization rate (expected positive relationship) and population density (expected positive relationship). Additionally, Table AP(6)-2 in Appendix 6 summarizes panel regression results in this respect. The graphical evidence (see Figure 5.4) suggests relatively strong relationships between IU and fixed-broadband network penetration rates, urbanization rate and gross domestic product *per capita*. Regarding the relationship between IU and fixed-broadband network penetration rates, we see that respective observations are well concentrated along the theoretical line, and the calculated correlation coefficient between these two variables is 0.87.[40] Not surprisingly, the latter suggests that the share of individuals using the Internet is massively conditioned by access to fixed-broadband infrastructure. Next, both gross domestic product *per capita* and the urbanization rate seem to be highly correlated with IU; the respective correlation coefficients are 0.49[41] and 0.33.[42] Henceforth, both economic wealth and living in highly urbanized regions are favorable conditions to use the Internet network. But, analogously to what we have found in the case of mobile-cellular telephony, neither costs—here approximated by fixed-broadband monthly subscription charge—nor population density seem to be important factors in explaining the changes in the number of people using the Internet network. These conclusions are drawn based on the graphical evidence presented in Figure 5.4 and are supported by the panel regression results in Table AP(6)-2 in Appendix 6. In each specification, the fixed-broadband penetration rate enters the regressions with the expected sign, and the results are statistically significant. Moreover, the value of the respective regression coefficients (see FE(1), FE(2) and FE(4)) suggests the relatively strong impact of this determinant on changes in the number of individuals using the Internet network in each of the examined countries. With regard to the remaining explanatory variables, the evidence seems to be rather 'scattered' and does not allow for drawing more concrete conclusions. In FE(1), the economic wealth is reported as statistically insignificant, while in the other two specifications, FE(3) and FE(6), despite the fact that the regressions coefficients results are statistically significant, their value is close to zero, suggesting no impact of gross domestic product *per capita* on Internet usage. In respect to other variables, the results are also ambiguous.

Final Remarks

The main targets of this chapter were threefold. First, we intended to identify the country-specific critical penetration rates (critical mass), critical years, technological take-offs and lengths of the pre-take-off stage among high-income and upper-middle-income economies between 1990 and 2015. By convention, this evidence referred exclusively to the process of diffusion of mobile-cellular telephony and the growing share of a country's population using the Internet network. Second, we aimed to answer the question of under which infrastructural, economic and institutional conditions the technological take-offs emerged in each of the analyzed countries. Third, using the panel regression approach, we examined the impact of arbitrarily selected factors on the process of ICT diffusion between 1990 and 2015. Our evidence shows that the 'average' ICT critical penetration rates do not vary significantly across countries or technologies. Similarly, the calculated 'average' lengths of the ICT pre-take-off stage are quite similar in both country income groups and for mobile-cellular telephony and Internet penetration rates. These findings confirm our conclusions drawn from the analysis of country-specific ICT diffusion trajectories (see Chapter 4) that the process of diffusion of new technologies follows the 'classical' S-shaped time path, and thus certain regularities may be traced in this respect. Moreover, we did not identify any 'common' infrastructural, economic and institutional prerequisites that would be critical to reach the ICT critical penetration rates. Countries where the ICT critical mass and the technological take-off took place varied hugely in multiple aspects. They differed not only in terms of economic performance but also in regard to infrastructural development, telecommunication market competition type and pricing policies, or, for instance, political freedoms and regimes. However, regardless of potentially unfavorable conditions, the technological take-offs were reported in all countries in the scope of our analysis.

Our major findings are remarkable, and they seem to confirm, at least partially, our main hypothesis that ICT diffusion is strongly endogenously driven, and it is mainly subjected to unveiled network externalities, which, once emerged, give strong impulse for the fast and self-sustainable spread of new technology. This is critical to fully understand the nature of new ICT.

Notes

1. See www.heritage.org/index/about.
2. See https://freedomhouse.org/report-types/freedom-world.
3. See www.itu.int/net4/itu-d/icteye/.
4. See http://iif.un.org/.
5. Compare results presented in Chapter 4.
6. Compare results presented in Chapter 4.
7. For methodological details, see Chapter 3.
8. If ICT marginal growths and ICT replication coefficients patterns intersect (converge), it indicates that the critical mass was achieved.
9. MCS marginal growths patterns are represented by solid lines, while MCS replication coefficients patterns are represented by dash lines.
10. MCS critical mass (or MCS critical penetration rate) designates the mobile-cellular telephony penetration rates in the critical year.
11. MCS critical year and mobile-cellular telephony critical year.
12. Lengths of the MCS pre-take-off stage and lengths of the pre-take-off stage along the mobile-cellular telephony diffusion curve.
13. MCS technological take-off and technological take-off identified along the mobile-cellular telephony diffusion curve.

14. Author's own calculations based on results summarized in Table 5.1.
15. Author's own calculations based on results summarized in Table in Appendix 4.
16. IU marginal growths patterns are represented by solid lines, while IU replication coefficients patterns by are represented by dash lines.
17. IU critical mass (or IU critical penetration rate) designates the mobile-cellular telephony penetration rates in the critical year.
18. IU critical year and mobile-cellular telephony critical year.
19. Lengths of the IU pre-take-off stage and lengths of the pre-take-off stage along mobile-cellular telephony diffusion curve.
20. IU technological take-off and technological take-off identified along mobile-cellular telephony diffusion curve.
21. In fact, the highest level of IU critical mass is observed for Serbia at 33.1%; this country is an outlier in the research country sample.
22. Author's own calculations based on results summarized in Table in Appendix 4.
23. See Section 5.1.
24. If data was not available for the critical year strictly, we used data from the 'nearest' year (if available, from the year *before* the critical year).
25. In terms of number of telecommunication market operators.
26. For data explanation and sources, see Sect. 5.1 in this chapter.
27. International Telecommunication Union provides comprehensive indicators on ICT affordability; it calculates Price Baskets for respective ICT services. However, these data are available since 2008 onwards and thus cannot be used in our research.
28. Author's calculations based on data summarized in Table 5.1.
29. Author's calculations based on data summarized in Table 5.1.
30. Author's own calculations based on data summarized in Table 5.2.
31. According to our calculations, the average value of GDP per capita during the IU critical years was 26,774 for high-income countries and 5,145 for upper-middle-income countries.
32. Refers to the price of the mobile postpaid plan in local currency for a mobile-broadband USB/dongle-based postpaid tariffs with 1GB volume of data (expressed in USD; see ITU 2016).
33. Refers to the price of mobile prepaid broadband USB_1GB in local currency for a mobile-broadband USB/dongle-based prepaid tariffs with 1GB volume of data (expressed in USD; see ITU 2016).
34. Refers to the price of the monthly subscription charge for mobile cellular service. Because of the variety of plans available in many countries, it is preferable to use the tariff with the cheapest initiation/connection charge. If prepaid services are used (for those countries that have more prepaid than postpaid subscribers), then the monthly subscription charge would be zero. If the plan includes free minutes and/or free SMS, this should be put in a note (see ITU 2016).
35. Refers to postpaid services.
36. See ITU Reports Measuring Information Society for various years.
37. Relying on the Hausman test specifications, we have estimated fixe effects regressions of a general form: $ICT_{i,y} = \alpha + \beta(x_{i,y}) + \mu_{i,y} + v_{i,y}$, where i denotes country, y denotes year, $x_{i,y}$ shows the iyth observations within the model, $x_{i,y}$ is the unobservable and time-invariant country-specific effect and $v_{i,y}$ accounts for observation-specific errors. To control for possible emerging heteroskedasticity or within-panel serial correlation, we use robust standard errors.
38. Author's calculations, number of observations 1,564.
39. Author's calculations, number of observations 1,962.
40. Author's calculations, number of observations 1,181.
41. Author's calculations, number of observations 1,824.
42. Author's calculations, number of observations 1,844.

References

Freedom House Reports (various years). Freedom House.

Heritage Foundation. (1995–2015). *Country rankings, different year (1995–2015)*. Heritage Foundation.

ITU. (various years). *Measuring information society reports*. ITU Geneva.

ITU World Telecommunication/ICT Indicators. (Edition 2016 and earlier). World Telecommunication Union.

Lechman, E. (2015). ICT diffusion in developing countries: Towards a new concept of technological takeoff. Springer.

United Nation Agency Integrated Implementation Framework. (2000–2010). United Nations.

World Development Indicators. (1990–2016). World Bank.

6   What Have We Learned From This Book?

ICT have triggered the profound transformation of economies and societies. The emergence of ICT has given rise to the emergence of totally new types of networks; thus, these technologies have reshaped the way that people communicate, work and live. The revolution that ICT have brought is deep and has far-reaching, long-term implications. This Digital Revolution has transformed the world faster and more extensively than any prior technological revolution has ever managed before. During the last four decades, the mobile telephony has reached almost every single person in the world; hardly anyone was left behind, and this is unprecedented in world history. Until the ICT Revolution began, multiple countries had never been offered many technological novelties and thus their economic isolation seriously grew through the ages. That is not to say that no technological progress had ever reached them, but their access to technological innovations was limited mainly because of financial, institutional and/or infrastructural and geographical constraints. Luckily, the ICT Revolution offers to the people technologies that may be adopted by materially deprived and poorly educated people living in physically isolated regions who suffer from infrastructural underdevelopment. ICT are cheap and easily distributable. It seems that, to a large extent, material poverty, unfavorable legal frameworks or poor infrastructures do not constitute barriers to rapid and unbounded ICT diffusion. As claimed by Hanna (2010), ICT are *opportunity windows* to all. Never before in human history have so many people been reached so fast by new and sophisticated technologies.

This book was designed to show the reader that new ICT, indeed, have rapidly diffused worldwide regardless of social, economic and institutional conditions encountered in examined high-income and upper-middle-income countries. Put differently, this extensive study was intended to demonstrate to the reader that today's world is undergoing an unprecedented next technological revolution—the Digital (ICT) Revolution. We have designed this study to unveil country-specific ICT diffusion patterns, to examine the dynamic of this process and its unique characteristics in each country in scope with our research. We have also aimed to show the unique process of reaching the critical mass along the technology diffusion trajectories, and the technological take-off that follows right after. Additionally, our aim was to answer the question, under what conditions do countries break out of technological stagnation into self-sustaining growth? Are these conditions 'common' for all countries? Or maybe each country follows its unique technology diffusion patterns, and we are unable to identify the bundle of prerequisites that enforce achieving critical mass and hence the emergence of the technological take-off. The question about the technological take-off prerequisites seems to be important, not only from the long-run economic policy perspective but also, above all, it gives us new knowledge on the nature of the process of new ICT dissemination worldwide. Achieving these goals was a challenging task, and we are fully aware that much work still needs to be done in this field of research.

What Have We Learnt From This Research?

First, we have learnt about the process of ICT diffusion across 47 high-income and 34 upper-middle-income countries between the period of 1980 and 2015. Here we have considered four core ICT indicators, which approximate access to and use of basic ICT. These are mobile-cellular telephony, fixed-broadband and wireless-broadband networks, and the share of population using the Internet (i. e. IU). Our research clearly demonstrates that between 1980 and 2015, ICT have diffused across all developed countries rapidly, and none of the examined economies has been omitted by the Digital Revolution. According to our calculations, the average mobile-cellular telephony penetration rates have increased from almost zero in 1990 to almost 130 per 100 inhabitants in 2015 in both country income groups. Regarding the process of deployment of fixed(wired) broadband networks, the results are less satisfactory, as, on average, only 30% and 11% of individuals had access to this type of ICT in 2015 in high-income and upper-middle-income countries, respectively. However, these relative 'shortages' in access to wired-broadband networks have been quickly compensated for by the extraordinary expansion of mobile (wireless) broadband technologies. Note that in 2015 in both country income groups, the average mobile-broadband penetration rates were close to 50%, thus half of society could enjoy access to this sophisticated telecommunication tool. The latter has enabled individuals in each country to access fixed- or mobile-broadband technologies, and thus respective statistics demonstrate relatively high usage of the Internet network (80% of individuals in high-income and 52% in upper-middle-income economies in 2015). Next, we have developed country-specific diffusion patterns in respect to mobile-cellular telephony, fixed-broadband and wireless-broadband networks, as well as the share of the population using the Internet and estimated parameters of the logistic growth model (for each individual country and for each ICT indicator separately). From the latter, we have learnt that ICT diffusion trajectories are very similar in shape in each of the examined countries. In fact, all ICT diffusion patterns are very homogenous, and they resemble the classical S-shaped time path. It is suggested that regardless of the external environment and conditions, new ICT diffuse in a similar way, passing analogous stages of development in each society (pre-take-off stage, exponential growth stage and stabilization (maturity) phase). This phenomenon of ICT diffusion paths' homogeneity shows that the process of ICT dissemination if endogenous in its nature and only if the specific critical mass of new users is reached, proceeds at an exponential rate, and the whole system inevitably heads towards full saturation to achieve maturity and stabilization. Additionally, we claim that from observations and empirical evidence, it can be easily concluded that the nature of the process of diffusion of new technologies speaks in support of the hypothesis of the existence of network effects (network externalities). These network effects are the seminal drivers of technology diffusion. On the one hand, they allow for the achievement of the critical mass along the technology diffusion path, and on the other hand, they enforce growth of a given technology network at an exponential rate, providing a solid background for its society- and economy-wide adoption.

Second, we have learnt that the phenomenally fast expansion of new ICT has enforced the emergence of another attractive process: *'fixed-to-mobile technological substitution'*. The *'fixed-to-mobile technological substitution'* mechanism demonstrates gradual switching from 'old' (here, fixed) technologies to 'new' (here, mobile/wireless) technologies. Confronting data on mobile-cellular telephony networks *versus* statistics on fixed (landline) telephony penetration rates, we have noted that across developed countries, the first ones are quickly evading national telecommunication markets, meaning that the role of 'old' telecommunication modes is radically diminishing. Evidently, in a great majority of countries in scope with our research, we have observed growing market shares possessed by mobile-cellular technology, which is happening at the expense of falling market shares possessed by traditional telephony. Interestingly, the analogous process of *'fixed-to-mobile technological substitution'* has been reported with regard to the Internet network infrastructure. Notably, fixed-broadband networks' importance in enabling connectivity with the Internet is gradually falling because of the fast spread of mobile (wireless) broadband solutions. Put shortly, we have demonstrated that in developed countries, 'new' technologies are used in place of 'old' ones. Furthermore, in the case of several specific countries, we also uncovered the technological leapfrogging effect,[1] demonstrating the process of the successful deployment of superior (more advanced) technologies in regions where their prior (old) versions have never been adopted, or their usage was negligible. Some countries have simply jumped over several stages of 'traditional' development and headed directly towards assimilation of the most advanced technological innovations. This unique process of technological leapfrogging was identified in countries where the adoption of landline telephony and/or the fixed-broadband network was negligible or even virtually nonexistent, and these countries have started to directly deploy mobile-cellular telephony and mobile-broadband networks, thus enabling them to connect with the outside world. As raised by Lee and Lim (2001) and Galperin (2005), this leapfrog-type development pattern is characteristic of those regions that—to some extent—have been 'forgotten' by past technological revolutions and until now did not have the opportunity to assimilate and benefit from technological progress. Today, the ongoing Digital Revolution offering wireless technologies has opened new opportunities for these technologically deprived regions, paving roads ahead to take advantage of new technologies. In that sense, new ICT are indeed revolutionary.

Third, we have learnt that in each of analyzed countries, the specific critical mass (critical penetration rate) was reached, which was followed by the emergence of the technological take-off. The latter shows that all examined countries managed to break out of the technological stagnation and take off into self-sustaining growth along ICT diffusion paths; henceforth, none of the examined countries remained virtually 'locked' in the early diffusion stage. The phenomenon of achieving the critical mass was explored by examining the country-specific diffusion patterns of mobile-cellular telephony as well as the development paths demonstrating growth of individuals using the Internet network in each analyzed economy. Table 6.1 outlines our general results regarding MCS/IU critical mass, critical year and length of the pre-take-off stage. Table 6.1 additionally summarizes critical conditions, which potentially might have enabled—or reversely hindered—entering the exponential growth phase along the MCS/IU diffusion path. A brief analysis of these findings gives rise to a few seminal conclusions. Despite the fact that across countries, the specific time periods (years) when the MCS critical penetration rates were achieved differed, the average lengths of the pre-take-off stage in both income groups are almost equal. Moreover, the average MCS critical mass also differs insignificantly between high-income and upper-middle-income economies. Very similar qualitative conclusions may be drawn when analyzing both average lengths of IU pre-take-off phase and the average levels of IU critical penetration rates; also, in this case, these values vary insignificantly between both country income groups. These findings support our initial supposition that technology diffusion follows the 'standard' sigmoid pattern and that the technology diffusion process demonstrates high endogeneity and, to a large extent, is driven by network externalities. To confirm the latter, we have also examined country-specific conditions (infrastructural, economic and institutional) that were identified during the MCS/IU critical years, which allowed for the contextualization of the emergence of the MCS/IU technological take-off.

Table 6.1 presents 'average' technological take-off critical conditions, which have been reported for both country income groups during MCS/IU critical years, while Figure 6.1 graphically displays the statistical relationships between the length of the MCS/IU pre-take-off phases *versus* technological take-off critical conditions in both country income groups.

Table 6.1 Technological take-offs critical conditions (average values). High-income and upper-middle-income economies. Period 1990–2015

	High-Income Economies	Upper-Middle-Income Economies
Mobile-cellular telephony		
Critical year	1996	2000
Critical mass (MCS penetration rate)	6.64	8.14
Length of pre-take-off phase (in years)	8.53	8.66
Fixed-telephony penetration rate	38.56	14.9
Prices of one-minute calls (peak, on net, in US dollars)	0.41	0.22
Prices of one SMS (peak, one net, in US dollars)	0.056	0.06
Type of competition on telecommunication market	FC 17	FC 12
	PC 10	PC 11
	M 2	M 5
		Duopoly 4
Economic freedom index	62.88	58.3
Investment freedom index	63.1	58.9
Country freedom status	Free 35	Free 11
	Partly free 4	Partly free 11
	Not free 4	Not free 10
GDP per capita	25,155	4,588
IU		
Critical year	1998	2004
Critical mass (IU penetration rate)	6.85	9.03
Length of pre-take-off phase (in years)	6.14	9.73
Fixed-broadband penetration rate	0.36	0.82
Active mobile-broadband penetration rate	0.99	9.72
Fixed-broadband subscription charge (in US dollars)	34.14	34.2
Type of competition on telecommunication market	FC 27	FC 24
	PC 4	PC 4
	M 2	M 4
Economic freedom index	65.16	59.19
Investment freedom index	64.87	52.74
Country freedom status	Free 35	Free 13
	Partly free 3	Partly free 10
	Not free 4	Not free 10
GDP per capita	26,774	5,145

Note: FC—full competition; PC—partial competition; M—monopoly.

Source: Author's elaboration.

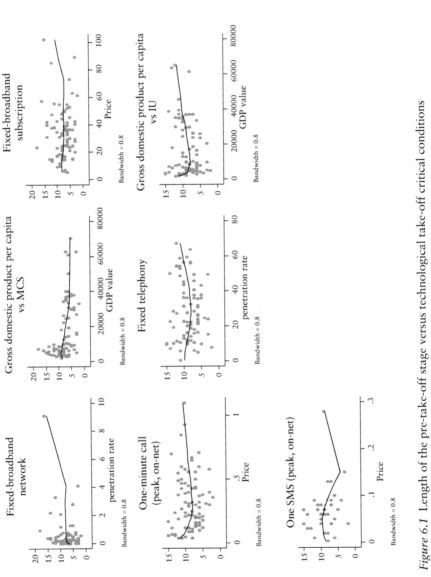

Figure 6.1 Length of the pre-take-off stage versus technological take-off critical conditions

Note: On the Y-axis, the length of the pre-take-off stage appears in years; not all values are logged. Data for high-income and upper-middle-income countries are included with bandwidth set as the default.

Source: Author's elaboration.

As we have already argued, diffusion is a dynamic process, and the in-time dynamism is its fundamental characteristic. Social, economic and institutional conditions differ across countries both at a certain moment of time and over time; therefore, we believe that learning what determines the diffusion pace and what are the prerequisites of the emergence of the technological take-off is essential to understanding it and analyzing it properly. In spite of similar previously identified average values of MCS/IU critical penetration rates and the MCS/IU average length pre-take-off phases in both country income groups, it might seem that the emergence of technological take-off took place under relatively unfavourable infrastructural, economic and institutional conditions. For instance, the average value of fixed-broadband or active mobile-broadband penetration rates were indecently low (compare respective data in Table 6.10). Additionally, in both income groups, the average FBS charge was relatively high (34 US$ dollars per month), thus this might potentially constitute an impeding factor of wide dissemination of wired Internet networks. When considering the FBS charge for each respective country (reported for IU critical years), we see that it ranges from 5.3 to 102.3 US$ dollars (sic!), while the calculated[2] correlation coefficient between the length of the IU pre-take-off phase and FBS charges results is 0.03, and it was statistically insignificant. The latter suggests that the price of monthly access to a fixed-broadband network is not a decisive factor which enforces or hinders the emergence of the IU technological take-off. This conclusion is additionally supported by the graphical evidence presented in Figure 6.1. We see that the fixed-broadband charges were extremely varied during the IU critical years. Analogous conclusions may be, however, derived in respect to other indicators, such as gross domestic product *per capita* and the telecommunication market competition type of the country freedom status. As summarized in Table 6.1, the IU technological take-off was reported even in 'not free' countries and/or in monopolized telecommunication markets. Additionally, these countries varied hugely in terms of economic (income) wealth. Note that in the best performing country, the GDP *per capita* was 70,477 US dollars, while in the worst performing country, it was only 2,052 US dollars. Interestingly, the correlation coefficient between the length of the IU pre-take-off stage and the GDP *per capita* (during the IU critical year) in −0.43 suggests that poorer countries take off earlier compared to wealthier ones. Results, similar in kind, are demonstrated with regard to critical conditions observed during the MCS critical years. Studying both data summarized in Table 6.1 and graphs displayed in Figure 6.1, we are not able to recognize (identify) any common and necessary conditions enabling the emergence of the MCS technological take-off. It seems that across the examined countries, the MCS technological take-off simply took place, regardless of the external (even hypothetically unfavourable) environment. Note that during the MCS critical years, the GDP *per capita* ranged from 1,761 to 65,115 US dollars, landline telephony penetration rates varied between 0.6 to 67.3 per 100 inhabitant and prices of one-minute calls ranged from

0.04 to 0.28 US dollars. Indeed, we did not find any statistically significant relationships between the length of the MCS pre-take-off stage and the values of selected indicators. Similar to what we have learnt from the analysis of IU technological take-off preconditions, the demand for mobile-cellular telephony was also boosted even in 'not free' countries and/or monopolized telecommunication markets.

The study of the process of ICT diffusion, as well as examining the country-unique conditions during their technological take-offs, was a challenging task. We have tried to establish whether the technological take-off is preconditioned by certain infrastructural, economic or institutional factors, or maybe it arrives at a specific point in time and is exclusively driven by the, social phenomenon, networks effects (externalities). Initially, we have hypothesized that there must exist a 'bundle' of prerequisites which enable societies and countries to break out of technological stagnation, leave the early diffusion phase characterized by spasmodic growth rates and take off into self-perpetuating (self-sustaining) growth. We believe that this assumption was rather rational. However, we have discovered that the process of diffusion of new ICT appears not to be sensitive to the changing environment and country-specific conditions. This is the reverse of what was expected; we did not diagnose the 'bundle of common conditions' which would constitute prerequisites for the emergence of the technological take-off. There is little evidence that technological take-off is driven by some specific critical conditions; it seems that it just happens regardless of the external conditions. Apparently, ICT demonstrate the unique ability to diffuse society- and economy-wide, irrespective of the external conditions. Technological take-offs were possible even in the absence of revolutionary institutional change in politically unfree countries across unfree telecommunication markets in materially deprived societies and regions suffering from permanent infrastructural backwardness. It is important to be aware of the fact that ICT are being quickly deployed, even under huge uncertainty. Most importantly, an impressive observation is that ICT diffusion becomes 'automatic' once a certain critical mass of new users is achieved. These are fundamental findings that contribute significantly to our understanding of the technology diffusion process. In fact, it seems to be astonishingly simply, endogenously strong and driven by interactions among social agents, which form a unique network of contacts. These social networks are a driving force for distributing new technologies, new ideas and new knowledge. However, is this type of endogeneity characteristic for all types of technology? Looking back at human history, it does not seem to be the case. Still many regions and societies are—to some extent—technologically backward, and they lack multiple achievements of past technological revolutions.

Throughout this study, we have managed to contextualize and integrate some facts and knowledge. We had confronted facts with suppositions. Although we are still some distance from knowing the exact mechanism, thanks to this study, we have moved at least one step ahead in understanding the complexity of the process of ICT dissemination worldwide, and this understanding is a necessary prerequisite that has been missing so that issues of economic change and growth can be tackled.

Notes

1. See for instance, Soete (1985), Steinmueller (2001) or Lee et al. (2005).
2. Author's calculations.

References

Galperin, H. (2005). Wireless networks and rural development: Opportunities for Latin America. *Information Technologies & International Development, 2*(3), 47.

Hanna, N. K. (2010). Transforming government and building the information society: Challenges and opportunities for the developing world. Springer Science & Business Media.

Lee, K., & Lim, C. (2001). Technological regimes, catching-up and leapfrogging: findings from the Korean industries. *Research Policy, 30*(3), 459–483.

Lee, K., Lim, C., & Song, W. (2005). Emerging digital technology as a window of opportunity and technological leapfrogging: Catch-up in digital TV by the Korean firms. *International Journal of Technology Management, 29*(1–2), 40–63.

Soete, L. (1985). International diffusion of technology, industrial development and technological leapfrogging. *World Development, 13*(3), 409–422.

Steinmueller, W. E. (2001). ICTs and the possibilities for leapfrogging by developing countries. *International Labour Review, 140*(2), 193–210.

Appendices

Appendix 1

Fixed-broadband network absolute changes in penetration rates. High-income and upper-middle-income economies. Periods 2005–2010 and 2010–2015

Country	FBS penetration rate change between 2010 and 2015—[A]	FBS penetration rate change between 2005 and 2010—[B]	Absolute difference between [B] and [A]	Country	FBS penetration rate change between 2010 and 2015—[A]	FBS penetration rate change between 2005 and 2010—[B]	Absolute difference between [B] and [A]
Argentina	6.10	7.58	1.48	Algeria	3.14	2.03	-1.11
Australia	3.26	14.77	11.51	Angola	0.57	0.06	-0.51
Austria	4.18	10.15	5.97	Azerbaijan	14.53	5.20	-9.33
Belgium	6.02	11.70	5.68	Belarus	13.79	17.54	3.76
Brunei Darussalam	2.58	3.21	0.63	Bosnia and Herzegovina	6.46	9.81	3.35
Canada	4.71	9.98	5.27	Botswana	1.18	0.52	-0.66
Chile	4.74	6.10	1.36	Brazil	5.01	5.49	0.47
Croatia	3.86	16.67	12.81	Bulgaria	7.19	13.07	5.88
Cyprus	4.76	14.53	9.77	China	9.27	6.46	-2.81
Czech Republic	6.47	14.49	8.02	Colombia	5.47	4.95	-0.51
Denmark	4.45	13.25	8.80	Costa Rica	2.68	7.45	4.76
Estonia	1.88	13.27	11.38	Dominican Republic	2.54	3.25	0.71
Finland	2.65	6.67	4.02	Ecuador	7.70	1.28	-6.42
France	7.60	18.33	10.73	Iran	9.54	1.30	-8.24

(Continued)

(Continued)

Country	FBS penetration rate change between 2010—[A]	FBS penetration rate change between 2005 and 2010—[B]	Absolute difference between [B] and [A]	Country	FBS penetration rate change between 2010 and 2015—[A]	FBS penetration rate change between 2005 and 2010—[B]	Absolute difference between [B] and [A]
Germany	5.68	18.65	12.97	Jamaica	1.57	2.58	1.01
Greece	10.45	18.83	8.37	Jordan	-0.38	4.09	4.47
Hungary	5.87	15.11	9.24	Kazakhstan	7.59	5.44	-2.15
Iceland	2.62	8.05	5.43	Lebanon	15.13	6.42	-8.71
Ireland	4.88	15.07	10.20	Macedonia	4.88	11.71	6.83
Israel	3.69	5.13	1.43	Malaysia	1.53	5.55	4.02
Italy	2.15	10.02	7.87	Maldives	1.70	3.68	1.98
Japan	3.71	8.43	4.72	Mauritius	8.11	7.19	-0.92
Korea (Rep.)	4.76	9.57	4.80	Mexico	2.67	7.24	4.57
Latvia	4.29	18.07	13.79	Namibia	1.29	0.43	-0.86
Lithuania	5.65	15.02	9.37	Panama	0.91	6.50	5.59
Malta	8.21	17.24	9.04	Paraguay	1.75	1.29	-0.46
Netherlands	3.64	12.94	9.30	Peru	3.23	1.91	-1.32
New Zealand	6.55	17.23	10.69	Romania	6.05	12.02	5.97
Norway	3.71	13.80	10.09	Serbia	5.88	10.46	4.58
Oman	3.52	1.56	-1.96	South Africa	3.81	1.10	-2.71
Poland	4.14	12.86	8.73	Suriname	6.60	2.66	-3.93
Portugal	9.53	8.99	-0.54	Thailand	4.34	4.05	-0.29
Qatar	1.72	5.21	3.49	Tunisia	-0.19	4.36	4.55
Russian Federation	7.84	9.83	1.98	Turkey	2.55	7.49	4.94

Saudi Arabia	5.73	6.00	0.27
Seychelles	6.87	6.36	-0.51
Singapore	0.10	11.76	11.66
Slovakia	7.20	12.77	5.57
Slovenia	4.73	13.07	8.35
Spain	5.24	11.46	6.22
Sweden	4.10	4.04	-0.05
Switzerland	7.58	14.68	7.09
United Arab Emirates	3.48	6.20	2.72
United Kingdom	6.87	14.44	7.57
United States	4.46	9.91	5.45
Uruguay	14.89	9.91	-4.98
Venezuela	2.48	4.43	1.94

Source: Author's calculations.

Appendix 2

Active mobile-broadband and fixed-broadband absolute changes in penetration rates. High-income and upper-middle-income economies. Period 2010–2015.

Country	Active mobile-broadband change	Fixed-broadband change	Country	Active mobile-broadband change	Fixed-broadband change
Argentina	62.29	6.10	Algeria	40.11	3.14
Australia	57.40	3.26	Angola	17.95	0.57
Austria	35.72	4.18	Azerbaijan	55.89	14.53
Belgium	57.08	6.02	Belarus	49.19	13.79
Brunei Darussalam	1.29	2.58	Bosnia and Herzegovina	28.17	6.46
Canada	26.94	4.71	Botswana	65.79	1.18
Chile	49.19	4.74	Brazil	78.06	5.01
Croatia	67.85	3.86	Bulgaria	46.36	7.19
Cyprus	25.34	4.76	China	52.57	9.27
Czech Republic	34.89	6.47	Colombia	38.58	5.47
Denmark	52.92	4.45	Costa Rica	88.28	2.68
Estonia	89.44	1.88	Dominican Republic	37.18	2.54
Finland	59.80	2.65	Ecuador	26.27	7.70
France	38.43	7.60	Iran	20.02	9.54
Germany	49.56	5.68	Jamaica	52.03	1.57
Greece	20.57	10.45	Jordan	35.48	-0.38
Hungary	32.04	5.87	Kazakhstan	36.73	7.59
Iceland	47.80	2.62	Lebanon	53.43	15.13
Ireland	45.86	4.88	Macedonia	37.81	4.88
Israel	23.72	3.69	Malaysia	80.82	1.53
Italy	44.35	2.15	Maldives	57.19	1.70
Japan	38.80	3.71	Mauritius	22.61	8.11

Country			Country		
Korea (Rep.)	12.01	4.76	Mexico	46.27	2.67
Latvia	37.38	4.29	Namibia	47.82	1.29
Lithuania	65.15	5.65	Panama	29.45	0.91
Malta	43.80	8.21	Paraguay	36.53	1.75
Netherlands	32.54	3.64	Peru	35.80	3.23
New Zealand	75.60	6.55	Romania	54.25	6.05
Norway	18.48	3.71	Serbia	53.77	5.88
Oman	52.07	3.52	South Africa	42.56	3.81
Poland	10.02	4.14	Suriname	75.85	6.60
Portugal	27.81	9.53	Thailand	75.28	4.34
Qatar	28.41	1.72	Tunisia	61.76	-0.19
Russian Federation	36.77	7.84	Turkey	40.93	2.55
Saudi Arabia	85.99	5.73			
Seychelles	17.58	6.87			
Singapore	43.83	0.10			
Slovakia	46.75	7.20			
Slovenia	27.90	4.73			
Spain	58.25	5.24			
Sweden	38.31	4.10			
Switzerland	67.55	7.58			
United Arab Emirates	78.63	3.48			
United Kingdom	44.63	6.87			
United States	49.17	4.46			
Uruguay	64.27	14.89			
Venezuela	21.55	2.48			

Source: Author's calculations

Appendix 3

MCS critical mass calculations. Marginal growths and replication coefficients. High-income and upper-middle-income economies. Period 1980–2015

High-income economies

Year	Argentina $\Omega_{i,t}$	Argentina $\phi_{i,t}$	Australia $\Omega_{i,t}$	Australia $\phi_{i,t}$	Austria $\Omega_{i,t}$	Austria $\phi_{i,t}$	Belgium $\Omega_{i,t}$	Belgium $\phi_{i,t}$	Brunei Darussalam $\Omega_{i,t}$	Brunei Darussalam $\phi_{i,t}$	Canada $\Omega_{i,t}$	Canada $\phi_{i,t}$	Chile $\Omega_{i,t}$	Chile $\phi_{i,t}$	Croatia $\Omega_{i,t}$	Croatia $\phi_{i,t}$	Cyprus $\Omega_{i,t}$	Cyprus $\phi_{i,t}$	Czech Republic $\Omega_{i,t}$	Czech Republic $\phi_{i,t}$
1986					0.12	1.95	0.03	1.90			0.18	4.94								
1987					0.09	1.37	0.12	2.65			0.14	1.62								
1988			0.16	7.03	0.14	1.40	0.12	1.60			0.38	2.03					0.16	7.87	0.03	3.74
1989			0.37	2.94	0.18	1.37	0.12	1.39			0.51	1.68					0.23	2.29	0.09	3.02
1990	0.03	5.14	0.52	1.93	0.30	1.45	0.08	1.20			0.85	1.67					0.24	1.59	0.16	2.17
1991	0.03	2.05	0.60	1.56	0.53	1.55	0.10	1.19	0.45	1.66	0.66	1.31	0.16	2.55	0.04	8.40	0.56	1.86	0.18	1.61
1992	0.06	1.83	1.15	1.69	0.72	1.48	0.06	1.10	0.36	1.32	0.85	1.31	0.20	1.75	0.09	3.14	0.65	1.53	1.47	4.10
1993	0.19	2.37	1.06	1.37	0.59	1.27	0.59	1.88	1.46	1.97	1.03	1.28	0.14	1.30	0.11	1.81	0.87	1.47	3.16	2.63
1994	0.37	2.12	2.91	1.75	0.70	1.25	1.05	1.83	2.46	1.83	1.79	1.38	0.20	1.33	0.22	1.92	2.46	1.90	4.28	1.84
1995	0.46	1.66	5.56	1.82	1.30	1.37	2.38	2.03	6.72	2.24	2.40	1.37	0.55	1.68	0.26	1.57	2.91	1.56	9.55	2.02
1996	0.72	1.62	9.39	1.76	2.67	1.56	4.85	2.03	2.22	1.18	2.98	1.34	0.81	1.59	0.68	1.95	2.22	1.27	23.46	2.24
1997	3.73	2.97	2.90	1.13	7.00	1.94	7.63	1.80	0.13	1.01	2.22	1.19	0.58	1.26	1.22	1.87	2.50	1.24	25.50	1.60
1998	1.76	1.31	1.51	1.06	14.16	1.98	13.93	1.81	0.96	1.07	3.69	1.26	3.64	2.32	1.39	1.53	3.56	1.28	16.40	1.24
1999	3.14	1.42	7.02	1.27	24.45	1.85	23.71	1.76	4.85	1.31	4.99	1.28	8.41	2.31	2.53	1.63	6.76	1.41	10.85	1.13
2000	7.04	1.66	11.27	1.34	23.19	1.44	19.90	1.36	8.29	1.41	5.71	1.25	7.20	1.49	16.54	3.53	9.55	1.41	10.48	1.11
2001	0.50	1.02	12.67	1.28	4.99	1.07	3.64	1.05	13.53	1.47	5.94	1.21	10.61	1.48	16.38	1.71	9.96	1.30	9.47	1.09
2002	-0.63	0.96	7.14	1.13	1.98	1.02	4.51	1.06	2.18	1.05	3.58	1.10	6.86	1.21	12.78	1.32	12.63	1.30	5.64	1.05
2003	3.20	1.18	7.64	1.12	6.09	1.07	4.59	1.06	5.79	1.13	4.12	1.11	5.97	1.15	5.27	1.10	9.52	1.17		
2004	14.61	1.70	9.61	1.13	8.21	1.09	3.94	1.05	5.96	1.12	4.99	1.12	11.84	1.26	6.93	1.12	10.98	1.17		
2005	22.05	1.62	8.25	1.10	7.63	1.08	1.60	1.02	7.20	1.13	5.70	1.12	7.41	1.13	18.71	1.29	7.00	1.09		
2006	23.49	1.41	4.94	1.06	6.95	1.07			17.11	1.27	4.73	1.09	10.74	1.17	17.22	1.21				

Year	Denmark		Estonia		Finland		France		Germany		Greece		Hungary		Iceland		Ireland		Israel	
	$\Omega_{i,t}$	$\phi_{i,t}$	$\Omega_{i,t}$	$\phi_{i,t}$	$\Omega_{i,t}$	$\phi_{i,t}$	$\Omega_{i,t}$	$\phi_{i,t}$	$\Omega_{i,t}$	$\phi_{i,t}$	$\Omega_{i,t}$	$\phi_{i,t}$	$\Omega_{i,t}$	$\phi_{i,t}$	$\Omega_{i,t}$	$\phi_{i,t}$	$\Omega_{i,t}$	$\phi_{i,t}$	$\Omega_{i,t}$	$\phi_{i,t}$
1981					0.10	1.20														
1982					0.11	1.19														
1983	0.17	2.24			0.17	1.24														
1984	0.28	1.90			0.20	1.23														
1985	0.30	1.51			0.31	1.29														
1986	0.22	1.25			0.35	1.26			0.03	21.99							0.03	4.99		
1987	0.39	1.34			0.41	1.24	0.05	4.31	0.03	2.04					0.95	1.87	0.06	2.32		
1988	0.47	1.31			0.65	1.30	0.10	2.49	0.06	2.02					0.58	1.29	0.08	1.82		
1989	0.43	1.22			1.04	1.37	0.14	1.81	0.08	1.65					0.52	1.20	0.21	2.16		
1990	0.47	1.19			1.35	1.35	0.18	1.58	0.13	1.66					0.80	1.26	0.32	1.84		
1991	0.53	1.18			1.20	1.23	0.16	1.32	0.32	1.94			0.06	3.21	1.08	1.27	0.20	1.28	0.16	1.46
1992	0.67	1.20	0.13	4.46	1.30	1.20	0.10	1.16	0.53	1.81			0.14	2.75	0.86	1.17	0.34	1.37	0.26	1.52
1993	2.81	1.69	0.32	2.95	2.00	1.26	0.23	1.30	0.97	1.81			0.22	1.96	0.77	1.13	0.47	1.38	0.54	1.72
1994	2.77	1.40	0.46	1.95	3.62	1.37	0.53	1.54	0.85	1.39	0.99	3.15	0.94	3.13	1.61	1.24	0.74	1.43	1.29	2.00
1995	6.05	1.63	1.18	2.25	7.06	1.53	0.72	1.47	1.47	1.49	1.11	1.77	1.18	1.85	3.30	1.40	1.92	1.78	5.77	3.23
1996	9.34	1.59	2.80	2.32	8.96	1.44	1.98	1.88	2.13	1.48	2.39	1.93	2.02	1.79	5.78	1.50	3.56	1.81	10.74	2.29
1997	2.31	1.09	5.40	2.10	12.77	1.44	5.73	2.35	3.30	1.50	3.71	1.75	2.27	1.50	6.63	1.38	6.92	1.87	10.61	1.56
1998	9.08	1.33	7.51	1.73	13.16	1.31	9.16	1.92	6.75	1.68	10.13	2.17	3.56	1.52	13.88	1.58	10.67	1.72	7.54	1.25
1999	12.97	1.36	10.30	1.58	8.15	1.15	17.27	1.90	11.42	1.69	16.87	1.90	5.47	1.53	24.17	1.64	19.19	1.75	11.64	1.31
2000	13.59	1.28	12.64	1.45	8.65	1.14	12.67	1.35	29.64	2.06	18.33	1.51	14.21	1.89	14.41	1.23	19.99	1.45	24.28	1.50
2001	10.95	1.17	7.23	1.18	8.45	1.12	13.01	1.27	9.43	1.16	18.32	1.34	18.63	1.62	10.94	1.14	12.13	1.19	16.57	1.23
2007	21.90	1.27	5.36	1.06	7.13	1.06	7.56	1.08	15.55	1.19	3.98	1.07	8.28	1.11	14.85	1.15	10.19	1.12	7.22	1.06
2008	14.50	1.14	2.13	1.02	10.40	1.09	4.72	1.05	6.80	1.07	4.73	1.08	4.19	1.05	-10.76	0.91	1.43	1.02	4.39	1.03
2009	13.90	1.11	-1.46	0.99	6.92	1.05	3.12	1.03	1.89	1.04	4.34	1.07	8.90	1.10	3.01	1.03	-4.76	0.95	-7.78	0.94
2010	10.25	1.07	-0.31	1.00	9.11	1.07	2.68	1.02	3.93	1.00	5.13	1.07	18.94	1.20	6.13	1.06	4.06	1.05	-2.01	0.98
2011	7.70	1.05	4.18	1.04	8.73	1.06	2.45	1.02	0.39	1.05	2.15	1.03	13.18	1.11	4.69	1.04	4.02	1.04	1.54	1.01
2012	7.47	1.05	0.98	1.01	6.11	1.04	-2.20	0.98	4.93	0.98	1.74	1.02	8.15	1.06	-2.89	0.98	0.69	1.01	2.75	1.02
2013	5.96	1.03	1.26	1.01	-4.31	0.97	-0.43	1.00	-1.73	0.95	1.04	1.01	-2.79	0.98	-5.36	0.95	-2.04	0.98	1.34	1.01
2014	-16.04	0.90	24.39	1.23	-4.32	0.97	3.37	1.03	-5.39	1.01	0.43	1.01	-1.05	0.99	-5.62	0.95	-0.02	1.00	1.35	1.01
2015	-2.57	0.98	1.57	1.01	5.50	1.04	1.42	1.01	1.31	1.01	0.89	1.01	-3.77	0.97	-0.66	0.99	-0.93	0.99	-0.33	1.00

(Continued)

(Continued)

Year	Denmark $\Omega_{i,t}$	Denmark $\phi_{i,t}$	Estonia $\Omega_{i,t}$	Estonia $\phi_{i,t}$	Finland $\Omega_{i,t}$	Finland $\phi_{i,t}$	France $\Omega_{i,t}$	France $\phi_{i,t}$	Germany $\Omega_{i,t}$	Germany $\phi_{i,t}$	Greece $\Omega_{i,t}$	Greece $\phi_{i,t}$	Hungary $\Omega_{i,t}$	Hungary $\phi_{i,t}$	Iceland $\Omega_{i,t}$	Iceland $\phi_{i,t}$	Ireland $\Omega_{i,t}$	Ireland $\phi_{i,t}$	Israel $\Omega_{i,t}$	Israel $\phi_{i,t}$
2002	9.44	1.13	17.37	1.36	6.38	1.08	2.18	1.04	3.51	1.05	12.16	1.17	19.00	1.39	3.41	1.04	-0.60	0.99	11.24	1.13
2003	5.16	1.06	13.04	1.20	4.20	1.05	4.64	1.07	6.68	1.09	-3.47	0.96	10.61	1.16	5.70	1.06	11.05	1.14	3.27	1.03
2004	7.15	1.08	15.87	1.20	4.34	1.05	4.12	1.06	7.72	1.11	3.49	1.04	7.92	1.10	2.48	1.03	7.21	1.08	7.40	1.07
2005	4.87	1.05	14.79	1.16	5.05	1.05	5.24	1.07	9.49	1.11	8.43	1.10	6.06	1.07	-3.54	0.96	8.22	1.09	5.81	1.05
2006	6.54	1.06	16.69	1.15	7.18	1.07	5.27	1.07	7.73	1.08	6.42	1.07	6.58	1.07	5.00	1.05	8.29	1.08	6.87	1.06
2007	8.25	1.08	2.31	1.02	7.25	1.07	5.45	1.07	12.86	1.13	11.75	1.12	10.74	1.11	6.52	1.06	4.87	1.04	4.12	1.03
2008	3.93	1.03	-3.87	0.97	13.54	1.12	3.69	1.04	11.42	1.10	13.41	1.12	12.05	1.11	1.96	1.02	0.15	1.00	-2.07	0.98
2009	4.40	1.04	-3.68	0.97	15.66	1.12	-0.58	0.99	-0.33	1.00	-4.71	0.96	-4.12	0.97	-0.64	0.99	-9.34	0.92	-2.35	0.98
2010	-8.03	0.94	6.75	1.06	12.22	1.08	-0.71	0.99	-19.74	0.84	-9.15	0.92	2.38	1.02	-1.01	0.99	-1.43	0.99	-1.25	0.99
2011	12.99	1.11	16.64	1.13	9.59	1.06	2.69	1.03	3.18	1.03	-1.57	0.99	-3.00	0.97	-0.40	1.00	3.24	1.03	-0.81	0.99
2012	1.62	1.01	16.48	1.11	6.43	1.04	3.30	1.04	1.93	1.02	11.02	1.10	-0.87	0.99	1.21	1.01	1.09	1.01	-1.29	0.99
2013	-5.15	0.96	-0.75	1.00	-35.74	0.79	1.12	1.01	9.33	1.08	-3.28	0.97	0.36	1.00	0.06	1.00	-4.09	0.96	2.16	1.02
2014	1.82	1.01	1.03	1.01	3.09	1.02	2.72	1.03	-0.50	1.00	-6.56	0.94	1.63	1.01	2.97	1.03	-0.41	1.00	-1.40	0.99
2015	1.39	1.01	-12.00	0.93	-4.16	0.97	1.40	1.01	-3.71	0.97	3.72	1.03	0.86	1.01	2.93	1.03	-1.36	0.99	12.02	1.10

Year	Italy $\Omega_{i,t}$	Italy $\phi_{i,t}$	Japan $\Omega_{i,t}$	Japan $\phi_{i,t}$	Korea (Rep.) $\Omega_{i,t}$	Korea (Rep.) $\phi_{i,t}$	Latvia $\Omega_{i,t}$	Latvia $\phi_{i,t}$	Lithuania $\Omega_{i,t}$	Lithuania $\phi_{i,t}$	Malta $\Omega_{i,t}$	Malta $\phi_{i,t}$	Netherlands $\Omega_{i,t}$	Netherlands $\phi_{i,t}$	New Zealand $\Omega_{i,t}$	New Zealand $\phi_{i,t}$	Norway $\Omega_{i,t}$	Norway $\phi_{i,t}$	Oman $\Omega_{i,t}$	Oman $\phi_{i,t}$
1982	0.00		0.01	1.48													0.23	6.60		
1983	0.01		0.01	1.36													0.30	2.12		
1984	0.03		0.01	1.48													0.37	1.66		
1985	0.06		0.02	1.52													0.58	1.61		
1986	0.35	1.41	0.03	1.53									0.07	3.17			0.57	1.38		
1987	0.53	1.83	0.05	1.58	0.01	1.43							0.06	1.57			0.78	1.37		
1988	0.38	2.03	0.08	1.61	0.02	1.96							0.06	1.36	0.23	4.14	0.75	1.26		
1989	0.74	1.97	0.20	2.01	0.04	1.93							0.15	1.69	0.56	2.87	0.35	1.10		
1990	1.81	4.03	0.31	1.77	0.09	1.99							0.15	1.40	0.73	1.85	0.67	1.17		
1991	2.95	2.13	0.41	1.58	0.20	2.06							0.24	1.45	0.51	1.32	0.86	1.18		
1992		1.38	0.27	1.24	0.24	1.62					0.31	1.52	0.33	1.43	0.76	1.36	1.10	1.20		
1993		1.54	0.33	1.24	0.45	1.72	0.11	3.76	0.03	4.67	0.45	1.50	0.32	1.29	1.17	1.41	2.02	1.31		
1994		1.85	1.77	2.02	1.09	2.02	0.18	2.24	0.09	3.65	0.55	1.40	0.68	1.48	2.57	1.64	4.96	1.58		
1995		1.75	5.92	2.70	1.51	1.70	0.27	1.82	0.28	3.30	0.81	1.43	1.40	1.67	3.33	1.50	8.93	1.66		

1996	4.39	1.64	12.15	2.29	3.40	1.93	0.56	1.92	1.01	3.47	0.41	1.15	3.05	1.87	3.32	1.33	6.25	1.28
1997	9.35	1.83	9.03	1.42	8.13	2.15	2.01	2.73	3.20	3.26	1.27	1.41	4.46	1.68	1.83	1.14	9.24	1.32
1998	15.41	1.75	7.17	1.23	15.61	2.03	3.77	2.19	2.91	1.63	1.17	1.27	10.36	1.94	5.79	1.38	8.67	1.23
1999	17.23	1.48	7.54	1.20	20.43	1.66	4.52	1.65	1.88	1.25	3.67	1.66	21.41	2.00	15.66	1.75	12.98	1.28
2000	20.86	1.39	7.82	1.17	7.08	1.14	5.46	1.48	5.58	1.59	18.83	3.03	25.05	1.59	3.43	1.09	12.13	1.20
2001	15.46	1.21	6.27	1.12	4.55	1.08	11.09	1.66	14.43	1.96	30.44	2.08	8.68	1.13	18.60	1.47	7.81	1.11
2002	4.67	1.05	4.86	1.08	6.83	1.11	11.57	1.41	18.69	1.64	8.93	1.15	−1.06	0.99	3.25	1.06	3.96	1.05
2003	3.84	1.04	4.24	1.07	2.39	1.03	13.73	1.35	14.13	1.29	2.98	1.04	6.39	1.08	2.83	1.05	5.51	1.07
2004	9.59	1.10	3.67	1.05	6.08	1.08	14.76	1.28	29.31	1.47	3.66	1.05	9.42	1.12	9.57	1.15	9.56	1.11
2005	14.17	1.13	3.83	1.05	3.35	1.04	15.95	1.23	40.92	1.45	4.04	1.05	5.89	1.06	11.18	1.15	4.20	1.04
2006	14.26	1.12	2.53	1.03	3.48	1.04	15.36	1.18	13.22	1.10	5.13	1.07	8.49	1.09	5.47	1.06	1.47	1.01
2007	14.84	1.11	5.83	1.07	8.27	1.10	2.92	1.03	8.30	1.06	4.79	1.06	11.67	1.11	9.58	1.11	2.42	1.02
2008	−0.08	1.00	2.35	1.03	2.01	1.02	5.20	1.05	5.81	1.04	3.61	1.04	7.70	1.07	7.55	1.08	2.36	1.02
2009	−1.38	0.99	4.61	1.05	4.27	1.04	1.56	1.01	0.16	1.00	8.17	1.09	−3.32	0.97	0.73	1.01	1.66	1.02
2010	5.29	1.04	5.49	1.06	5.23	1.05	1.26	1.01	−0.55	1.00	7.45	1.07	−6.23	0.95	−0.90	0.99	3.74	1.03
2011	3.35	1.02	7.47	1.08	2.97	1.03	1.05	1.01	2.83	1.02	15.11	1.14	3.55	1.03	1.37	1.01	1.34	1.01
2012	1.48	1.01	6.63	1.06	1.69	1.02	16.32	1.15	2.83	1.02	2.05	1.02	−1.01	0.99	1.16	1.01	0.28	1.00
2013	−0.81	0.99	5.41	1.05	1.57	1.01	−2.92	0.98	−13.71	0.92	5.33	1.04	−1.81	0.98	−4.59	0.96	0.18	1.00
2014	−4.53	0.97	3.92	1.03	4.71	1.04	−7.96	0.94	−9.48	0.94	−2.77	0.98	0.27	1.00	6.28	1.06	−0.14	1.00
2015	−2.97	0.98	4.82	1.04	2.75	1.02	10.18	1.09	−2.34	0.98	2.31	1.02	7.12	1.06	9.78	1.09	−2.56	0.98

Year	*Poland*		*Portugal*		*Qatar*		*Russian Federation*		*Saudi Arabia*		*Seychelles*		*Singapore*		*Slovakia*		*Slovenia*		*Spain*	
	$\Omega_{i.t}$	$\phi_{i.t}$	$\Omega_{i.t}$	$\phi_{i.t}$	$\Omega_{i.t}$	$\phi_{i.t}$	$\Omega_{i.t}$	$\phi_{i.t}$	$\Omega_{i.t}$	$\phi_{i.t}$	$\Omega_{i.t}$	$\phi_{i.t}$	$\Omega_{i.t}$	$\phi_{i.t}$	$\Omega_{i.t}$	$\phi_{i.t}$	$\Omega_{i.t}$	$\phi_{i.t}$	$\Omega_{i.t}$	$\phi_{i.t}$
1987																			0.01	2.47
1988																			0.02	2.76
1989													0.52	2.38					0.05	2.56
1990			0.04	2.34									0.82	1.92					0.06	1.83
1991			0.06	1.93	0.04	1.05			0.00	1.00			0.93	1.54					0.14	1.98
1992			0.25	2.95	0.03	1.03	0.00	19.97	0.00	1.00			1.12	1.42	0.03	12.87	0.15	6.70	0.18	1.66
1993	0.04	7.14	0.64	2.71	0.01	1.01	0.00	1.67	0.00	0.98			1.68	1.45	0.03	2.03	0.15	1.86	0.19	1.42
1994	0.06	2.48	0.71	1.70	1.46	2.67	0.01	2.78	0.00	0.98			1.51	1.28	0.05	1.90	0.49	2.52	0.39	1.60
1995	0.09	1.92	1.65	1.96	1.36	1.58	0.04	3.19	0.00	0.98			1.83	1.26	0.12	2.07	0.55	1.67	1.35	2.29
1996	0.37	2.89	3.17	1.94	1.93	1.52	0.09	2.52	0.93	11.74	1.30	20.60	3.29	1.37	0.30	2.32	0.70	1.51	5.19	3.16

(Continued)

(Continued)

Year	Poland $\Omega_{i,t}$	Poland $\phi_{i,t}$	Portugal $\Omega_{i,t}$	Portugal $\phi_{i,t}$	Qatar $\Omega_{i,t}$	Qatar $\phi_{i,t}$	Russian Federation $\Omega_{i,t}$	Russian Federation $\phi_{i,t}$	Saudi Arabia $\Omega_{i,t}$	Saudi Arabia $\phi_{i,t}$	Seychelles $\Omega_{i,t}$	Seychelles $\phi_{i,t}$	Singapore $\Omega_{i,t}$	Singapore $\phi_{i,t}$	Slovakia $\Omega_{i,t}$	Slovakia $\phi_{i,t}$	Slovenia $\Omega_{i,t}$	Slovenia $\phi_{i,t}$	Spain $\Omega_{i,t}$	Spain $\phi_{i,t}$
1997	1.55	3.75	8.26	2.26	2.60	1.46	0.18	2.18	0.73	1.72	1.55	2.13	11.16	1.92	3.19	6.97	2.64	2.27	3.37	1.44
1998	2.91	2.38	15.28	2.03	3.74	1.46	0.18	1.54	1.51	1.87	3.75	2.29	6.08	1.26	4.92	2.32	3.42	1.73	5.25	1.48
1999	5.29	2.05	15.44	1.51	2.80	1.23	0.42	1.84	1.01	1.31	14.06	3.11	13.36	1.46	3.68	1.43	23.62	3.91	21.36	2.32
2000	7.29	1.71	19.15	1.42	5.61	1.38	1.29	2.39	2.57	1.60	11.82	1.57	27.46	1.64	10.75	1.87	29.36	1.92	22.68	1.60
2001	8.52	1.48	12.40	1.19	8.73	1.43	3.08	2.38	5.27	1.77	12.69	1.39	4.24	1.06	16.77	1.73	12.78	1.21	12.53	1.21
2002	10.20	1.39	6.33	1.08	13.27	1.46	6.80	2.28	10.84	1.90	8.91	1.20	5.74	1.08	14.41	1.36	9.89	1.13	8.33	1.11
2003	9.19	1.25	12.42	1.15	14.68	1.35	12.84	2.06	8.73	1.38	4.31	1.08	3.97	1.05	14.03	1.26	3.56	1.04	7.49	1.09
2004	14.93	1.33	5.07	1.05	11.04	1.19	26.14	2.05	6.82	1.22	4.95	1.08	7.14	1.08	11.06	1.16	5.35	1.06	1.84	1.02
2005	15.92	1.26	8.02	1.08	19.22	1.28	32.29	1.63	18.88	1.49	4.12	1.06	6.32	1.07	4.87	1.06	-4.74	0.95	7.97	1.09
2006	19.87	1.26	7.13	1.07	7.77	1.09	21.47	1.26	20.28	1.35	12.22	1.18	6.24	1.06	6.45	1.08	2.62	1.03	5.36	1.05
2007	12.17	1.13	11.64	1.10	14.64	1.15	14.33	1.14	31.94	1.41	6.96	1.09	21.41	1.21	21.59	1.24	4.89	1.05	4.65	1.04
2008	6.64	1.06	5.24	1.04	-4.52	0.96	19.69	1.17	26.95	1.25	17.28	1.20	7.11	1.06	-10.32	0.91	5.64	1.06	1.27	1.01
2009	2.29	1.02	-21.44	0.84	19.42	1.18	21.23	1.15	30.89	1.23	18.21	1.18	6.39	1.05	-0.59	0.99	1.65	1.02	1.90	1.02
2010	5.60	1.05	3.83	1.03	0.37	1.00	5.40	1.03	21.74	1.13	6.74	1.06	6.71	1.05	7.71	1.08	0.55	1.01	-0.30	1.00
2011	8.38	1.07	1.09	1.01	-4.48	0.96	-23.45	0.86	5.34	1.03	8.98	1.07	4.72	1.03	0.93	1.01	1.87	1.02	1.79	1.02
2012	10.25	1.08	-4.00	0.97	6.38	1.05	3.28	1.02	-7.15	0.96	9.90	1.07	2.01	1.01	1.93	1.02	3.22	1.03	-4.70	0.96
2013	7.53	1.05	0.65	1.01	25.79	1.20	7.51	1.05	-3.16	0.98	-0.46	1.00	3.80	1.02	2.00	1.02	1.82	1.02	-1.48	0.99
2014	-0.19	1.00	-0.92	0.99	-6.88	0.95	2.31	1.02	-4.65	0.97	14.85	1.10	-9.04	0.94	3.03	1.03	1.87	1.02	1.06	1.01
2015	-0.18	1.00	-1.70	0.98	7.82	1.05	4.81	1.03	-2.97	0.98	-4.07	0.97	-0.75	0.99	5.37	1.05	1.14	1.01	-0.05	1.00

Year	Sweden $\Omega_{i,t}$	Sweden $\phi_{i,t}$	Switzerland $\Omega_{i,t}$	Switzerland $\phi_{i,t}$	United Arab Emirates $\Omega_{i,t}$	United Arab Emirates $\phi_{i,t}$	United Kingdom $\Omega_{i,t}$	United Kingdom $\phi_{i,t}$	United States $\Omega_{i,t}$	United States $\phi_{i,t}$	Uruguay $\Omega_{i,t}$	Uruguay $\phi_{i,t}$	Venezuela $\Omega_{i,t}$	Venezuela $\phi_{i,t}$
1982	0.08	1.34			0.09	1.45								
1983	0.11	1.33			0.09	1.32								
1984	0.26	1.59			0.20	1.52								
1985	0.18	1.26			0.20	1.33	0.14	2.60	0.10	3.68				
1986	0.47	1.54			0.12	1.15	0.28	2.23	0.14	1.98				
1987	0.71	1.53							0.22	1.79				

Year														
1988	0.82	1.40	0.38	5.59	-0.05	0.95	0.47	1.93	0.33	1.66				
1989	1.23	1.43	0.63	2.35	0.60	1.70	0.72	1.74	0.56	1.68			0.01	2.00
1990	1.29	1.31	0.77	1.70	0.40	1.27	0.24	1.14	0.68	1.49			0.02	1.96
1991	1.21	1.22	0.72	1.38	0.40	1.21	0.25	1.13	0.86	1.42			0.04	2.18
1992	0.97	1.15	0.57	1.22	0.18	1.08	0.42	1.19	1.31	1.45			0.30	4.62
1993	1.30	1.17	0.58	1.19	0.90	1.37	1.31	1.50	1.85	1.44	0.10	2.88	0.48	2.27
1994	6.85	1.77	1.03	1.28	0.77	1.23	2.88	1.73	3.00	1.49	0.06	1.36	0.61	1.71
1995	7.04	1.45	1.60	1.34	1.40	1.34	3.08	1.45	3.50	1.38	1.02	5.80	0.35	1.24
1996	5.41	1.24	3.01	1.47	2.35	1.43	2.57	1.26	3.63	1.29	1.18	1.96	0.75	1.41
1997	7.61	1.27	5.34	1.57	4.01	1.51	2.69	1.22	3.90	1.24	0.61	1.25	2.08	1.81
1998	10.60	1.30	9.15	1.62	6.06	1.61	10.27	1.68	4.75	1.24	1.56	1.52	3.90	1.84
1999	11.46	1.25	18.96	1.79	10.85	1.64	20.87	1.82	5.69	1.23	5.05	2.10	7.25	1.85
2000	13.99	1.24	21.89	1.51	18.43	1.29	27.42	1.59	7.89	1.26	2.73	1.28	6.51	1.41
2001	8.93	1.12	8.53	1.13	13.77	1.24	4.49	1.06	6.22	1.16	3.26	1.26	3.71	1.17
2002	8.45	1.10	5.95	1.08	14.35	1.17	4.63	1.06	4.16	1.09	-0.20	0.99	-0.20	0.99
2003	9.22	1.10	5.69	1.07	12.91	1.14	8.05	1.10	6.00	1.12	-0.47	0.97	1.37	1.05
2004	-0.61	0.99	0.53	1.01	12.45	1.09	8.62	1.09	7.70	1.14	3.08	1.21	4.87	1.18
2005	3.00	1.03	6.81	1.08	8.62	1.04	9.09	1.09	5.77	1.09	16.69	1.92	14.69	1.46
2006	4.87	1.05	7.14	1.08	3.92	1.18	7.01	1.06	7.98	1.12	35.23	2.01	22.35	1.48
2007	4.76	1.05	9.13	1.09	20.16	1.03	5.50	1.05	5.77	1.08	20.03	1.29	17.03	1.25
2008	-2.02	0.98	7.73	1.07	4.28	1.00	1.08	1.01	3.15	1.04	14.75	1.16	11.36	1.13
2009	3.69	1.03	4.15	1.04	0.63	0.94	1.77	1.01	3.41	1.04	17.61	1.17	0.90	1.01
2010	5.03	1.04	2.76	1.02	-8.84	1.02	-0.33	1.00	2.69	1.03	9.24	1.08	-2.40	0.98
2011	4.06	1.03	4.22	1.03	1.97	1.14	-0.02	1.00	3.13	1.03	9.02	1.07	1.57	1.02
2012	3.35	1.03	4.67	1.04	18.24	1.15	1.16	1.01	1.57	1.02	6.52	1.05	4.49	1.05
2013	0.96	1.01	4.72	1.04	22.23	1.04	-0.15	1.00	1.07	1.01	7.49	1.05	-0.44	1.00
2014	2.31	1.02	-0.10	1.00	6.19	1.05	-1.03	0.99	13.13	1.14	6.18	1.04	-2.66	0.97
2015	2.54	1.02	5.34	1.04	9.29		2.17	1.02	7.38	1.07	-0.59	1.00	-5.98	0.94

(Continued)

Year	Algeria $\Omega_{i,t}$	Algeria $\phi_{i,t}$	Angola $\Omega_{i,t}$	Angola $\phi_{i,t}$	Azerbaijan $\Omega_{i,t}$	Azerbaijan $\phi_{i,t}$	Belarus $\Omega_{i,t}$	Belarus $\phi_{i,t}$	Bosnia and Herzegovina $\Omega_{i,t}$	Bosnia and Herzegovina $\phi_{i,t}$	Botswana $\Omega_{i,t}$	Botswana $\phi_{i,t}$	Brazil $\Omega_{i,t}$	Brazil $\phi_{i,t}$	Bulgaria $\Omega_{i,t}$	Bulgaria $\phi_{i,t}$	China $\Omega_{i,t}$	China $\phi_{i,t}$	Colombia $\Omega_{i,t}$	Colombia $\phi_{i,t}$
Upper-Middle-Income Economies																				
1989																	0.00	2.98		
1990																	0.00	1.84		
1991	0.02	9.92											0.00	9.88			0.00	2.56		
1992	0.00	0.98											0.02	4.70			0.01	3.67		
1993	0.00	0.98											0.10	5.60			0.04	3.56		
1994	-0.01	0.28	0.01	1.61			0.01	5.33					0.24	3.11	0.07	6.58	0.08	2.43		
1995	0.01	3.41	0.00	1.06	0.07	11.85	0.04	3.43					0.43	2.21	0.17	3.25	0.17	2.29	0.51	3.11
1996	0.02	2.45	0.01	1.61	0.14	2.80	0.01	1.11					0.73	1.91	0.07	1.28	0.26	1.87	0.65	1.87
1997	0.02	1.46	0.03	2.08	0.29	2.33	0.02	1.25	0.21	5.91			1.21	1.79	0.53	2.66	0.50	1.92	1.93	2.38
1998	0.00	1.02	0.02	1.36	0.31	1.61	0.04	1.49	0.44	2.72			1.62	1.60	0.71	1.83	0.83	1.79	1.33	1.40
1999	0.17	3.94	0.10	2.38	3.78	5.65	0.11	1.94	0.71	2.03	4.44	5.94	4.39	2.01	2.78	2.78	1.52	1.80	0.34	1.07
2000	0.04	1.18	0.01	1.04	0.58	1.13	0.26	2.12	1.03	1.74	7.32	2.37	4.55	1.52	4.89	2.13	3.26	1.96	0.64	1.13
2001	0.04	1.15	0.34	2.81	3.73	1.72	0.90	2.82	9.03	4.71	5.97	1.47	2.96	1.22	10.31	2.12	4.59	1.69	2.39	1.42
2002	1.07	4.44	0.42	1.80	0.68	1.08	3.30	3.37	7.75	1.68	-0.26	0.99	3.20	1.20	13.47	1.69	4.66	1.41	3.10	1.39
2003	3.00	3.17	1.33	2.41	3.04	1.32	6.73	2.43	8.38	1.44	5.91	1.32	6.07	1.31	11.84	1.36	4.82	1.30	3.62	1.32
2004	10.21	3.33	2.36	2.04	4.58	1.36	11.61	2.02	8.62	1.31	3.91	1.16	10.14	1.40	16.23	1.36	4.83	1.23	9.68	1.66
2005	25.64	2.76	5.11	2.10	8.98	1.52	19.38	1.84	4.88	1.13	1.87	1.07	10.66	1.30	20.21	1.33	4.29	1.17	26.14	2.07
2006	20.62	1.51	8.10	1.83	12.17	1.46	19.53	1.46	7.62	1.19	13.36	1.44	6.80	1.15	26.99	1.33	4.92	1.16	17.29	1.34
2007	17.68	1.29	10.17	1.57	13.17	1.34	10.66	1.17	14.62	1.30	16.73	1.39	10.56	1.20	22.59	1.21	6.25	1.18	8.39	1.12
2008	-2.87	0.96	8.97	1.32	22.23	1.43	12.45	1.17	18.99	1.30	16.70	1.28	14.88	1.23	8.11	1.06	6.74	1.16	15.34	1.20
2009	14.29	1.19	5.86	1.16	12.56	1.17	16.63	1.20	2.20	1.03	19.19	1.25	8.99	1.11	1.43	1.01	7.54	1.16	0.44	1.00
2010	-1.51	0.98	5.25	1.12	13.74	1.16	7.19	1.07	-3.66	0.96	23.99	1.25	13.34	1.15	-2.37	0.98	7.87	1.14	3.72	1.04
2011	5.87	1.07	11.72	1.24	9.91	1.10	4.30	1.04	1.73	1.02	25.97	1.22	18.12	1.18	4.81	1.03	8.90	1.14	2.37	1.02
2012	3.21	1.03	1.58	1.03	-1.20	0.99	0.35	1.00	4.97	1.06	7.80	1.05	6.00	1.05	5.28	1.04	8.69	1.12	4.72	1.05
2013	3.27	1.03	0.47	1.01	-1.15	0.99	5.27	1.05	3.52	1.04	6.86	1.04	10.30	1.08	-2.94	0.98	7.95	1.10	1.23	1.01
2014	7.65	1.08	1.61	1.03	3.29	1.03	3.71	1.03	0.18	1.00	6.66	1.04	3.65	1.03	-12.8	0.91	3.57	1.04	9.00	1.09
2015	4.59	1.04	-2.64	0.96	0.38	1.00	1.13	1.01	-1.13	0.99	1.71	1.01	-12.36	0.91	-3.08	0.98	0.89	1.01	2.66	1.02

Year	Costa Rica $\Omega_{i,t}$	$\phi_{i,t}$	Dominican Rep. $\Omega_{i,t}$	$\phi_{i,t}$	Ecuador $\Omega_{i,t}$	$\phi_{i,t}$	Iran $\Omega_{i,t}$	$\phi_{i,t}$	Jamaica $\Omega_{i,t}$	$\phi_{i,t}$	Jordan $\Omega_{i,t}$	$\phi_{i,t}$	Kazakhstan $\Omega_{i,t}$	$\phi_{i,t}$	Lebanon $\Omega_{i,t}$	$\phi_{i,t}$	Macedonia $\Omega_{i,t}$	$\phi_{i,t}$	Malaysia $\Omega_{i,t}$	$\phi_{i,t}$
1987																			0.04	1.56
1988																			0.05	1.52
1989																			0.06	1.40
1990																			0.25	2.14
1991			0.03	1.74							0.00	0.96							0.22	1.46
1992			0.02	1.26					0.22	3.09	0.00	0.95							0.35	1.50
1993	0.04	1.47	0.04	1.41					0.31	1.98	0.00	0.94							0.68	1.65
1994	0.07	1.50	0.13	1.99					0.44	1.70	0.00	0.95							1.10	1.64
1995	0.33	2.62	0.43	2.62	0.31	2.81	0.01	1.71	0.76	1.71	0.24	7.87	0.03	11.65					2.02	1.71
1996	0.77	2.42	0.32	1.45	0.04	1.08	0.07	3.71	0.37	1.20	0.27	1.98	0.03	2.16	2.49	1.63			2.30	1.47
1997	0.46	1.35	0.70	1.69	0.55	2.07	0.28	3.91	0.43	1.20	0.45	1.83	0.01	1.16	5.64	1.88	0.57	11.59	2.02	1.28
1998	1.14	1.65	0.78	1.45	0.94	1.88	0.23	1.60	0.47	1.18	0.79	1.80	0.13	2.69	4.14	1.34	0.87	2.41	0.67	1.07
1999	0.70	1.24	2.48	1.99	1.10	1.55	0.14	1.24	2.54	1.82	0.74	1.42	0.14	1.69	3.64	1.22	0.90	1.60	3.22	1.33
2000	1.79	1.50	3.17	1.64	0.73	1.23	0.70	1.93	8.57	2.52	5.64	3.24	1.02	4.01	3.10	1.16	3.25	2.35	8.81	1.67
2001	2.76	1.51	6.29	1.77	2.87	1.75	1.66	2.14	8.74	1.61	9.74	2.19	2.64	2.95	-0.13	0.99	5.17	1.92	9.00	1.41
2002	4.13	1.51	4.60	1.32	5.26	1.78	0.24	1.08	24.45	2.07	6.97	1.39	3.03	1.76	-0.79	0.97	6.80	1.63	6.22	1.20
2003	6.39	1.52	4.03	1.21	6.08	1.51	1.67	1.50	12.15	1.26	1.72	1.07	2.00	1.28	-0.49	0.98	19.6	2.12	7.61	1.21
2004	3.08	1.17	4.46	1.19	8.14	1.45	2.29	1.45	9.38	1.16	5.30	1.20	7.40	1.82	1.39	1.06	9.96	1.27	12.91	1.29
2005	3.75	1.17	11.26	1.41	19.14	1.73	4.81	1.66	4.94	1.07	27.99	1.88	19.41	2.18	1.97	1.09	6.86	1.15	18.03	1.31
2006	7.38	1.29	9.81	1.25	15.17	1.33	9.55	1.79	10.49	1.14	20.11	1.34	15.23	1.43	2.20	1.09	6.25	1.12	-1.70	0.98
2007	0.92	1.03	8.75	1.18	9.16	1.15	19.78	1.91	14.76	1.17	4.37	1.05	28.97	1.57	3.32	1.12	25.2	1.42	13.14	1.18
2008	7.83	1.23	16.62	1.29	10.85	1.16	17.72	1.43	1.04	1.01	5.52	1.07	15.74	1.20	3.65	1.12	8.16	1.10	14.43	1.17
2009	0.76	1.02	13.36	1.18	9.22	1.11	12.28	1.21	8.13	1.08	7.41	1.08	12.61	1.13	22.19	1.65	-1.24	0.99	6.97	1.07
2010	24.61	1.58	1.47	1.02	8.80	1.10	1.13	1.02	7.77	1.07	5.26	1.05	13.48	1.12	9.68	1.17	9.93	1.11	11.27	1.10
2011	20.67	1.31	-2.35	0.97	2.03	1.02	1.71	1.02	-9.14	0.92	8.60	1.08	34.93	1.29	11.22	1.17	2.76	1.03	7.73	1.06
2012	24.26	1.28	0.51	1.01	5.66	1.06	1.79	1.02	-8.87	0.92	17.01	1.15	29.03	1.19	3.62	1.05	0.97	1.01	13.85	1.11
2013	34.05	1.30	1.50	1.02	-0.58	0.99	8.15	1.11	4.19	1.04	13.62	1.11	-1.13	0.99	-0.24	1.00	0.01	1.00	3.39	1.02
2014	-3.79	0.97	-9.57	0.89	-1.75	0.98	3.55	1.04	5.15	1.05	6.01	1.04	-12.50	0.93	7.78	1.10	-0.67	0.99	4.11	1.03
2015	8.48	1.06	3.72	1.05	-24.47	0.76	5.59	1.06	4.13	1.04	31.63	1.21	14.98	1.09	-1.28	0.99	-0.12	1.00	-4.92	0.97

(Continued)

(Continued)

Year	Maldives		Mauritius		Mexico		Namibia		Panama		Paraguay		Peru		Romania		Serbia		South Africa	
	$\Omega_{i,t}$	$\phi_{i,t}$	$\Omega_{i,t}$	$\phi_{i,t}$	$\Omega_{i,t}$	$\phi_{i,t}$	$\Omega_{i,t}$	$\phi_{i,t}$	$\Omega_{i,t}$	$\phi_{i,t}$	$\Omega_{i,t}$	$\phi_{i,t}$	$\Omega_{i,t}$	$\phi_{i,t}$	$\Omega_{i,t}$	$\phi_{i,t}$	$\Omega_{i,t}$	$\phi_{i,t}$	$\Omega_{i,t}$	$\phi_{i,t}$
1989					0.01	5.55														
1990					0.06	7.37													0.00	1.39
1991			0.03	1.12	0.11	2.47							0.02	3.39					0.00	1.22
1992			0.03	1.15	0.17	1.90							0.07	3.71					0.01	1.72
1993			0.10	1.37	0.07	1.21					0.04	2.21	0.06	1.65					0.07	3.12
1994			0.14	1.39	0.19	1.44					0.09	2.21	0.06	1.41	0.01	3.49			0.74	8.30
1995			0.53	2.03	0.11	1.19					0.17	2.02	0.09	1.38	0.03	3.28			0.45	1.54
1996			0.79	1.76	0.33	1.46	0.18	1.84			0.34	2.03	0.52	2.68	0.03	1.88			0.97	1.75
1997	0.50	63.0	1.86	2.02	0.71	1.67	0.32	1.83	0.57	3.28	1.01	2.51	0.88	2.06	0.81	11.89			2.02	1.90
1998	0.11	1.22	1.50	1.41	1.57	1.89	0.37	1.52	2.11	3.58	2.83	2.69	1.24	1.73	1.96	3.22			3.38	1.79
1999	0.48	1.78	3.50	1.67	4.23	2.27	0.54	1.50	4.85	2.66	3.80	1.84	1.01	1.34	3.18	2.12			4.08	1.53
2000	1.71	2.56	6.51	1.75	6.00	1.79	2.71	2.67	5.66	1.73	7.03	1.85	0.94	1.24	5.13	1.85			6.86	1.58
2001	4.00	2.43	7.65	1.50	7.10	1.52	1.20	1.28	1.81	1.13	5.72	1.37	1.90	1.39	6.07	1.54			5.11	1.27
2002	8.02	2.18	6.15	1.27	3.64	1.18	2.14	1.39	1.30	1.09	8.86	1.42	1.83	1.27	5.73	1.33			5.97	1.25
2003	8.29	1.56	9.41	1.32	3.56	1.15	3.63	1.47	4.82	1.29	1.23	1.04	2.19	1.25	8.74	1.38			6.31	1.21
2004	15.60	1.68	6.92	1.18	7.30	1.26	2.99	1.26	16.78	1.79	-0.96	0.97	4.11	1.38	14.39	1.45			7.85	1.22
2005	29.71	1.77	8.84	1.20	7.41	1.21	7.86	1.55	13.81	1.36	1.77	1.06	5.21	1.35	14.29	1.31	19.83	1.42	26.58	1.61
2006	21.08	1.31	9.33	1.17	6.85	1.16	7.51	1.34	11.47	1.22	21.79	1.68	12.40	1.62	12.08	1.20	14.44	1.22	10.67	1.15
2007	12.21	1.14	12.63	1.20	9.22	1.19	8.80	1.30	22.82	1.36	22.89	1.43	21.89	1.67	20.19	1.28	23.02	1.28	4.20	1.05
2008	37.08	1.36	8.35	1.11	6.87	1.12	11.38	1.30	23.94	1.28	16.22	1.21	18.77	1.34	18.74	1.20	15.34	1.15	4.24	1.05
2009	4.40	1.03	4.12	1.05	5.96	1.09	26.28	1.53	57.60	1.52	-4.34	0.95	12.17	1.17	3.14	1.03	4.57	1.04	1.73	1.02
2010	8.58	1.06	8.19	1.09	6.06	1.08	13.38	1.18	12.92	1.08	3.14	1.04	14.13	1.17	-3.11	0.97	0.90	1.01	6.65	1.07
2011	8.01	1.05	8.02	1.08	1.72	1.02	9.46	1.11	-0.62	1.00	7.67	1.08	10.12	1.10	-4.04	0.96	4.95	1.04	25.30	1.26
2012	5.83	1.04	15.07	1.14	4.11	1.05	-3.94	0.96	-16.66	0.91	2.26	1.02	-11.61	0.89	-2.40	0.98	-12.4	0.90	7.36	1.06
2013	15.57	1.09	3.37	1.03	3.91	1.05	23.42	1.25	-2.85	0.98	2.10	1.02	0.08	1.00	0.59	1.01	1.62	1.01	15.09	1.12
2014	8.19	1.05	9.01	1.07	-2.61	0.97	-4.68	0.96	-2.51	0.98	1.91	1.02	5.53	1.06	0.33	1.00	2.74	1.02	3.55	1.02
2015	17.27	1.09	8.32	1.06	0.65	1.01	-11.65	0.90	16.14	1.10	-0.21	1.00	6.26	1.06	1.23	1.01	-1.61	0.99	10.08	1.07

Time	Suriname $\Omega_{i,t}$	$\phi_{i,t}$	Thailand $\Omega_{i,t}$	$\phi_{i,t}$	Tunisia $\Omega_{i,t}$	$\phi_{i,t}$	Turkey $\Omega_{i,t}$	$\phi_{i,t}$
1987							0.01	13.71
1988							0.01	1.89
1989			0.04	2.24	0.00		0.01	1.56
1990			0.04	1.56	0.00		0.03	2.00
1991			0.10	1.93	0.00		0.03	1.48
1992			0.22	2.01	0.01		0.02	1.26
1993			0.28	1.64	0.00		0.04	1.35
1994	0.07	1.27	0.55	1.77	0.00	1.17	0.15	2.04
1995	0.07	1.20	0.94	1.75	0.00	1.16	0.44	2.46
1996	0.16	1.41	0.90	1.41	0.04	2.01	0.61	1.82
1997	-0.04	0.92	0.56	1.18	0.01	1.16	1.31	1.97
1998	0.82	2.62	-0.41	0.89	0.33	5.03	3.05	2.14
1999	2.48	2.87	0.55	1.17	0.17	1.40	7.33	2.28
2000	4.99	2.31	1.11	1.29	0.66	2.13	12.49	1.96
2001	9.59	2.09	7.07	2.44	2.78	3.23	5.00	1.20
2002	4.19	1.23	15.38	2.28	1.86	1.46	5.33	1.17
2003	12.04	1.53	6.17	1.23	13.58	3.31	6.42	1.18
2004	8.52	1.25	7.91	1.24	18.08	1.93	9.63	1.23
2005	3.47	1.08	5.03	1.12	18.96	1.50	12.45	1.24
2006	16.74	1.36	14.44	1.31	15.72	1.28	12.36	1.19
2007	11.10	1.18	19.27	1.32	4.10	1.06	12.44	1.16
2008	53.05	1.71	13.26	1.17	6.45	1.08	4.37	1.05
2009	19.36	1.15	6.08	1.07	10.42	1.13	-5.43	0.94
2010	-47.5	0.68	8.51	1.09	11.33	1.12	-2.50	0.97
2011	1.43	1.01	8.31	1.08	10.66	1.10	3.78	1.04
2012	5.75	1.06	10.96	1.09	2.90	1.03	2.05	1.02
2013	54.61	1.51	12.76	1.10	-2.50	0.98	1.50	1.02
2014	9.51	1.06	4.39	1.03	12.88	1.11	1.83	1.02
2015	10.11	1.06	-18.63	0.87	1.45	1.01	1.23	1.01

Source: Author's calculations.

Appendix 4

IU critical mass calculations. Marginal growths and replication coefficients. High-income and upper-middle-income economies. 1990–2015.

Year	Argentina		Australia		Austria		Belgium		Brunei Darussalam		Canada		Chile		Croatia		Cyprus		Czech Republic	
	$\Omega_{i,t}$	$\phi_{i,t}$	$\Omega_{i,t}$	$\phi_{i,t}$	$\Omega_{i,t}$	$\phi_{i,t}$	$\Omega_{i,t}$	$\phi_{i,t}$	$\Omega_{i,t}$	$\phi_{i,t}$	$\Omega_{i,t}$	$\phi_{i,t}$	$\Omega_{i,t}$	$\phi_{i,t}$	$\Omega_{i,t}$	$\phi_{i,t}$	$\Omega_{i,t}$	$\phi_{i,t}$	$\Omega_{i,t}$	$\phi_{i,t}$
High-income economies																				
1991			0.51	1.88	0.13	1.99	0.02	19.94			0.21	1.58								
1992			0.67	1.61	0.38	2.48	0.08	4.98			0.35	1.61								
1993	0.03	9.87	0.21	1.12	0.12	1.19	0.10	1.99			0.27	1.29	0.04	1.96	0.17	2.76	0.01	1.13	0.68	2.17
1994	0.01	1.48	0.26	1.13	0.63	1.82	0.50	3.49			1.19	2.01	0.07	1.97	0.25	1.92	0.05	1.97	0.19	1.15
1995	0.04	1.97	0.53	1.24	0.50	1.36	0.30	1.42			1.78	1.75	0.21	2.46	0.34	1.67	0.30	3.69	0.49	1.33
1996	0.06	1.65	0.52	1.19	5.02	3.66	1.98	2.99	2.29	3.25	2.60	1.62	0.34	1.97	0.87	2.01	0.26	1.64	0.98	1.50
1997	0.14	1.97	13.09	5.00	2.62	1.38	1.97	1.66	1.53	1.46	8.31	2.23	0.37	1.55	1.54	1.89	3.70	6.50	0.98	1.34
1998	0.55	2.96	14.44	1.88	5.89	1.62	2.95	1.60	1.45	1.30	9.83	1.65	0.61	1.57	1.13	1.35	4.51	2.03	2.94	1.75
1999	2.45	3.95	9.97	1.32	7.62	1.49	5.89	1.75	1.39	1.22	11.29	1.45	2.44	2.47	2.24	1.51	2.45	1.28	2.95	1.43
2000	3.75	2.14	5.97	1.15	10.69	1.46	15.66	2.14	1.33	1.17	15.11	1.42	12.50	4.05	4.91	1.74	3.91	1.34	4.92	1.50
2001	2.74	1.39	5.93	1.13	5.46	1.16	1.86	1.06	3.92	1.44	8.90	1.17	2.50	1.15	6.20	1.54	3.56	1.23	9.23	1.63
2002	1.10	1.11			-2.63	0.93	15.04	1.48	2.41	1.19	1.39	1.02	3.00	1.16	4.99	1.28	9.50	1.50	10.37	1.43
2003	1.03	1.09			6.14	1.17	3.64	1.08	4.27	1.28	2.61	1.04	3.37	1.15	8.16	1.36	1.77	1.06	1.20	1.03
2004	4.12	1.35			11.58	1.27	3.89	1.08	10.12	1.52	1.76	1.03	2.70	1.11	2.23	1.07	3.74	1.12	-0.23	0.99
2005	1.68	1.11			3.72	1.07	1.96	1.04	6.75	1.23	5.70	1.09	3.00	1.11	4.84	1.15	-1.02	0.97	12.66	1.36
2006	3.21	1.18	3.00	1.05	5.60	1.10	3.90	1.07	5.72	1.16	0.74	1.01	3.32	1.11	3.46	1.09	3.02	1.09	4.00	1.08
2007	5.02	1.24	3.45	1.05	5.77	1.09	4.72	1.08	2.49	1.06	0.80	1.01	1.40	1.04	2.80	1.07	4.94	1.14	11.04	1.21
2008	2.17	1.08	2.22	1.03	3.50	1.05	1.56	1.02	1.32	1.03	3.50	1.05	1.40	1.04	6.34	1.14	1.54	1.04	1.46	1.02
2009	5.89	1.21	2.58	1.04	0.58	1.01	4.00	1.06	3.00	1.07	3.60	1.05	4.26	1.11	5.97	1.12	7.50	1.18	4.39	1.07
2010	11.00	1.32	1.75	1.02	1.72	1.02	5.00	1.07	4.00	1.08	0.00	1.00	3.44	1.08	1.24	1.02	3.18	1.06	1.67	1.02
2011	6.00	1.13	3.49	1.05	3.57	1.05	6.61	1.09	3.00	1.06	2.70	1.03	7.25	1.16	4.15	1.07	3.87	1.07	2.94	1.04
2012	4.80	1.09	-0.49	0.99	1.29	1.02	-0.89	0.99	4.27	1.08	0.00	1.00	2.80	1.05			3.83	1.07	0.68	1.01

	$\Omega_{i,t}$	$\phi_{i,t}$	$\Omega_{i,t}$	$\phi_{i,t}$	$\Omega_{i,t}$	$\phi_{i,t}$	$\Omega_{i,t}$	$\phi_{i,t}$	$\Omega_{i,t}$	$\phi_{i,t}$	$\Omega_{i,t}$	$\phi_{i,t}$	$\Omega_{i,t}$	$\phi_{i,t}$	$\Omega_{i,t}$	$\phi_{i,t}$	$\Omega_{i,t}$	$\phi_{i,t}$	$\Omega_{i,t}$	$\phi_{i,t}$
2013	4.10	1.07	4.45	1.06	0.59	1.01	1.45	1.02	4.23	1.07	2.80	1.03	2.95	1.05	4.81	1.08	4.76	1.08	5.60	1.08
2014	4.80	1.08	0.55	1.01	0.38	1.00	2.83	1.03	4.27	1.07	1.32	1.02	3.11	1.05	1.82	1.03	3.88	1.06	1.59	1.02
2015	4.70	1.07	0.56	1.01	2.93	1.04	0.05	1.00	2.43	1.04	1.35	1.02	3.18	1.05	1.23	1.02	2.39	1.03	0.68	2.17

Year	Denmark		Estonia		Finland		France		Germany		Greece		Hungary		Iceland		Ireland		Israel	
	$\Omega_{i,t}$	$\phi_{i,t}$	$\Omega_{i,t}$	$\phi_{i,t}$	$\Omega_{i,t}$	$\phi_{i,t}$	$\Omega_{i,t}$	$\phi_{i,t}$	$\Omega_{i,t}$	$\phi_{i,t}$	$\Omega_{i,t}$	$\phi_{i,t}$	$\Omega_{i,t}$	$\phi_{i,t}$	$\Omega_{i,t}$	$\phi_{i,t}$	$\Omega_{i,t}$	$\phi_{i,t}$	$\Omega_{i,t}$	$\phi_{i,t}$
1991	0.10	1.99			1.00	3.48	0.09	2.65	0.12	1.99	0.00	0.99	0.04	14.29	1.03	3.05	0.11	2.99	0.10	1.94
1992	0.19	1.99			0.49	1.35	0.14	1.99	0.19	1.74	0.14	3.96	0.15	4.00	1.13	1.73	0.11	1.66	0.10	1.45
1993	0.19	1.49	0.24	4.59	0.68	1.36	0.31	2.12	0.03	1.07	0.19	1.98	0.29	2.50	4.13	2.55	0.28	1.99	0.09	1.28
1994	0.77	2.32	0.86	3.86	2.35	1.91	0.31	1.52	0.46	1.99	0.37	1.98	0.19	1.40	4.42	1.65	0.55	1.99	0.18	1.45
1995	2.48	2.85	1.62	2.40	8.99	2.83	0.74	1.82	0.92	1.99	0.65	1.86	0.29	1.43	3.59	1.32	1.09	1.98	0.35	1.61
1996	1.89	1.49	0.75	1.27	2.88	1.21	0.95	1.58	1.22	1.66	0.45	1.33	0.97	2.00	12.67	1.86	1.89	1.86	1.24	2.33
1997	5.67	1.99	2.18	1.62	2.68	1.16	1.67	1.65	3.66	2.20	1.37	1.74	1.95	2.01	8.79	1.32	4.01	1.98	2.23	2.03
1998	11.29	1.99	5.09	1.89	5.99	1.31	2.06	1.49	3.17	1.47	3.66	2.13	1.96	1.50	5.03	1.14	2.84	1.35	5.91	2.34
1999	7.92	1.35	3.70	1.34	6.84	1.27	2.81	1.44	10.97	2.11	2.26	1.33	1.14	1.19	3.18	1.08	6.92	1.63	3.13	1.30
2000	8.58	1.28	14.08	1.97	4.95	1.15	5.18	1.57	9.37	1.45	1.80	1.20	7.53	2.08	4.92	1.11	5.29	1.30	7.44	1.55
2001	3.79	1.10	2.95	1.10	5.86	1.16	12.02	1.84	1.43	1.05	3.73	1.34	2.14	1.15	29.73	1.60	2.71	1.12	-3.50	0.83
2002	21.29	1.50	9.99	1.32	19.32	1.45	3.85	1.15	17.17	1.54	3.13	1.21	4.96	1.30	4.02	1.05	8.46	1.33	0.39	1.02
2003	12.01	1.19	3.80	1.09	6.79	1.11	5.96	1.20	7.08	1.15	3.62	1.20	6.11	1.28	0.74	1.01	2.68	1.08	1.83	1.10
2004	4.67	1.06	7.88	1.17	3.17	1.05	3.01	1.08	8.83	1.16	2.58	1.12	11.23	1.40	3.12	1.04	4.62	1.12	3.18	1.16
2005	1.81	1.02	8.25	1.16	2.09	1.03	3.72	1.10	3.98	1.06	8.25	1.34	8.09	1.21	2.51	1.03	13.21	1.32	2.42	1.11
2006	3.91	1.05	2.06	1.03	5.18	1.07	4.00	1.09	3.45	1.05	3.63	1.11	6.24	1.13	1.09	1.01	6.34	1.12	2.69	1.11
2007	-1.62	0.98	2.68	1.04	1.12	1.01	19.22	1.41	3.00	1.04	2.32	1.06	7.70	1.14	0.40	1.00	4.18	1.07	20.25	1.73
2008	-0.01	1.00	4.39	1.07	2.89	1.04	4.59	1.07	2.84	1.04	4.20	1.11	1.00	1.02	2.00	1.02	2.04	1.03	11.26	1.23
2009	1.82	1.02	1.92	1.03	-1.18	0.99	0.90	1.01	1.00	1.01	2.00	1.05	3.00	1.05	0.39	1.00	2.47	1.04	3.73	1.06
2010	1.88	1.02	1.60	1.02	4.40	1.05	5.70	1.08	3.00	1.04	7.25	1.16	3.02	1.05	1.43	1.02	5.04	1.07	4.38	1.07
2011	1.09	1.01	2.40	1.03	1.82	1.02	0.54	1.01	-0.73	0.99	3.42	1.07	2.56	1.04	1.39	1.01	2.03	1.03	1.37	1.02
2012	2.45	1.03	1.89	1.02	1.17	1.01	3.62	1.05	1.08	1.01	4.80	1.09	2.06	1.03	0.34	1.00	1.33	1.02	1.93	1.03
2013	2.37	1.03	1.01	1.01	1.63	1.02	0.48	1.01	1.82	1.02	3.34	1.06	3.49	1.05	1.61	1.02	1.44	1.02	-0.55	0.99
2014	1.36	1.01	4.84	1.06	0.87	1.01	1.83	1.02	2.02	1.02	3.62	1.06	-3.30	0.96	0.04	1.00	0.43	1.01	4.77	1.07
2015	0.34	1.00	4.17	1.05	0.27	1.00	0.94	1.01	1.40	1.02									3.87	1.05

(Continued)

(Continued)

Year	Italy		Japan		Korea (Rep.)		Latvia		Lithuania		Malta		Netherlands		New Zealand		Norway		Oman	
	$\Omega_{i,t}$	$\phi_{i,t}$	$\Omega_{i,t}$	$\phi_{i,t}$	$\Omega_{i,t}$	$\phi_{i,t}$	$\Omega_{i,t}$	$\phi_{i,t}$	$\Omega_{i,t}$	$\phi_{i,t}$	$\Omega_{i,t}$	$\phi_{i,t}$	$\Omega_{i,t}$	$\phi_{i,t}$	$\Omega_{i,t}$	$\phi_{i,t}$	$\Omega_{i,t}$	$\phi_{i,t}$	$\Omega_{i,t}$	$\phi_{i,t}$
1991	0.02	2.00	0.02	1.99	0.02	1.98								1.58			0.70	1.99		
1992	0.03	2.00	0.06	2.39	0.05	2.13							0.20	2.49			0.81	1.57		
1993	0.05	1.75	0.30	4.15	0.15	2.54							0.79	1.49	0.35	2.21	0.57	1.26		
1994	0.07	1.57	0.40	1.99	0.06	1.25							0.65	1.66	2.54	5.02	1.37	1.49		
1995	0.33	2.73	0.79	1.99	0.51	2.63							1.29	1.99	1.72	1.54	2.27	1.55		
1996	0.50	1.95	2.78	2.74	0.80	1.98					0.83	4.67	3.22	1.49	3.16	1.65	11.83	2.84		
1997	1.25	2.22	4.79	2.10	1.98	2.22	1.24	2.53	0.70	3.53	2.87	3.73	3.18	1.46	6.56	1.82	2.17	1.12		
1998	2.28	2.00	4.25	1.46	3.18	1.88	1.26	1.61	0.99	2.02	2.58	1.66	4.42	1.58	17.03	2.17	2.14	1.10	0.42	1.96
1999	9.82	3.15	7.98	1.59	16.77	3.47	1.07	1.32	0.95	1.48	1.26	1.19	8.18	1.76	9.86	1.31	17.44	1.77	1.65	2.92
2000	8.73	1.61	8.60	1.40	21.15	1.90	1.93	1.44	3.50	2.20	5.35	1.69	16.93	1.12	5.89	1.14	12.00	1.30	1.00	1.40
2001	4.11	1.18	8.54	1.28	11.90	1.27	0.90	1.14	0.75	1.12	4.76	1.36	4.81	1.12	5.86	1.12	12.00	1.23	2.37	1.67
2002	0.82	1.03	8.06	1.21	2.80	1.05	14.72	3.04	10.51	2.46	11.04	1.62	5.39	1.12	5.84	1.11	8.84	1.14	0.98	1.17
2003	1.00	1.04	1.84	1.04	6.10	1.10	5.04	1.23	8.22	1.46	2.72	1.09	11.92	1.24	1.88	1.03	5.29	1.07	0.38	1.06
2004	4.20	1.14	13.96	1.29	7.20	1.11	11.60	1.43	5.32	1.21	2.98	1.09	3.06	1.05	0.89	1.01	-0.44	0.99	-0.50	0.93
2005	1.76	1.05	4.53	1.07	0.80	1.01	7.42	1.19	4.99	1.16	6.62	1.19	4.17	1.06	0.87	1.01	4.30	1.06	-0.08	0.99
2006	2.99	1.09	1.76	1.03	4.60	1.06	7.63	1.17	7.68	1.21	-0.83	0.98	12.48	1.18	6.28	1.10	0.56	1.01	1.62	1.24
2007	2.80	1.07	5.61	1.08	0.70	1.01	5.54	1.10	6.00	1.14	6.49	1.16	2.70	1.03	0.76	1.01	4.38	1.05	8.38	2.01
2008	3.74	1.09	1.10	1.01	2.20	1.03	4.24	1.07	5.32	1.11	3.18	1.07	2.12	1.03	2.27	1.03	3.64	1.04	3.32	1.20
2009	4.30	1.10	2.60	1.03	0.60	1.01	3.43	1.05	4.54	1.08	8.78	1.18	1.60	1.02	7.67	1.11	1.51	1.02	6.80	1.34
2010	4.85	1.10	0.21	1.00	2.10	1.03	1.58	1.02	2.36	1.04	4.14	1.07	2.21	1.03	0.76	1.01	1.31	1.01	9.03	1.34
2011	0.71	1.01	0.84	1.01	0.06	1.00	1.33	1.02	1.52	1.02	5.02	1.08	1.09	1.01	0.77	1.01	0.10	1.00	12.17	1.34
2012	1.44	1.03	0.44	1.01	0.31	1.00	3.37	1.05	3.59	1.06	0.18	1.00	0.70	1.02	0.77	1.01	1.16	1.01	12.00	1.25
2013	2.63	1.05	8.72	1.11	0.70	1.01	2.11	1.03	1.22	1.02	0.71	1.01	1.44	1.01	0.78	1.01	0.40	1.00	6.45	1.11
2014	3.50	1.06	0.89	1.01	3.10	1.04	0.60	1.01	3.68	1.05	4.26	1.06	1.10	1.01	2.72	1.03	1.25	1.01	3.77	1.06
2015	3.61	1.06	4.22	1.05	2.03	1.02	3.37	1.04	-0.75	0.99	3.01	1.04	-0.79	0.99	2.72	1.03	0.51	1.01	3.95	1.06

Year	Poland		Portugal		Qatar		Russian Federation		Saudi Arabia		Seychelles		Singapore		Slovakia		Slovenia		Spain	
	$\Omega_{i,t}$	$\phi_{i,t}$	$\Omega_{i,t}$	$\phi_{i,t}$	$\Omega_{i,t}$	$\phi_{i,t}$	$\Omega_{i,t}$	$\phi_{i,t}$	$\Omega_{i,t}$	$\phi_{i,t}$	$\Omega_{i,t}$	$\phi_{i,t}$	$\Omega_{i,t}$	$\phi_{i,t}$	$\Omega_{i,t}$	$\phi_{i,t}$	$\Omega_{i,t}$	$\phi_{i,t}$	$\Omega_{i,t}$	$\phi_{i,t}$
1991																			0.01	2.00
1992	0.05	9.97	0.15	2.50							0.31	2.92							0.05	2.99
1993	0.08	2.49	0.20	1.80			0.01	19.99			0.29	1.62							0.05	1.66
1994	0.26	2.99	0.27	1.60			0.04	4.00			0.42	1.55	0.19	2.49	0.66	2.61	0.66	2.61	0.15	2.19
1995	0.26	1.66	0.78	2.08			0.09	2.75			1.69	2.42	0.20	1.64	1.83	2.71	1.83	2.71	0.10	1.36
1996	0.65	2.00	1.49	1.99	0.74	4.89	0.12	1.82	0.02	2.44	5.48	2.91	0.26	1.50	2.17	1.75	2.17	1.75	0.95	3.50
1997	0.78	1.60	1.97	1.66	2.15	3.32	0.20	1.75	0.03	1.95	5.12	1.61	0.39	1.50	2.52	1.50	2.52	1.50	1.47	2.10
1998	2.03	1.98	4.92	1.99	0.44	1.14	0.34	1.72	0.05	1.95	6.12	1.45	1.52	2.29	2.51	1.33	2.51	1.33	1.56	1.56
1999	1.35	1.33	4.87	1.49	0.55	1.16	0.21	1.25	0.39	4.87	4.56	1.23	2.75	2.02	2.51	1.25	2.51	1.25	2.72	1.62
2000	1.83	1.34	1.69	1.11	0.79	1.19	0.96	1.94	1.72	4.48	11.84	1.49	3.99	1.73	2.50	1.20	2.50	1.20	6.54	1.92
2001	2.62	1.36	1.66	1.10	1.31	1.27	0.97	1.49	2.47	2.12	5.67	1.16	3.10	1.49	15.07	2.00	15.07	2.00	4.52	1.33
2002	11.25	2.14	1.28	1.07	4.06	1.66	1.18	1.40	1.70	1.36	5.33	1.13	27.61	1.33	-2.34	0.92	-2.34	0.92	2.24	1.12
2003	3.72	1.18	10.30	1.53	9.02	1.88	4.17	2.01	1.62	1.25	6.84	1.15	2.90	3.20	4.02	1.14	4.02	1.14	19.54	1.96
2004	7.66	1.31	2.11	1.07	1.46	1.08	4.56	1.55	2.23	1.28	8.16	1.15	9.85	1.07	8.96	1.28	8.96	1.28	4.08	1.10
2005	6.28	1.19	3.21	1.10	4.03	1.19	2.37	1.18	2.47	1.24	-1.00	0.98	2.30	1.23	6.00	1.15	6.00	1.15	3.87	1.09
2006	5.77	1.15	3.02	1.09	4.24	1.17	2.80	1.18	6.75	1.53	-2.00	0.97	0.89	1.04	7.20	1.15	7.20	1.15	2.49	1.05
2007	4.02	1.09	4.08	1.11	8.03	1.28	6.64	1.37	10.54	1.54	10.90	1.18	5.72	1.02	2.73	1.05	2.73	1.05	4.74	1.09
2008	4.53	1.09	2.04	1.05	7.30	1.20	2.17	1.09	6.00	1.20	-0.90	0.99	4.25	1.10	1.26	1.02	1.26	1.02	4.49	1.08
2009	5.84	1.11	4.14	1.09	8.80	1.20	2.17	1.08	2.00	1.06	0.00	1.00	3.95	1.07	6.00	1.10	6.00	1.10	2.80	1.05
2010	3.35	1.06	5.03	1.10	15.90	1.30	14.00	1.48	3.00	1.08	2.00	1.03	5.71	1.06	6.00	1.09	6.00	1.09	3.40	1.05
2011	-0.37	0.99	1.95	1.04	0.00	1.00	6.00	1.14	6.50	1.16	0.00	1.00	-1.27	1.08	-2.66	0.96	-2.66	0.96	1.80	1.03
2012	0.36	1.01	5.09	1.09	0.30	1.00	14.80	1.30	6.50	1.14	1.00	1.01	2.27	0.98	1.01	1.01	1.01	1.01	2.21	1.03
2013	0.54	1.01	1.76	1.03	16.00	1.23	4.17	1.07	6.50	1.12	8.90	1.12	1.17	1.03	4.33	1.06	4.33	1.06	1.83	1.03
2014	3.75	1.06	2.49	1.04	6.19	1.07	2.55	1.04	4.21	1.07	-1.87	0.98	2.10	1.02	-1.09	0.99	-1.09	0.99	4.55	1.06
2015	1.40	1.02	4.04	1.06	1.39	1.02	2.89	1.04	4.90	1.08	3.07	1.04	5.04	1.06	1.51	1.02	1.51	1.02	2.50	1.03

(Continued)

(Continued)

Year	Sweden $\Omega_{i,t}$	Sweden $\phi_{i,t}$	Switzerland $\Omega_{i,t}$	Switzerland $\phi_{i,t}$	United Arab Emirates $\Omega_{i,t}$	United Arab Emirates $\phi_{i,t}$	United Kingdom $\Omega_{i,t}$	United Kingdom $\phi_{i,t}$	United States $\Omega_{i,t}$	United States $\phi_{i,t}$	Uruguay $\Omega_{i,t}$	Uruguay $\phi_{i,t}$	Venezuela $\Omega_{i,t}$	Venezuela $\phi_{i,t}$
1991	0.58	1.99	0.58	1.98			0.09	1.99	0.38	1.48				
1992	0.34	1.29	0.57	1.48			0.09	1.50	0.56	1.48				
1993	0.22	1.15	0.42	1.24			0.26	1.99	0.55	1.32			0.03	3.44
1994	1.70	1.99	0.55	1.26			0.52	1.99	2.59	2.14			0.01	1.33
1995	1.69	1.49	0.83	1.31			0.86	1.83	4.37	1.90	0.25	4.96	0.07	2.20
1996	3.95	1.77	1.00	1.28	0.27	3.65	2.23	2.18	7.18	1.78	1.54	5.96	0.13	2.03
1997	14.68	2.62	10.55	3.32	2.92	8.78	3.26	1.79	5.20	1.32	1.52	1.82	0.14	1.57
1998	9.74	1.41	9.70	1.64	3.61	2.10	6.28	1.85	8.48	1.39	3.62	2.08	0.99	3.54
1999	7.97	1.24	9.20	1.37	8.03	2.16	7.62	1.56	5.76	1.19	2.99	1.43	1.46	2.05
2000	4.25	1.10	13.10	1.39	8.68	1.58	5.53	1.26	7.23	1.20	0.57	1.06	0.52	1.18
2001	6.08	1.13	8.00	1.17	2.65	1.11	6.66	1.25	6.00	1.14	0.58	1.06	1.28	1.38
2002	18.80	1.36	6.30	1.11	2.04	1.08	23.00	1.69	9.70	1.20	0.30	1.03	0.27	1.06
2003	8.56	1.12	3.70	1.06	1.16	1.04	8.34	1.15	2.91	1.05	4.52	1.40	2.59	1.53
2004	4.76	1.06	2.70	1.04	0.65	1.02	0.79	1.01	3.06	1.05	1.13	1.07	0.90	1.12
2005	0.94	1.01	2.30	1.03	9.87	1.33	4.39	1.07	3.21	1.05	3.03	1.18	4.15	1.49
2006	2.93	1.03	5.60	1.08	12.00	1.30	-1.18	0.98	0.96	1.01	9.31	1.46	2.67	1.21
2007	-5.75	0.93	1.50	1.02	9.00	1.17	6.27	1.09	6.07	1.09	4.60	1.16	5.61	1.37
2008	7.99	1.10	2.00	1.03	2.00	1.03	3.30	1.04	-1.00	0.99	5.30	1.16	5.05	1.24
2009	1.00	1.01	2.10	1.03	1.00	1.02	5.17	1.07	-3.00	0.96	2.50	1.06	6.82	1.26
2010	-1.00	0.99	2.60	1.03	4.00	1.06	1.44	1.02	0.69	1.01	4.60	1.11	4.67	1.14
2011	2.77	1.03	1.29	1.02	10.00	1.15	0.38	1.00	-1.96	0.97	5.00	1.11	2.85	1.08
2012	0.41	1.00	0.01	1.00	7.00	1.09	2.10	1.02	4.97	1.07	3.05	1.06	8.83	1.22
2013	1.60	1.02	1.14	1.01	3.00	1.04	2.36	1.03	-3.30	0.96	3.24	1.06	5.85	1.12
2014	-2.26	0.98	1.06	1.01	2.40	1.03	1.77	1.02	1.60	1.02	3.77	1.07	2.10	1.04
2015	-1.91	0.98	0.57	1.01	0.84	1.01	0.39	1.00	1.55	1.02	3.14	1.05	4.87	1.09

Year	Algeria		Angola		Azerbaijan		Belarus		Bosnia and Herzegov- ina		Botswana		Brazil		Bulgaria		China		Colombia	
	$\Omega_{i,t}$	$\phi_{i,t}$	$\Omega_{i,t}$	$\phi_{i,t}$	$\Omega_{i,t}$	$\phi_{i,t}$	$\Omega_{i,t}$	$\phi_{i,t}$	$\Omega_{i,t}$	$\phi_{i,t}$	$\Omega_{i,t}$	$\phi_{i,t}$	$\Omega_{i,t}$	$\phi_{i,t}$	$\Omega_{i,t}$	$\phi_{i,t}$	$\Omega_{i,t}$	$\phi_{i,t}$	$\Omega_{i,t}$	$\phi_{i,t}$
Upper-middle-income countries																				
1992													0.01	3.94						
1993													0.01	1.97						
1994													0.01	1.48	0.02	8.35	0.00	6.93	0.08	1.75
1995	0.00	4.90			0.00	1.44	0.00	6.01					0.07	2.79	0.10	6.13	0.00	4.24	0.14	1.75
1996	0.00	0.98			0.00	3.09	0.03	10.03					0.35	4.29	0.61	6.06	0.01	2.64	0.22	1.67
1997	0.01	5.91	0.00	7.31	0.02	3.96	0.02	1.67	0.04	3.93	0.09	2.44	0.34	1.74	0.49	1.68	0.02	2.48	0.58	2.05
1998	0.01	1.97	0.01	3.25	0.01	1.49	0.02	1.51	0.08	2.42	0.15	1.95	0.69	1.88	0.63	1.51	0.14	5.20	0.57	1.51
1999	0.18	9.86	0.05	3.90	0.06	2.65	0.42	6.70	0.05	1.35	0.29	1.96	0.56	1.38	1.06	1.58	0.54	4.20	0.51	1.30
2000	0.29	2.46	0.03	1.46	0.05	1.49	1.37	3.76	0.89	5.57	0.52	1.86	0.83	1.41	2.46	1.85	1.07	2.51	0.65	1.29
2001	0.15	1.31	0.03	1.29	0.16	2.07	2.44	2.31	0.12	1.11	1.78	2.59	1.66	1.58	2.24	1.42	0.86	1.49	1.75	1.61
2002	0.95	2.46	0.13	1.99	4.69	16.36	4.65	2.08	1.45	2.21	0.53	1.18	4.62	2.02	1.47	1.19	1.96	1.74	2.79	1.61
2003	0.60	1.38	0.10	1.37	1.50	1.30	1.25	1.14	1.32	1.50	-0.04	0.99	4.06	1.44	2.96	1.33	1.60	1.35	1.73	1.23
2004	2.44	2.11	0.09	1.25	0.70	1.11	2.60	1.25	11.50	3.90	-0.04	0.99	5.87	1.44	6.09	1.51	1.10	1.18	1.89	1.21
2005	1.21	1.26	0.68	2.46	0.83	1.12	2.10	1.16	5.86	1.38	-0.04	0.99	1.95	1.10	1.84	1.10	1.22	1.17	4.33	1.39
2006	1.53	1.26	0.36	1.31	3.96	1.49	1.30	1.09	3.80	1.18	1.03	1.31	7.16	1.34	7.12	1.36	2.00	1.23	6.46	1.42
2007	2.08	1.28	0.20	1.13	2.55	1.21	3.50	1.22	2.80	1.11	0.99	1.23	2.70	1.10	6.55	1.24	5.48	1.52	3.80	1.17
2008	0.73	1.08	0.20	1.12	2.54	1.17	3.30	1.17	6.74	1.24	0.97	1.18	2.95	1.10	6.03	1.18	6.60	1.41	4.40	1.17
2009	1.05	1.10	0.40	1.21	10.32	1.60	4.43	1.19	3.08	1.09	-0.10	0.98	5.39	1.16	5.33	1.13	6.30	1.28	6.50	1.22
2010	1.27	1.11	0.50	1.22	18.60	1.68	4.37	1.16	5.01	1.13	-0.15	0.98	1.43	1.04	1.23	1.03	5.40	1.19	3.85	1.11
2011	1.50	1.12	0.30	1.11	4.00	1.09	7.85	1.25	5.02	1.12	2.00	1.33	5.04	1.12	1.75	1.04	4.00	1.12	8.63	1.21
2012	1.23	1.09	3.40	2.10	4.20	1.08	7.26	1.18	5.01	1.10	3.50	1.44	2.87	1.06	3.92	1.08	4.00	1.10	2.72	1.06
2013	1.27	1.08	2.40	1.37	18.8	1.35	7.26	1.15	5.01	1.09	3.50	1.30	2.48	1.05	1.16	1.02	3.50	1.08	0.87	1.02
2014	8.50	1.52	1.30	1.15	2.00	1.03	4.85	1.09	3.01	1.05	3.50	1.23	3.51	1.07	2.43	1.05	2.10	1.05	3.33	1.06
2015	13.20	1.53	2.20	1.22	2.00	1.03	3.21	1.05	4.27	1.07	9.00	1.49	4.53	1.08	1.17	1.02	2.40	1.05	0.08	1.75

(Continued)

(Continued)

Year	Costa Rica		Dominican Rep.		Ecuador		Iran		Jamaica		Jordan		Kazakhstan		Lebanon		Macedonia		Malaysia	
	$\Omega_{i,t}$	$\phi_{i,t}$	$\Omega_{i,t}$	$\phi_{i,t}$	$\Omega_{i,t}$	$\phi_{i,t}$	$\Omega_{i,t}$	$\phi_{i,t}$	$\Omega_{i,t}$	$\phi_{i,t}$	$\Omega_{i,t}$	$\phi_{i,t}$	$\Omega_{i,t}$	$\phi_{i,t}$	$\Omega_{i,t}$	$\phi_{i,t}$	$\Omega_{i,t}$	$\phi_{i,t}$	$\Omega_{i,t}$	$\phi_{i,t}$
1993	0.08	73.21			0.01	3.20	0.00	10.24	0.07	2.97									0.02	24.37
1994	0.20	3.43			0.02	2.12	0.01	3.79	0.48	5.40									0.07	3.90
1995	0.14	1.49			0.01	1.26	0.03	2.95	0.21	1.35			0.01	21.69					0.05	1.46
1996	0.42	2.02	0.06	4.35	0.04	1.97	0.05	2.13	1.18	2.48	0.02	1.93	0.02	2.82	0.07	1.96	0.04	1.87	0.71	5.85
1997	0.80	1.95	0.07	1.90	0.02	1.28	0.28	3.79	0.38	1.19	0.55	13.34	0.03	2.03	1.10	8.85	0.43	6.63	1.46	2.71
1998	1.03	1.63	0.09	1.64	0.02	1.14	0.56	2.47	0.76	1.32	0.71	2.18	0.03	2.03	1.48	2.19	0.50	1.99	4.44	2.93
1999	1.24	1.46	0.87	4.72	0.70	6.57	0.55	1.59	0.75	1.24	1.22	1.94	0.07	2.03	2.65	1.98	0.49	1.49	5.55	1.82
2000	1.90	1.49	2.60	3.35	0.64	1.78	3.14	3.12	2.24	1.58	0.10	1.04	0.33	3.54	2.58	1.48	0.99	1.66	9.08	1.74
2001	3.76	1.65	0.72	1.20	1.21	1.83	2.31	1.50	1.70	1.28	2.08	1.79	0.20	1.44	-1.17	0.85	0.98	1.40	5.31	1.25
2002	10.34	2.08	2.39	1.54	1.59	1.60	0.56	1.08	2.20	1.28	1.32	1.28	0.34	1.50	0.22	1.03	13.8	5.00	5.64	1.21
2003	0.44	1.02	1.07	1.16	0.20	1.05	0.61	1.08	2.80	1.28	2.44	1.41	0.67	1.66	1.00	1.14	1.74	1.10	2.63	1.08
2004	0.46	1.02	0.97	1.12	0.37	1.08	0.66	1.08	3.60	1.28	3.19	1.38	0.33	1.19	1.00	1.13	5.37	1.28	7.28	1.21
2005	1.28	1.06	2.62	1.30	1.16	1.24	0.71	1.08	4.70	1.29	1.27	1.11	0.65	1.32	1.14	1.13	2.01	1.08	6.38	1.15
2006	3.03	1.14	3.36	1.29	1.21	1.20	2.55	1.27	2.50	1.12	0.93	1.07	0.31	1.12	4.86	1.48	2.17	1.08	3.01	1.06
2007	3.30	1.13	2.82	1.19	3.60	1.50	1.78	1.15	0.70	1.03	6.13	1.44	0.31	1.10	3.74	1.25	7.68	1.27	4.06	1.08
2008	3.89	1.14	3.16	1.18	8.00	1.74	2.10	1.15	3.37	1.14	3.00	1.15	0.75	1.23	3.79	1.20	9.74	1.27	0.10	1.00
2009	2.04	1.06	6.90	1.33	5.80	1.31	3.10	1.19	9.77	1.35	3.00	1.13	6.98	2.74	7.61	1.34	5.73	1.12	0.10	1.00
2010	2.17	1.06	3.68	1.13	4.43	1.18	3.73	1.20	-3.65	0.90	1.20	1.05	7.20	1.65	13.54	1.45	0.13	1.00	0.40	1.01
2011	2.71	1.07	6.60	1.21	2.34	1.08	7.22	1.32	3.31	1.10	7.70	1.28	13.40	1.74	8.32	1.19	4.80	1.09	4.70	1.08
2012	8.29	1.21	4.32	1.11	3.77	1.12	9.40	1.31	3.30	1.09	2.10	1.06	19.00	1.60	9.25	1.18	0.75	1.01	4.80	1.08
2013	-1.54	0.97	3.58	1.08	5.14	1.15	4.73	1.12	2.77	1.07	4.40	1.12	2.72	1.05	9.25	1.15	7.79	1.14	-8.74	0.87
2014	7.04	1.15	3.68	1.08	5.31	1.13					4.80	1.12	9.68	1.18	2.50	1.04	2.82	1.04	6.61	1.12
2015	6.76	1.13	2.35	1.05	3.35	1.07					7.20	1.16	3.00	1.05	1.00	1.01	2.32	1.03	7.40	1.12

Year	Maldives $\Omega_{i,t}$	Maldives $\phi_{i,t}$	Mauritius $\Omega_{i,t}$	Mauritius $\phi_{i,t}$	Mexico $\Omega_{i,t}$	Mexico $\phi_{i,t}$	Namibia $\Omega_{i,t}$	Namibia $\phi_{i,t}$	Panama $\Omega_{i,t}$	Panama $\phi_{i,t}$	Paraguay $\Omega_{i,t}$	Paraguay $\phi_{i,t}$	Peru $\Omega_{i,t}$	Peru $\phi_{i,t}$	Romania $\Omega_{i,t}$	Romania $\phi_{i,t}$	Serbia $\Omega_{i,t}$	Serbia $\phi_{i,t}$	South Africa $\Omega_{i,t}$	South Africa $\phi_{i,t}$
1992					0.01	2.94													0.03	2.93
1993					0.01	1.64													0.07	2.93
1994					0.02	1.53									0.02	7.10			0.13	2.17
1995					0.06	2.37			0.05	7.35			0.02	3.93	0.05	2.85			0.43	2.74
1996					0.10	1.95	0.00	1.46	0.16	3.92			0.21	7.37	0.15	2.96			0.17	1.24
1997	0.08	1.36	0.29	2.59	0.43	3.13	0.05	6.50	0.32	2.45	0.08	4.89	0.16	1.64	0.22	2.01			0.79	1.94
1998	0.26	1.84	2.09	5.39	0.64	2.02	0.23	4.88	2.21	5.10	0.10	1.96	0.79	2.95	1.79	5.02			1.27	1.78
1999	0.55	1.97	2.09	1.81	0.59	1.47	0.05	1.17	1.09	1.39	0.19	1.96	0.76	1.64	0.46	1.21			1.21	1.42
2000	1.08	1.97	2.63	1.57	3.22	2.74	1.31	4.89	2.72	1.71	0.37	1.96	1.12	1.58	0.92	1.34			1.23	1.30
2001	1.41	1.64	1.50	1.21	1.96	1.39	0.77	1.47	0.71	1.11	0.35	1.47	4.50	2.46	0.92	1.26			1.00	1.19
2002	1.73	1.48	1.47	1.17	4.86	1.69	0.22	1.09	1.25	1.17	0.70	1.63	1.39	1.18	2.04	1.45			0.36	1.06
2003	0.63	1.12	1.93	1.19	1.00	1.08	0.73	1.28	1.47	1.17	0.32	1.18	2.63	1.29	2.32	1.35			0.30	1.04
2004	0.61	1.10	1.50	1.12	1.20	1.09	0.44	1.13	1.15	1.12	1.34	1.63	2.50	1.22	6.10	1.69			1.42	1.20
2005	0.28	1.04	1.48	1.11	3.11	1.22	0.21	1.05	0.34	1.03	4.45	2.29	3.00	1.21	6.50	1.43	2.80	1.12	-0.94	0.89
2006	4.17	1.61	1.53	1.10	2.31	1.13	0.39	1.10	5.87	1.51	0.06	1.01	3.60	1.21	3.16	1.15	0.90	1.03	0.12	1.02
2007	5.26	1.48	3.52	1.21	1.29	1.07	0.44	1.10	4.94	1.28	3.25	1.41	4.50	1.22	3.64	1.15	5.95	1.22	0.46	1.06
2008	6.90	1.42	1.59	1.08	0.90	1.04	0.49	1.10	11.53	1.52	3.06	1.27	5.37	1.21	4.12	1.15	2.45	1.07	0.36	1.05
2009	1.60	1.07	0.70	1.03	4.63	1.21	1.17	1.22	5.26	1.16	4.63	1.32	3.37	1.03	4.18	1.13	2.50	1.07	1.57	1.19
2010	1.73	1.07	5.82	1.26	4.71	1.18	5.10	1.78	1.02	1.03	0.90	1.05	0.83	1.11	3.33	1.09	2.80	1.07	14.00	2.40
2011	7.47	1.28	6.62	1.23	6.13	1.20	0.40	1.03	2.60	1.06	4.96	1.25	1.24	1.04	0.08	1.00	1.30	1.03	9.97	1.42
2012	4.93	1.15	0.47	1.01	2.57	1.07	0.94	1.08	-2.40	0.94	4.58	1.18	2.19	1.06	5.87	1.15	5.90	1.14	7.03	1.21
2013	5.17	1.13	4.70	1.13	3.71	1.09	0.96	1.07	3.73	1.09	7.56	1.26	1.00	1.03	3.88	1.08	5.35	1.11	5.50	1.13
2014	5.18	1.12	4.69	1.12	0.93	1.02	0.94	1.07	0.89	1.02	6.10	1.17	1.00	1.03	4.32	1.09	8.62	1.16	2.50	1.05
2015	5.18	1.11	5.34	1.12	13.0	1.29	7.47	1.50	6.29	1.14	1.38	1.03	0.70	1.02	1.68	1.03	3.24	1.05	2.92	1.06

(Continued)

(Continued)

Year	Suriname		Thailand		Tunisia		Turkey	
	$\Omega_{i,t}$	$\phi_{i,t}$	$\Omega_{i,t}$	$\phi_{i,t}$	$\Omega_{i,t}$	$\phi_{i,t}$	$\Omega_{i,t}$	$\phi_{i,t}$
1992			0.00	6.58				
1993			0.01	39.51				
1994			0.03	2.84			0.04	5.90
1995			0.04	1.94	0.00	1.52	0.03	1.64
1996	0.11	1.97	0.04	1.54	0.02	2.47	0.11	2.36
1997	0.78	4.43	0.25	3.12	0.02	1.58	0.28	2.46
1998	0.67	1.67	0.73	3.03	0.06	2.47	0.23	1.48
1999	0.22	1.13	1.34	2.22	1.49	14.85	1.59	3.28
2000	0.61	1.32	1.26	1.52	1.15	1.72	1.47	1.64
2001	0.56	1.22	1.87	1.51	1.55	1.56	1.43	1.38
2002	1.10	1.36	1.97	1.36	0.95	1.22	6.19	2.19
2003	0.56	1.13	1.77	1.23	1.24	1.24	0.95	1.08
2004	1.36	1.29	1.38	1.15	2.04	1.31	2.25	1.18
2005	0.33	1.05	4.35	1.41	1.13	1.13	0.88	1.06
2006	3.10	1.48	2.13	1.14	3.33	1.35	2.78	1.18
2007	4.61	1.49	2.87	1.17	4.11	1.32	10.39	1.57
2008	6.95	1.49	-1.83	0.91	10.4	1.61	5.74	1.20
2009	10.30	1.49	1.90	1.10	6.54	1.24	2.03	1.06
2010	0.23	1.01	2.30	1.11	2.73	1.08	3.42	1.09
2011	0.41	1.01	1.27	1.06	2.30	1.06	3.25	1.08
2012	2.68	1.08	2.79	1.12	2.34	1.06	2.06	1.05
2013	2.72	1.08	2.48	1.09	2.36	1.06	1.12	1.02
2014	2.68	1.07	5.95	1.21	2.36	1.05	4.79	1.10
2015	2.68	1.07	4.43	1.13	2.36	1.05	2.70	1.05

Source: Author's calculations.

Appendix 5
Critical mass visualization

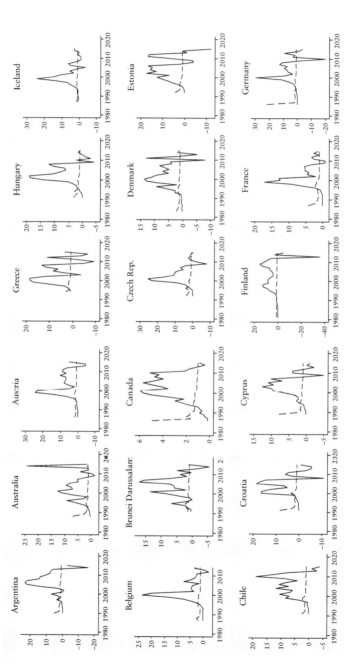

Figure AP(5)-1 Technology replication coefficients (dash line) and marginal growth in technology adoption (solid line) in country-specific patterns for mobile-cellular telephony. High-income economies

Note: On the Y-axis, there are raw values of technology replication coefficients and marginal growth in technology adoption.

Source: Author's elaboration.

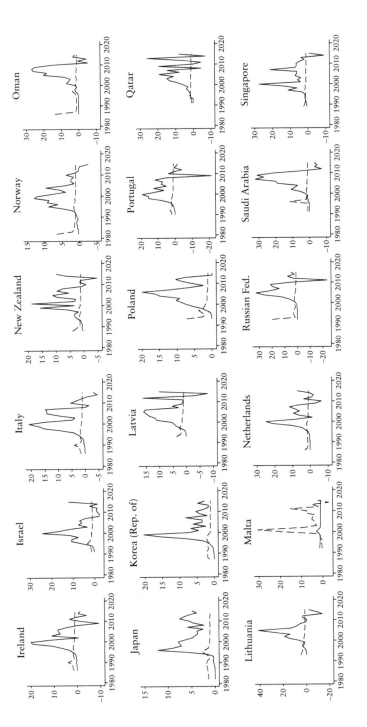

Figure AP(5)-1 (Continued)

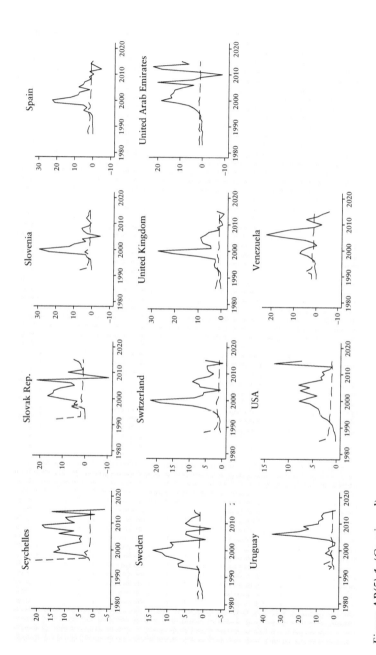

Figure AP(5)-1 (Continued)

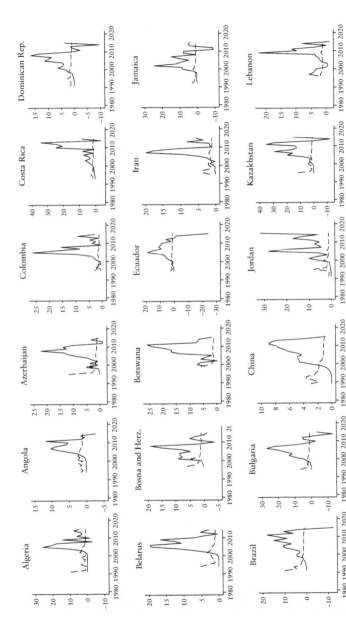

Figure AP(5)-2 Technology replication coefficients (dash line) and marginal growth in technology adoption (solid line) in country-specific patterns for mobile-cellular telephony. Upper-middle-income economies

Note: On the Y-axis, there are raw values of technology replication coefficients and marginal growth in technology adoption.

Source: Author's elaboration.

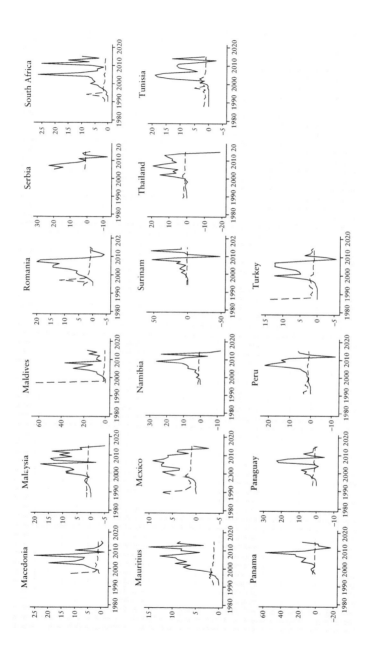

Figure AP(5)-2 (Continued)

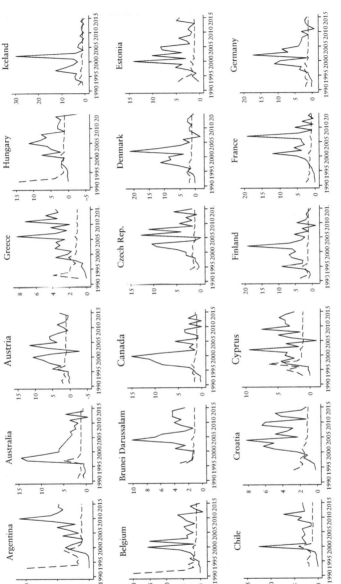

Figure AP(5)-3 Technology replication coefficients (dash line) and marginal growth in technology adoption (solid line) country-specific patterns for Internet penetration rates. High-income economies

Note: On the Y-axis, there are raw values of technology replication coefficients and marginal growth in technology adoption.

Source: Author's elaboration.

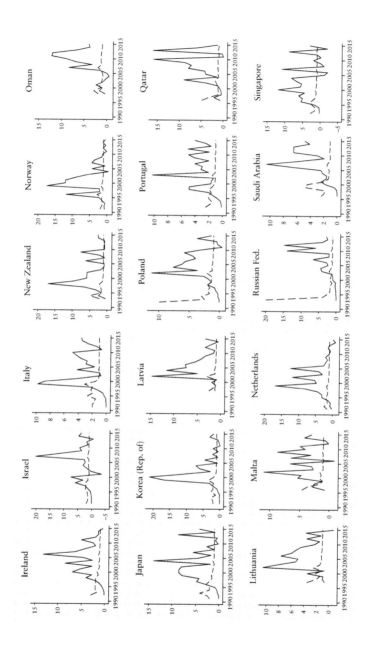

Figure AP(5)-3 (Continued)

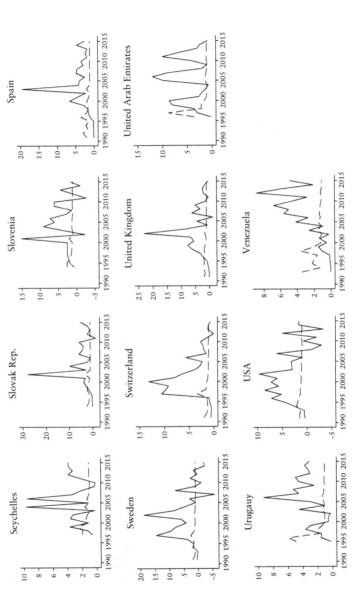

Figure AP(5)-3 (Continued)

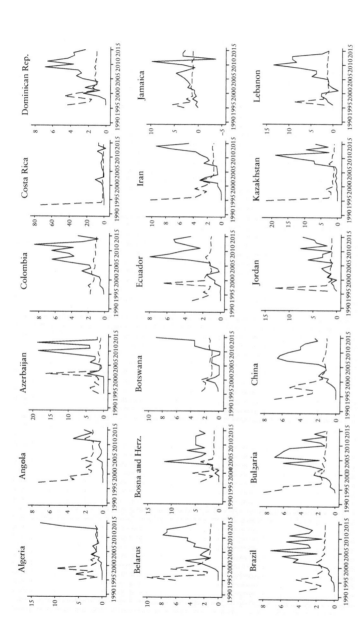

Figure AP(5)-4 Technology replication coefficients (dash line) and marginal growth in technology adoption (solid line) in country-specific patterns for Internet penetration rates. Upper-middle-income economies

Note: On the Y-axis, there are raw values of technology replication coefficients and marginal growth in technology adoption.

Source: Author's elaboration.

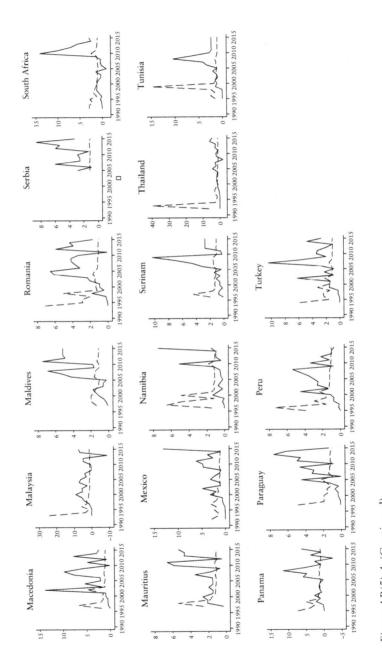

Figure AP(5)-4 (Continued)

Appendix 6

ICT and its selected determinants. Panel regression results.

Table AP(6)-1 Mobile-cellular subscriptions. Fixed effects regression estimates. High-income and upper-middle-income economies (*full sample*). Period 1990–2015

Explanatory variables	FE (1)	FE (2)	FE (3)	FE (4)	FE (5)	FE (6)	FE(7)	FE(8)
$FTL_{i,y}$	0.00 [0.48]	0.24 [0.73]		1.18 [0.71]				
$Min_{i,y}$	-3.52 [2.19]	-6.78 [4.86]			-6.91 [4.81]			
$GDP_{i,y}$	0.006 [0.00]		0.006 [0.00]			0.007 [0.001]		
$Urb_{i,y}$	7.88 [1.40]		7.05 [1.30]				9.41 [1.03]	
$Pop_{i,y}$	0.012 [0.022]		0.012 [0.02]					0.08 [0.32]
R-sq. (within)	0.55	0.00	0.54	0.01	0.00	0.37	0.34	0.04
ρ (rho)	0.97	0.10	0.96	0.11	0.11	0.92	0.92	0.60
F-test (Prob>F)	48.25 [0.00]	1.13 [0.32]	62.5 [0.00]	2.79 [0.09]	2.06 [0.15]	19.9 [0.00]	82.8 [0.00]	7.44 [0.00]
Mean VIF	1.30	1.09	1.07	—	—	—	—	—
# of obs.	1550	1588	1939	1988	1588	1949	1988	1978
# of countries	81	81	81	81	81	81	81	81

Note: Estimates account for fixed effects. Panel balanced. Constant included, not reported. Robust standard errors reported below coefficients. In bold, results are statistically significant at 5% level of significance.

Source: Author's estimates.

Table AP(6)-2 IU. Fixed effects regression estimates. High-income and upper-middle-income economies (*full sample*). Period 1990–2015

Explanatory variables	FE (1)	FE (2)	FE (3)	FE (4)	FE (5)	FE (6)	FE(7)	FE(8)
$FBS_{i,y}$	1.62 [0.17]	1.86 [0.17]		1.78 [0.08]				
$FBSSub_{i,y}$	-0.11 [0.04]	-0.12 [0.03]			-0.30 [0.06]			
$GDP_{i,y}$	-0.000 [0.00]		0.004 [0.00]			0.004 [0.001]		
$Urb_{i,y}$	2.32 [0.57]		3.01 [0.71]				4.72 [0.58]	
$Pop_{i,y}$	0.003 [0.00]		-0.002 [0.012]					0.04 [0.01]
R-sq. (within)	0.68	0.63	0.62	0.71	0.12	0.62	0.28	0.03
ρ (rho)	0.96	0.72	0.97	0.47	0.82	0.97	0.90	0.61
F–test (Prob>F)	43.45 [0.00]	75.9 [0.00]	87.01 [0.00]	396.9 [0.00]	23.17 [0.00]	87.01 [0.00]	64.83 [0.00]	8.79 [0.00]
Mean VIF	1.53	1.00	1.08	—	—	—	—	—
# of obs.	694	697	1839	1199	966	1839	1869	1859
# of countries	81	81	81	81	81	81	81	

Note: estimates account for fixed effects. Panel—balanced. Constant included—not reported. Robust standard errors reported below coefficients. In bolds—results statistically significant at 5% level of significance.

Source: Author's estimates.

Index

For Product Safety Concerns and Information please contact our EU
representative GPSR@taylorandfrancis.com
Taylor & Francis Verlag GmbH, Kaufingerstraße 24, 80331 München, Germany

www.ingramcontent.com/pod-product-compliance
Ingram Content Group UK Ltd.
Pitfield, Milton Keynes, MK11 3LW, UK
UKHW020939180425
457613UK00019B/473

* 9 7 8 0 3 6 7 8 8 9 5 7 9 *